A VISION SHARED

(AMERICAN SAMOA REVISITED)

by
Hugh Neems

ISBN 978-1-234-56789-1

A VISION SHARED

Hugh Neems

Without some sense of the dignity of man, some perception of the higher uses of life, some inward conscience of right, some outward vision of truth, without something imperative because it is great, and not because it is pleasant, our path is into darkness.

John Oman. Vision and Authority. 1902

Acknowledgement
I am grateful to my friends George Lambert and Paul Wood for their valuable help in the production of this book.

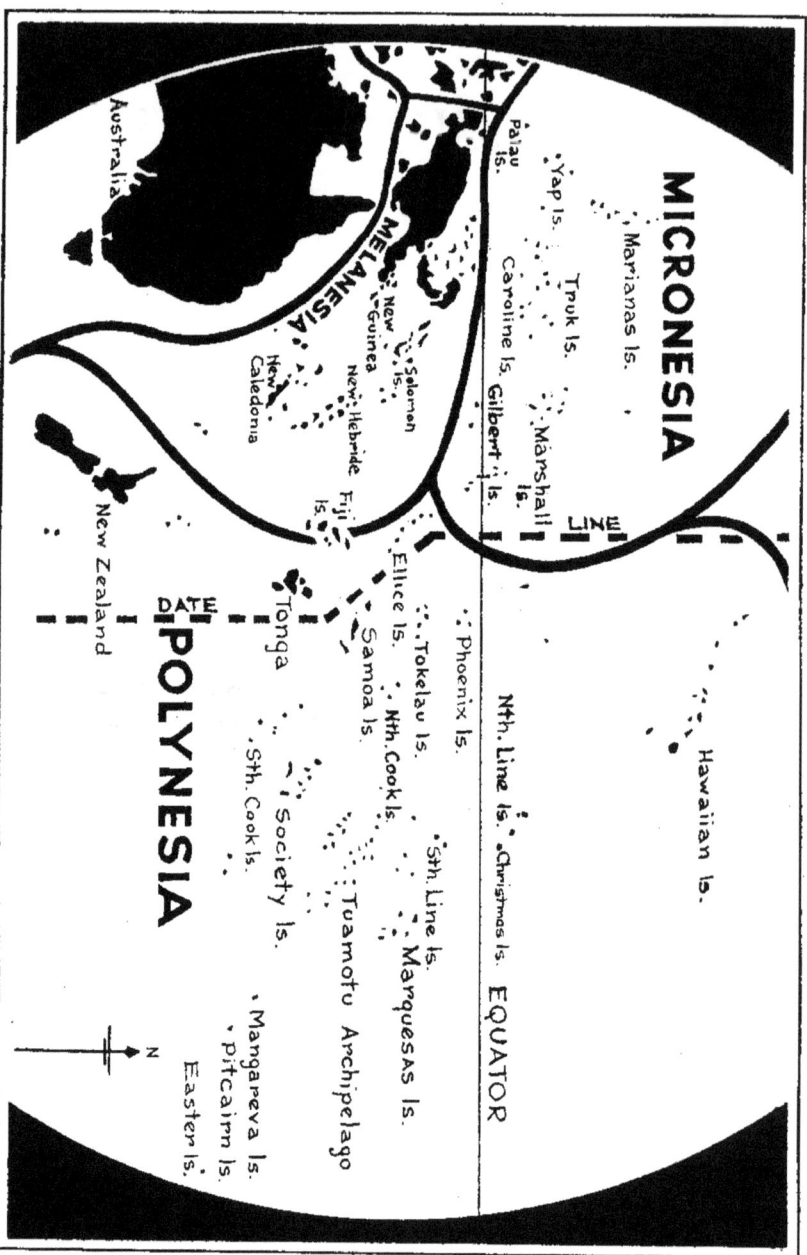

This map shows the Equator, the Date Line and the three areas of Micronesia, Melanesia and Polynesia.

UNION OF S.S. REPUBLICS

CHINA

JAPAN

ALASKA

CANADA

UNITED STATES OF AMERICA

Hongkong

Manila

PHILIPPINES

INDONESIA

AUSTRALIA

Sydney

New Guinea

Pt. Moresby

New Caledonia

Norfolk I.

NEW ZEALAND

Wellington

Yap

Palau Is.

Caroline Is.

Guam

Marianas

Truk

Ponape

Marshall

Nauru

Ocean Is.

Solomons

New Hebrides

Loyalty Is.

Fiji

Tonga

Santa Cruz

Samoa

W. Samoa

Tokelau Is.

Ellice Is.

Phoenix Is.

Gilbert Is.

Majuro

Hawaii

S. Francisco

Christmas I.

Niue

Cook Is.

Rarotonga

Society Is.

Tahiti

Tuamotu Is.

Marquesas Is.

Pitcairn I.

Easter I.

Valparaiso

SOUTH AMERICA

Panama

1595

1766

2225

1251

2396

825

710

2074

3900

3160

2370

2395

5160

4896

iii

A VISION SHARED

Introduction to Parts 1 and 2

Part One 'From the beginning' (p1-60) is about the settlement of the Pacific Islands by the Polynesians beginning three thousand years ago. The earliest voyagers discovered mainly uninhabited islands as they explored the largest watery space on earth. Their ancestors were a sea-going people originating from Taiwan and the South China Sea, who navigated their way north of Australia to make a home along the coast of the large island of New Guinea. After long occupation these communities provided launch pads for further migratory journeys into the Pacific Ocean's immensity. They voyaged eastwards towards the rising sun, the 'Great Unknown' and South America.

Many centuries later around 1500 AD European navigators such as Roggeveen, La Perouse and James Cook sailed westwards with the setting sun behind them, from the tip of South America in the direction of S.E. Asia. They 'discovered' islands such as Hawai'i and Aotearoa (New Zealand). Four thousand miles apart, these were the names of islands given to them by Polynesians migrating from the coast lands of New Guinea. The impact made by the White Man on Pacific people by whalers, traders, missionaries and empire builders is described in Chapters 1-7. Part One ends by focusing on a group of islands which came into being in 1900 with the name of American Samoa. This development was one example among many of major colonial powers defining their spheres of influence before the outbreak of World War 1 in 1914.

Part Two 'Beyond Colonialism' (p61-219) is concerned with the fortunes of the Samoan people as they absorbed the major upheaval caused by the Pacific War from 1941-1946. The achievement of Independence in Western Samoa in 1961, and President Kennedy's 'New Frontier Programme' of economic aid for American Samoa in the 1960's, brought about disturbance and realignments in the culture and traditions of the Samoan people in both territories. Divided into five chapters, Part Two begins with 'Green bananas' as a chapter heading,leading to an experience of Falling apart' followed by 'Well done the rowers', the encouraging shout of a longboat crew crossing over the reef. Behind the fourth chapter heading 'Proceed with caution' lies the experience of a foreigner working in partnership with local leaders. 'A Durable Network', the final chapter is about the growing pains of a world-wide multi-racial community.

A VISION SHARED

Part 1: In the beginning

The wind blew over the face of the waters, and the first wave began a world wide movement. So begins a Polynesian creation story. A wind blowing (Fa'amatagi), can also refer to telling a story from the beginning. Part One of this book relies on the image of giant waves rolling across ocean depths. These unpredictable surges are not to be confused with surface waves that are affected by local weather conditions. They are enormous swells produced by the confluence of several wide swathes of sea water moving inexorably across thousands of miles of ocean floor. Using the imagery of an over-riding force of nature, it is suggested that seven powerful movements of human activity shaped the character and disposition of South Pacific people. A description of these formative agencies is divided into seven chapters, culminating in the creation of nations with new names after the disastrous typhoon of 1898. The 20th Century began, with four colonial powers America, Germany, France and Britain apparently in control of the Pacific Islander's destiny.

First Wave - Polynesian settlement

The first wave carried explorers in large outrigger canoes towards the sunrise in the general direction of South America. They colonised many fertile islands and bare coral strands to create a distinctive culture in an ocean area known today as the Polynesian Triangle. Their origins, tools, trade, hierarchical social structure and oral traditions are issues raised.

Second Wave - Voyagers from outer space

Polynesians called the first Europeans 'Papalagi', meaning 'Those who broke through the horizon'. (Heaven). After several centuries of relative isolation, relieved by inter-island trade, the descendents of the early settlers were required to respond to visitors from the 'White Man's world'. Explorers, traders and empire builders belonged to the second wave,who arrived in the Pacific from Europe from 1520 onwards.

Third Wave - Trade Mission

Protestant Christians from London were next on the scene. Admired as heroic pioneers, or disliked for their interference in the Islanders way of life, the British missionary enterprise in the South Seas is seen to be an essential element in the story of Pacific people. The link with British commercial interests is examined.

Fourth Wave - Rough diamonds

In 1797 the ship 'Duff' arrived in Tahiti with 30 artisan/ tradesmen missionaries on board. They had left England with little idea of what they would find. Twenty years passed before any interest was shown in their teaching. At one point surviving pioneers supplied a warring chief with guns. After a hard won victory he publicly embraced Christianity, and the mass conversion of the Tahitian people took place. It is a record of angels with dirty faces.

Fifth Wave - Book-Eaters

The written word was a curiosity to Pacific Islanders who were quick to learn the printer's skills. Reading and owning a Bible became the way to enter the New Dispensation. Learning to speak and write in the language of the elite in Tahitian society, the printer-missionaries became students of South Sea life and manners. Light was thrown on life in Ancient Polynesia. Meanwhile the recently formed Tahitian Mission extended its work to Samoa and other Polynesian islands, which acted as spring boards for recent converts to venture into 'darkest' Melanesia.

Sixth Wave - Do or die

The people of Melanesia suffered at the hands of brutal dealers in sandal-wood, and 'Blackbirders' who sold them into slavery on the Queensland sugar plantations. Revenge led to murder and cannibalism against the White Man, guilty and innocent alike. Burns poem 'Scots Wha Hae wi Wallace bled' applied to several of his countrymen who lived and died alongside many Polynesian colleagues.

Seventh Wave Big Business / Gun-boats / Self- rule

An ocean swell that left an indelible mark along many Pacific shorelines was created by Big Business, gunboat imperialism and the movement towards self government. Between 1850 and 1900 the major international powers, Britain, France,Germany and the USA were involved in a struggle for colonial assets. Tahiti and other Society Islands were annexed by France.

A typhoon in 1898, which destroyed six armed warships led to the partition of Samoa,and a growing demand for self determination in government and church . One consequence was a Treaty in which the U.S. Navy inherited a magnificent harbour and Coaling Station in Pago Pago, American Samoa.

The port of Pango Pango
A vessel lies at the Station Wharf and a Matson liner is anchored off it

A Vision Shared

Chapter One:
First Wave - Settlement

Polynesian village

There are more islands in the Pacific Ocean than the six thousand stars seen on a clear night with the naked eye. The awe inspiring array of stars is matched by ten thousand islands, large as New Guinea, or small as Pitcairn, the two separated by four thousand miles of water. Molten rock spouting unexpectedly from the ocean floor remind Islanders that they inhabit the tops of mountain chains, which erupt occasionally to create tsunamis. The corridor created by the islands of Indonesia and New Guinea on one side, and the Australian Barrier Reef on the other, opens out into the Great Ocean with the rising sun beckoning intrepid voyagers to move on.

More than ten thousand years ago people from south-east Asia migrated towards New Guinea, and the area known today as Melanesia, dark islands. Later arrivals moved on much further to other landfalls, which became known as Micronesia, or minute islands. Polynesia (many islands), is the name given to the largest area, with territory north and south of the Equator, and east of the International Date Line. The distribution of the Melanesians around the coast of New Guinea suggests that they travelled on catamarans or outrigger

1

canoes. Later arrivals developed these craft into larger and more versatile vessels through improved hull and sail design. These outriggers made it possible for a sea-going people to seek settlement across unknown waters.

Comparing the size of New Guinea and the Solomon Islands in Melanesia with Australia reveals that these are large islands. Samoa, Tahiti, and the Cook Islands in Polynesia rising to a few thousand feet are of medium size, whereas the Caroline and Marshall islands in Micronesia, are no more than strips of sand covering coral reefs, which cling to the highest point of submerged volcanic rock. Present day inhabitants of these atolls are threatened by a rise in sea levels, due to global warming.

The Polynesians were great seafarers long before the European explorer Magellan (1519), voyaged westwards from South America across the Pacific Ocean. More than a thousand years earlier, navigators sailing east towards the Americas in successive waves had found and colonised every island in what came to be known as The Polynesian Triangle. Hawai'i was its apex, and a base line extended from New Zealand to Easter Island, a distance of 4,000 miles.

Reasons advanced for their migration, such as fishermen blown off course in a storm, or vanquished warriors hurriedly escaping invaders to find sanctuary elsewhere, do not adequately explain the careful planning that went into journeys expected to be long and arduous. The migrating voyagers included women, who did not take part in deep sea fishing expeditions. Intending to make new settlements, they took with them domestic animals, cultivated plants, drinking water and other provisions. Often compared with the renowned Nordic navigators of the Northern Hemisphere, 'The Vikings of the Sunrise' made their home in the islands of the Southern Hemisphere.

Halfway across the Pacific between New Guinea and Peru in South America a group of islands,which includes Tahiti, became the centre of a expanding Polynesian universe. Ra'iatea, an island 125 miles from Tahiti, known originally as Havai'i was regarded as the birthplace of many lands. (fanau fa'a fanua). The colonisation of the Pacific islands by Polynesians began here. Known nowadays as The Society Islands, their configuration resembles the head of an octopus (Tahiti), with tentacles reaching out into the surrounding ocean.

From these central Pacific Islands such as Havai'i and Uporu, the Polynesian cultural identity and language spread through the voyages of seasoned mariners to create sister settlements with similar sounding names. Hawai'i

2,000 miles to the north, Savai'i and Upolu in the Samoan group, 700 miles to the west, are examples of a common ancestry. Tonga and Raratonga, (700 miles to the southwest] also became home to kith and kin, whilst 2,000 miles further on, another branch of the Polynesian family became the Maori people in New Zealand.

Navigational skills of the highest order were needed to scour the vast uncharted waters. The helmsman, whilst making use of contrary as well as following winds, kept a sharp lookout for the movement of stars, and the pull of the moon. These navigators noticed the differences in the seascape as the hours of daylight increased or decreased. Sea watchers, (matatai) on board considered the flight pattern of the migratory albatross or frigate bird. The presence or absence of dolphins, whales and shoals of various fish seen during the different seasons of the year were features providing important clues for maintaining contact with what were becoming familiar sea-lanes. They noticed smells carried on the breeze, distinctive cloud clusters over some islands, detecting slight changes in the temperature, or salinity of sea water. Shunting, sailing and rowing their craft, their progress was based on careful observation, but was also open to supernatural explanation.

Particular stars that followed a predetermined trajectory appeared to beckon them to a meeting with their destiny beyond the horizon. Though not literally true, the catamaran remained steady under a brilliant white star, such as Sirius, whilst their destination moved steadily towards them. It sounds a bit spooky, yet early aviators spoke of 'flying by the seat of their pants' when they lacked the help of instruments. Confidence that all will turn out well was a large part of this 'sixth sense', which operated alongside the other five senses. Polynesians preferred to speak of a supernatural Being, or beings who kept them on course, - nevertheless it mattered that their navigator was able to read the messages found in the 'signs and seasons'. Orientation that was aware of the larger picture, was balanced by an attention to small details.

The deep and lasting impression made on the psyche of Polynesian people as they found their way across the Pacific Ocean, cannot be overstated. Trying to understand the tremendous forces behind the salt spray constantly drenching their craft lying low in the water, observing laws of life on the ocean wave, they were constantly aware of supernatural agencies determining their sense of direction. Both sea and land were haunted by aitu (demons) who could distract the unwary traveller, yet at the same time other spirits could be relied on to be helpful guides. Samoan proverbs show that early navigators in Oceania acted on the assumption that there was an overlap between the natural and the supernatural. The cautionary saying, 'Ne'i afe se atua a le ala'(Beware of evil spirits haunting the way), was matched by an adventurous antidote. 'E le sili le tai i lo le tapua'i'. ('Know how', is not superior to spiritual awareness). Sacred songs and chants were a powerful aid to the memory of priestly pathfinders as they remembered their star maps.

Ancient maritime knowledge continues to inform the subtlety of a talking chief's oratory, and even throw away lines on a bus going to market in the 21st Century, reflect a preoccupation with the thrill of travel. 'Malo le tautai!'(fa'auli) is the cry that goes up from the passengers when a bus driver negotiates a hairpin bend.(Well done the navigator). His response, 'Fa'afetai tapua'i means 'Thanks for your encouragement'. For many generations the sea was not so much a barrier to be overcome, but a means of 'keeping in touch' with life in other island communities, of celebrating a common ancestry, confirming religious beliefs, of developing variations in language expression. The sea was to be respected, loved and feared. The experience encouraged reliance on travelling companions, some of whom were regarded as equals, whereas others had a superior quality because of gifts granted to them by superior beings (gods). On land an hierarchical social order reflected the dominant features of a nautical organisation that had served Polynesians well in deep and dangerous waters.

(Tala o le Vavau) (Legends) and genealogies (Gafa) also provide further information about Polynesian migratory patterns. A condensed racial history (Fa'alupega), recited regularly in Samoan gatherings, reinforced the rights and privileges of separate families through their chiefs. A roll call of titles clarified the extent of inherited land, and thereby indicated status in their hierarchical society. It is a Samoan version of 'Who's Who'! The authority of family heads is confirmed by unchanging rituals of the village and district community, such as the drinking of the common cup of kava.

One set of traditions, found throughout Polynesia refers to Ra'iatea (Tahiti), as being at the heart of their universe. Another tradition mentions the names of famous navigators who led the earliest exploratory voyages. Their names, as well as those given to the sturdy vessels in which the heroes sailed, were passed on through particular families to be regarded as sacred idols (tupua) or role models worthy of veneration.

Common linguistic patterns as well as religious and social customs were found in island groups such as Tonga and Samoa, but significant differences began to emerge. However recent archeological evidence shows that trade and exchange in stone age tools and implements continued between these groups, and others, for two thousand five hundred years before recorded history. This knowledge came to light through a study of volcanic stone quarries less than a mile from my old home in Tutuila, Eastern Samoa. Excavations revealed that high quality stone tools (to'i ma'a) adzes (matau),chisels and scrapers, were made from the unusually fine grained basalt peculiar to the island of Tutuila, during the first millennium B.C. An adze, a stone blade lashed to a wooden handle by twine made from the husk of the coconut, was used for carving wood, and as a weapon of war.

On the mountain side above the village of Leone, piles of basalt flakes and fragments quarried from a large outcrop, had been discarded at various stages in the making of different tools. The site covering 50 acres, had been the scene of intense industrial activity. Sharpening and finishing these products was carried out close to streams on the coast at the present day locations of Sogi and Atauloma. Clearly visible I often gazed at the hand worn bowl- shaped depressions in the volcanic lava, which bear witness to their craftsmanship, and the organisation of skilled and unskilled labour.

Depressions made in sharpening adze heads

The same scientists,working on what is known as the Tataga-matau Quarry near Leone, compared basalt adzes recovered in Ofu, Manu'a and Mangaia in the Cook Islands group, with adzes made in Tutuila. In both cases, they were able to demonstrate that basalt quarried in Tutuila, was used in the manufacture of adzes imported into Ofu, a distance of 60 miles away,and to Mangaia, a distance of 1,000 miles. Radio carbon dating of local raw material, adzes and adze flakes, found in Ofu and Mangaia confirmed that all of the fine grained artefacts originated in Tutuila.

Later studies have shown that Tonga, Fiji and the Solomon Islands were included in an extensive trade and exchange network in fine stone tools made in Tutuila. Several stone adzes were also found in the Seuao Cave at Safata in Upolu. Wooden bowls and canoes were some of the goods exchanged. Clear evidence shows that long distance ocean travel and commerce was the inescapable backdrop to the Polynesian way of life. Going on a journey (malaga) was written large into their genes.

The longest journey of all was to 'Pulotu', or nether regions, the Polynesian Chief's spiritual homeland at the time of death. Just as their 'elite' forefathers had set out on the trail of the rising sun, so the setting sun in the west is still a powerful symbol for a chief 'going home' at the end of life on earth. Traditional departure places for this supernatural form of travel, including the one at Falealupo in Savai'i, Western Samoa, are always found at the western extreme of island groups throughout Polynesia. They indicate that the chief's last journey was in the direction of South East Asia.

Twenty miles from the International Dateline, Falealupo is arguably the last place on earth to see the sunset each day, and explains why a BBC television crew was present to capture the moment when the village entered the 21st Century. According to Samoan folklore, Le Fafa at Falealupo, is the 'jumping off' point for the spirit (aitu) of a chief on his way to Pulotu. Going home meant retracing the various stages in a long distance journey leading back to the Polynesian's place of origin.

In 1947, the Kon Tiki expedition led by Thor Heyerdahl, sought to demonstrate that the Polynesians began their migration to the central Pacific from the opposite direction to the one already considered. Botanical science had provided evidence that the sweet potato, found throughout the islands, came from South America in the east, and not from Asia in the west. Heyerdahl claimed that beginning in Peru, the ancient voyagers had drifted westwards on strong currents across the South Pacific towards the setting sun.

On April 28 Heyerdahl and a crew of five left Callao harbour on their raft made of balsa logs strapped together, to begin an epic voyage first to the Marquesas, a distance of 4,000 miles, arriving there on July 21. They finally ran aground on a small coral atoll at Raroia, 500 miles east of Tahiti on August

7th. A successful outcome to their voyage showed that the east-west migration was a practical possibility. Moreover, it was asserted that drift voyages put a question mark against the navigational skills needed by Polynesian navigators heading towards the rising sun.

The use of computer models furthered the discussion. Different scenarios revealed that thousands of random drift voyages ended in oblivion. Their waywardness served to support the alternative explanation, that Polynesians possessing outstanding gifts of seamanship, migrated across the Pacific from southeast Asia. This is the view of most researchers engaged in Oceanic studies. Added grist to their mill was provided by a study conducted in 2004 into the DNA of rats brought to Polynesia by the earliest settlers. Tests indicated that the islands were colonised by people from southeast Asia, accompanied by faithful 'Ratty'. Further research suggests that links with Peru in South America came about after the migrants from S.E. Asia had settled in the Marquesas. Two way traffic between the far reaches of Eastern Polynesia and distant Peru became possible with canoes of improved design. The long distance travelled without a land-fall has encouraged continued debate among Oceania scholars with regard to the significance of the Kon Tiki expedition.

Voyage over

Chapter Two

Second Wave - From outer space

Papalagi is a Polynesian word meaning 'heaven breakers'. It refers to the first white skinned visitors to burst into the Pacific Ocean.

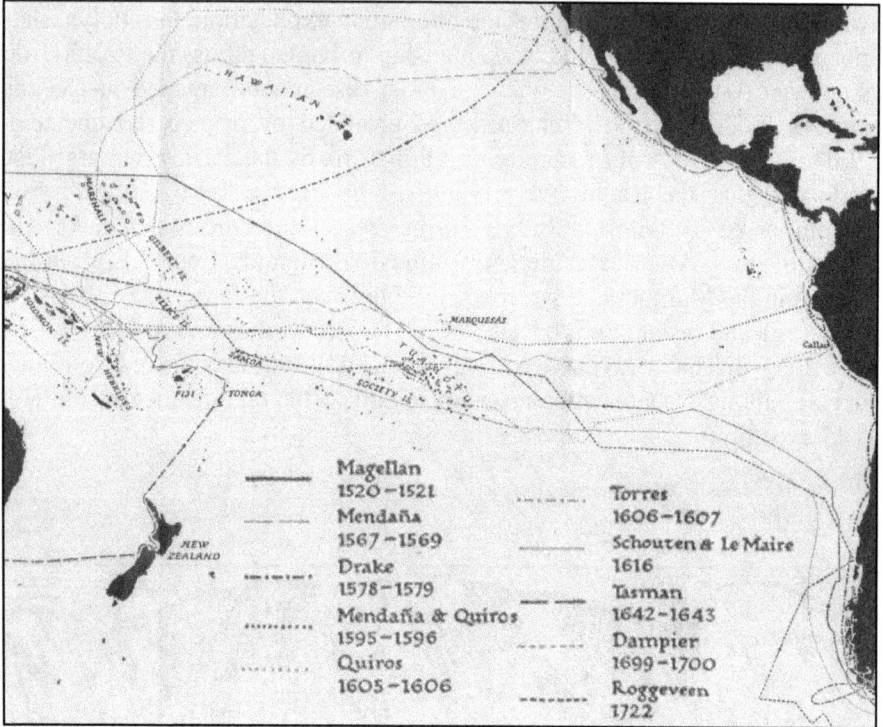

Magellan 1520 –1521		Torres 1606 –1607	
Mendaña 1567 –1569		Schouten & Le Maire 1616	
Drake 1578 –1579		Tasman 1642 –1643	
Mendaña & Quiros 1595 –1596		Dampier 1699 –1700	
Quiros 1605 –1606		Roggeveen 1722	

In 1520 Ferdinand Magellan, the Portuguese explorer, was the leader of the European expedition of 5 ships searching for a westward route to Asia, and a lucrative spice trade. Of the 257 men who set out, 18 completed the voyage. Magellan died in Indonesia.

Two hundred years after Magellan, a Dutch expedition of three ships arrived off the 3,153 feet high easternmost island of Ta'u, in the Samoan group on June 22nd 1722. One of Roggeveen's crew wrote in a ships journal 'Three outrigger canoes came out to meet them in which there sat a man of obvious authority, and a girl wearing a blue coral necklace. The men who had spears, bows and arrows, were extensively tattooed with a belt round their waists, to which were attached long and wide leaves, or rushes.' After this peaceful first

8

meeting between the 'Papalagi' (heaven breakers) and the people of Samoa, Roggeveen and his company then sailed to Tutuila, about 50 miles west, continued to Upolu for a similar distance, but did not go ashore.

In 1736 Wilkes the American explorer enthused about the natural harbour named Pago Pago, in E. Samoa. He also wrote that 'Polynesians remind me of maniacs in the utmost frenzy. On the death of a paramount chief, war broke out between district alliances, each supporting a rival claimant to the succession'. Generally speaking the first European settlers found the Islanders to be friendly and hospitable, but they were left in no doubt after witnessing heads hacked off, that tribal conflict had to be avoided.

Thirty two years passed before two French ships, under the command of Louis Bougainville, became the next European vessels to be seen by the Samoans. In 1768 they appeared first in Manu'a, and afterwards in Tutuila. Impressed by the considerable coastal traffic, and the number of canoes Bourganville saw engaged in fishing, he named the group the Navigators Islands. A further nineteen years passed before another Frenchman, La Perouse, leading an expedition of two ships, arrived on the north coast of Tutuila in December 1787. Two French parties landed on Samoan soil, one at Fagasa and the other at A'asu, a few miles away. Here they attempted to record the name of the homeland given to them by the inhabitants. Maunga, the high chief's name, was incorrectly applied to the island of Tutuila. They were nearly correct in hearing Pola, rather than Upolu, as the name of the next Samoan island on their itinerary sailing westwards. ((Map p64)

On Tutuila Island a violent scuffle broke out as fresh food and water was being taken on board at A'asu, resulting in thirty seven Samoans and several French sailors being killed. The cause of this incident is unknown, but A'asu villagers blamed warriors from the A'ana district of Upolu, 60 miles away, said to be exercising their right as overlords of Tutuila. Samoans allowed on board the French ships to replenish victuals, possibly tried to barter for highly desirable iron tools and fittings. Misunderstanding about contrasting methods of bargaining was the probable cause of violent quarrels.

After these brief encounters with long intervals separating them, La Perouse was reported as saying that Pacific inhabitants were 'wild beasts'. From his logbooks it is known 'that for two days the captain tried to get near enough to bombard the village of A'asu as a reprisal, but on the third day he accepted his losses, and moved on west to Upolu'. Islanders did not forget aggressive European behaviour, and later took revenge on white visitors.

9

One of these was Captain Cook, who sailed from Whitby in North Yorkshire on the first of his global voyages in 1748. His ship entered the Pacific by way of Cape Horn, the southern tip of South America. Sailing west in warm seas, 45 degrees south, Cook came to Tahiti, one of the Society Islands named after the Royal Society in London, the sponsor of the expedition. Cook was sent to observe the planet Venus as it passed between the Earth and the Sun. On the unlit side Venus could be seen as a small black circle moving across the face of the Sun. It was hoped that observations would lead to more accurate projections concerning the distance of Venus from the Sun, and the distances between the other planets. Pacific explorers depended on such measurements in calculating their ship's position.

Four years later on his second epic journey, he sailed first to the bottom of the African continent, on through the broken ice of the southern Indian Ocean to New Zealand. Setting sail again, this time going eastwards in the 'Forty's' (40 degrees south), the ship moved northwards to the warmer seas of Tahiti. Cook was impressed when he saw the Tahitian pahi, a double hulled craft carrying more than 100 people, and similar to the Samoan alia, for it was much faster than 'The Endeavour' and said to be capable of travelling 120 miles in a day.

On this second expedition Cook had the help of the newly developed chronometer, Harrison's instrument for measuring longitude. During the three years long voyage Cook sailed between sixty and seventy thousand miles. One year after his return to Portsmouth he was off again, this time with two ships, to New Zealand, and then Tahiti, before going north across the equator, when for the first recorded time, Europeans saw the Islands of Hawai'i. Initially Cook was regarded as a superior being, but after a series of violent disputes between members of his crew and the Islanders about metal from the ship, Captain Cook was murdered.

The age of major European exploration came to an end with the death of Cook. Although some parts of the ocean remained unvisited, and some islands undiscovered, the main outlines of the Pacific had been mapped out. Besides providing minute details about coastlines, winds, tides and sunken reefs, Cook and his colleagues described the geography of the islands, their people and food resources.

In England the explorers raised expectations among traders and whalers. The government thought about adding colonies to the crown, and evangelists began to remind their hearers of the reason for their existence 'to take the

Good News of Jesus Christ to 'all peoples everywhere'. (Matt. 28) Within a few years whaling and trading captains, missionaries and white settlers, were placing rough charts of many little known atolls and reefs in the hands of professional cartographers. Behind the 'opening-up' of the Pacific by the Europeans, is an exceptionally ugly story.

In the Antarctic seas Cook had come across a land extraordinarily rich in small forms of marine life,which sustained an enormous number and variety of animals and birds. Every year hundred-foot blue whales would come down south in thousands to feed on minute shrimps, and in March when they had grown fat and encased in blubber, the whole horde would turn north to warmer seas. (Whilst living in Samoa I happened to look out to sea one morning as I was shaving, and could not believe my eyes when I saw the unmistakable humpback of a whale making water spouts as it moved across Leone Bay, a short distance beyond the reef in front of our home.

Cook's account of this amazing 'Sea World' was of great interest to traders in the northern hemisphere, who were attempting to satisfy their customers need for grease to protect rope, and more particularly to lighten the long darkness of the winter months using oil lamps and candles. The clubbing to death of millions of seals over the next 50 years beggars description. Slaughter continued as easy profits were made for ship owners by men working in dehumanising conditions. It is not surprising that Pacific Island people were not favourably impressed by some of these representatives of the white race first thought to have descended from heaven

Sealers came first, and then it was the turn of the whalers as the slaughter went on. Towed ashore, the blubber was peeled off carcasses like the skin of an orange, and rendered down into oil in furnace-heated vats on the beach. The whaling ship named Gypsy left London in 1839, to return 3 years 5 months later having caught 71 whales, and obtained 1,773 barrels of oil. Returning sailors reported 'The Sea turned red with their blood as they died in their scores, butchered as they floundered in the shallows'. Brutal work produced many unsavoury characters who settled in the Islands.

The deception and brutal treatment of Pacific people by British sandalwood traders, was a particular disgrace. Murderous characters gave 'The White Man' an odious reputation throughout Melanesia. In addition Blackbirder ships searched isolated islands and found hundreds of men, forcing them to leave everything to become indentured labour on sugar plantations in Queensland, Australia, where they were kept as prisoners.

Missionaries and colonial servants brought these concerns to the attention of the British Government, which prompted Parliament to pass a bill in 1817 'for the speedy trial of offences committed in distant countries, or upon the sea'. The preamble to the Act make its intention very plain ; 'that grievous murders and manslaughters have been committed in the South Pacific Ocean by masters and crew, deserters, who live amongst island inhabitants, where - by great violence has been done and a general scandal and prejudice raised against the name and character of British and other European traders. They were to be caught and punished'. On the other side of the world, dark deeds continued throughout the 19th Century.

Conflicting stories about life in the South Seas circulated in England. A rosy picture was provided by the publication of the diaries of Captain Cook, and the drawings of the Royal Society's President, Joseph Banks. He had been Cook's chief naturalist on board ship and his romantic version of life in remote tropical islands released a flood of imaginative travel writing about ' the noble savage'. William Hodges, an artist on Cook's second voyage, sensitively captured the shimmering Southern light. The romanticised Tahitian women he portrayed, were based on voluptuous Venetian libertines devoid of sexual inhibition. Powerful evocative images captured the hearts and minds of Europeans living through cold winters.

The glamorous image was reinforced by a commission given to Captain Bligh by the Royal Society in London.. He was sent to Tahiti in 1787 to collect breadfruit seedlings and transport them to the West Indies where they were intended to provide a staple diet for the Negro slaves. Bligh had to wait in Tahiti for five months until the seedlings were sufficiently mature to be stowed away in his large cabin. During that time relationships formed between crew members and Tahitian women were more than casual, so that when it came to the time to sail away, many of the mariners, such as Fletcher Christian, found it hard to tear themselves away from the easy life. Europeans generally came to think of Tahiti, and other Pacific Islands, as a paradise of free love, abundant alcohol and little work.

When Bligh returned to Tahiti in 1792 he reported that a disastrous change had overtaken Tahiti since Cook's last visit 15 years earlier. 'Whaling ships had begun to call there, many of the islanders were addicted to drink, and venereal disease was steadily gaining ground. Elegant clothing was discarded in favour of dirty shirts and trousers given to them by the sailors. They do not speak their own language but mixed it up with English jargon.' Other sea captains confirmed in 1791 the reports of the Tahitian's unhappy condition. In 'enlightened' France, as well as in England, there were second thoughts about the Polynesians being charming children of nature.

Julian Crozet wrote in a similar vein when he returned to Europe after a South Pacific voyage. 'I have noticed them to change from childish delight to deepest gloom, from complete calmness to the greatest heights of rage, and then to burst into immoderate laughter the moment afterwards, one moment caressing, and menacing the next, but they were never long in the same mood and struck me as having dangerous and deceitful tendencies'.

The Breadfruit

However it was not only Pacific Islanders who suffered from mood swings. The earlier European fantasy of a far away land where idyllic love and natural goodness flourished, was overtaken by one in which Polynesians were regarded as thieves, sexual predators, murderers, cannibals and idolaters. The Pacific Islands became another Sodom and Gomorrah, not the Garden of Eden. Incomprehension about a culture very different from their own was deep rooted.

Tropical islands created by a lively imagination had long fascinated educated English people wanting stories of adventure. In a popular novel by Daniel Defoe, written in 300 years ago (1720), an English castaway named Robinson Crusoe was marooned on a remote island for 28 years. Surrounded by the delights of an exotic paradise, the hero Crusoe continued to replicate life in England at that time. In particular,Defoe through Crusoe revealed an Englishman's insatiable interest in trade,and a desire to propagate a Puritan style religion. Crusoe's main aim however was to exploit the wealth found in the island's abundant resources.

In the novel Crusoe rescues a prisoner captured by cannibals .Named Friday, he is converted to the Christian faith and becomes Crusoe's trusted servant. In a similar manner his tropical island home is referred to as a colony. Robinson

Crusoe became a powerful symbol of unwearied diligence and application associated with the descendents of 17th Century Puritans. They were driven by an evangelical fervour drawing strength from a generous Providence. Whereas those involved in the First Wave of discovery had a respect, often fear of the vast expanse of Oceania, many who were borne along on the Second Wave, wanted to exploit her resources. Considerable economic benefits were the result, but at a terrible cost.

Fatal impact

Chapter Three

Third Wave - Trade Mission.

World-wide trade

Tradesmen who were Calvinistic Methodists or Independents were the next group to cause a stir in the Pacific. To understand the lasting impression they made on Pacific Island people it is important to know where they were coming from. Originally the group had been part of the Established Church of England,who wanted to be more outspoken in their Christian witness. They had responded with fervour to the Revival or Awakening, a religious movement led by the Wesley brothers, and George Whitefield, which affected all sections of British society in the 18th Century. Whitefield, had an extraordinary talent for theatrical performance, shown in his dramatic presentation of biblical events. David Garrick (1717-1779), a famous London actor and theatre manager said, 'I would give a thousand guineas if I could say 'Oh' like Mr Whitefield. The preacher had a similar emotional effect on crowds as the Beatles of the 20th Century. 'Help' was the listeners cry as they struggled with the down-pull of a vividly described whirlpool of inner conflict, before reaching out for the helping hand of Jesus.

Revivalism was not all froth, and no substance. The harsh conditions in which illiteracy was overcome in Wales was brought about by the Circulating Schools. Born as a result of spiritual revival first in the Anglican Church,and later through the Methodist Movement, the Welsh people became literate long before their English neighbours. Thomas Charles of Bala, a Calvinistic Methodist, who had been an Anglican vicar, was instrumental in creating the Sunday School movement, and founding the influential Bible Society with its world wide influence. Their zeal in relieving poverty and providing education prepared the way for 'ordinary people' to have their moment in the sun. Many from their ranks were destined to be in the vanguard of Empire expansion, commercial growth, colonial service and overseas missionary service. Meantime the aristocracy called the tune.

Salena, the Countess of Huntingdon (1707-91), was deeply moved by the preaching of George Whitefield (1714-70). She became the founder of a network of Calvinistic Methodist chapels in and around Cambridge, which extended to North Wales, and centred on Bala. Some of her 'upper crust' friends such as Sir Joseph Banks, President of the Royal Society, were attracted by the intellectual rigour and precision of Calvinist thought.'The Study of Natural History' written by Banks describing unfolding laws and patterns in nature,were said to confirm God's reliable laws in creation.

Salena's other friends included Bligh of the Bounty, Dr. David Bogue, an influential classical scholar from Edinburgh, and the Reverend Thomas Haweis, her personal chaplain, a former physician, who was well connected to nobility. Bogue and Haweis, believed that because the British people had benefited from 'overseas' Christians , they too had a moral responsibility to pass on the Faith to other nations. Whereas Bogue stressed intellectual rigour as an integral element in the Gospel's appeal, Haweis emphasized the need for a change of heart. The creative tension between these two attitudes shaped the formation of The Mission Society.

The published sermons of Haweis show him looking into every nook and cranny of scripture to buttress a compelling vision of God's sovereign power and love reaching out to all mankind. Preaching that nothing happens apart from His will, he claimed that a willingness to respond, or to deny the Supreme Being's claim on our lives, were both found within Providence. Reading his detailed expositions he comes across as a person with personal warmth and enthusiasm for other's welfare, rather than someone with intellectual curiosity. Genuine freedom, Haweis believed, was possible when self sufficiency was questioned. 'So far as we can, let us forget ourselves' was his guiding precept. 'We are God's, so let His wisdom inform and guide our lives,in order that we may be recreated (born again)'.

Haweis revealed his indebtedness to Calvin and the Reformed tradition with regard to civil government. Christians were to endure patiently the rulers set over them, because God could possibly be working through them. However civil disobedience was obligatory if tyrannical leaders, or degrading social systems rejected Christian standards. His observation that God could be found at work in the customs and behaviour of other races was a novel insight for someone of his generation. God would make Himself known in new ways, not being bound by ancient truths. 'The Lord has yet more truth to break forth from his word' was a Puritan watchword. This cursory glance at Reformed Church thinking throws some light on the attitudes and actions of the early missionaries as they embarked on a world-wide adventure.

Haweis moved easily among a burgeoning British meritocracy. This group had begun to create unease among the aristocratic land owning class. Newcomers were making big money as merchants, bankers, and industrialists. Soon they were joined by botanists and astronomers interested in undiscovered wealth in the South Pacific. Being a friend of Banks, Haweis was particularly interested to hear about his voyages with Captain Cook, to gather exotic plants, some of which found a new home in London's Kew Gardens. Shortly before Countess Salena's death, Haweis persuaded her to fund a mission to what seemed to be captivating islands. Two missionaries were to travel with Captain Bligh, but the project collapsed in 1791, after Bishop Porteous of London refused to ordain them. Three years later Haweis was writing articles in The Evangelical Magazine, printed in London, intended to prepare the way for the foundation of a society for overseas mission.

Dr. David Bogue, who had been a guest Seminary lecturer in France, Germany and New England, began in 1780 to direct the studies of men preparing for the Independent (Congregational) Ministry. Subsequently he became the Principal of Gosport Academy. (Before 1871 a university education was restricted to men willing to conform to the beliefs of the Established Church). Bogue and Haweis held contrasting views about ministerial training. Bogue agreed with the free enquiry encouraged at the Independent Northampton Academy. One of the students of that Academy, Joseph Priestley, the discoverer of oxygen, pursued scientific interests along with theology. All sides of a question were examined with the aim, it was said by Northampton's Principal, Philip Doddridge (1702-51), 'to arm against that zeal which is not according to knowledge'. Several Independent Academies such as Gosport and Northampton softened the unyielding metal of Calvinism. Boswell said that Homerton Academy had a tutor who was Samuel Johnson's anvil. Their encounters on the subject of predestination and human freedom made the sparks fly.

In Dr. Bogue's Independent Academy at Gosport the curriculum included linguistics, history, biblical studies, writing and publishing books. Legal guidance on the setting up of Civil Government in foreign lands was a subject introduced later. Encouraged by Bogue to maintain a lifelong discipline of study, 115 of his students became Christian missionaries in India, China and the Pacific Islands. One of Bogue's students Robert Morrison (1782-1835), first studied medicine and astronomy, and later in China became proficient in both Mandarin and Cantonese dialects. He translated the whole Bible into Chinese and laid the foundation for educational and medical work in China based on European methods. Aaron Buzzacott (18001864) of Takamoa College in the Cook Islands, also studied under Bogue, and used lecture notes to prepare Polynesian teachers for missionary service in Oceania.

Academies recognised that Britain's growing commercial interest in overseas markets presented an opportunity for Christians to use their trade routes and bases in the service of world wide missionary enterprise. The Reverend-John Eyre M. A., an evangelical Anglican, who was the first Principal of Hackney, a non-denominational Academy, was also deeply involved in the Society's inauguration in 1795. Eyre's portrait in the dining hall at New College, London reminded students like myself, that the college grew out of an amalgamation of several Academies, including Hackney, Homerton, Cambridge and the one at Gosport, with Bogue as its Principal. Mainstream Anglicans, uneasy about a fresh outbreak of divisive Puritan extremism, similar to that which occurred in the English Civil War (1642-1649), dismissed overseas mission as the misguided enthusiasm of people 'in trade'.

Haweis, Bogue and Eyre were aware that there was seething discontent among the labouring class in Britain as the 18th century drew to an end. Violent Bread Riots threatened the nation's stability as the possibility of war with France increased. Numerous Acts of Enclosure by Parliament caused the eviction of hordes of workers from the land. In this uncertain economic climate,some artisans looking for work were willing to accept an unpredictable future. A small group came forward for missionary work overseas. At the same time manufacturers of the 'middling sort' were looking for new markets as the nation's industrial and economic strength expanded. Influential commercial interests were therefore sympathetic to a missionary movement grounded in the Protestant Work ethic.

Sharing a common interest in the development of closer links with the South Pacific Haweis, Bogue and Sir Joseph Banks saw that the time was right for action in Tahiti. Ports of call such as Papaete in Tahiti met the need for 'Refreshment'. This was an expression which described the onshore activities of seafarers restricted by many months spent on long voyages. Refreshment meant the chance to indulge in heavy drinking, to visit women for sexual pleasure, said to be freely available. It was also true that for others an opportunity was given to observe Tahitian etiquette, to experience warm hospitality, and observe unusual customs whilst enjoying healthy fresh food. The harsh reality of the South Seas was the increase in the number of desertions from whaling ships and sealers in the 18th Century. The introduction of guns and gunpowder, of sexual diseases, together with the so-called childhood sicknesses of measles, mumps and jaundice caused great distress. Large numbers of Pacific Islanders died as a consequence of the White Man's fatal impact. Trading taking place in firearms, liquor, and knives was responsible for increasing lawlessness.

These debilitating conditions increased a sense of urgency among those in England who linked business opportunities with restraining evil, and building societies based on Christian values. Haweis, the driving force among the Directors of the nascent missionary society,was persuaded that the climate and settled life of Polynesia promised success for clean and healthy living. The simplicity of the language, when compared with the languages of India and China, was an added attraction. Absence of nation-wide organised governments to throw out the missionaries before they could settle, was another important advantage. As a result of these considerations the Board of Directors readily accepted the view of Haweis, that Tahiti, one of the Society Islands should become the centre for evangelism in the South Pacific.

Advice was sought from Banks and Bligh for someone with nautical skills to lead the expedition. Captain James Wilson was suggested. Son of a ship's navigator in Newcastle, born in 1760, he had served as mate, later master of a ship, protecting English soldiers against the American colonists at Bunker Hill, near Boston, in 1775. Later, when seconded to the East India Company as a ship's Master, he was in the thick of hostilities with the French in colonial wars, was imprisoned several times by Indian rulers in fortresses similar to the notorious Black Hole of Calcutta, but escaped each time. Returning to England in his mid forties as a merchant, he retired in financial comfort to live in the home of his niece, who was an ardent Calvinist. His adventurous life caught the popular mood for romantic stories about distant lands, serialised in magazines for the upwardly mobile middle classes.

Wilson caused a stir when he turned his back on his previously held belief that using reason alone led to belief in a Supreme Being. Having been dismissive of faith and organised religion, he suddenly became a 'born again' Calvinistic Methodist. Haweis accepted Wilson's dramatic conversion, and saw him as 'God's Man', uniquely qualified to be a 'Captain Courageous' engaged in a missionary enterprise. Wilson offered his services without payment to captain the missionary vessel, and to bring proposals for the purchase of a suitable boat. It was later agreed that the return voyage would include China and the East Indies, presenting the captain with an opportunity to bring back to England a lucrative consignment of tea.

Wilson supervised the procurement of a river built, copper bottomed ship named 'The Duff', built two years earlier. 'Duyfhen' is a Dutch word meaning 'little dove' and subsequently 'The Messenger of Peace',(referring to The Flood described in Genesis), became a distinctive symbol of the London Missionary Society. The ship weighed three hundred tons, and cost £5,650. Wilson also took responsibility for appointing three principle officers, a surgeon, a gunner, carpenter,a sail-maker and fifteen deckhands. The selection of missionaries was guided by the forceful opinion of Dr. Haweis, who maintained that skilled manual workers of firm Christian conviction, living upright moral lives whilst accepting the Bible as an infallible guide, were to be preferred to educated men. The view of Haweis and his supporters that 'Change of heart' rather than the 'intellectual rigour' of Bogue and his supporters became the majority view in the selection of the first missionary candidates. (The second batch came mainly from the other wing of the missionary dove.)

Thirty were selected, six of whom were married and had small children. They came from small business enterprises in which tradesmen usually served long apprenticeships such as in printing, weaving, tailoring, leather and ironwork. Henry Nott was a bricklayer/builder, whereas Jefferson had been a teacher and part-time actor before he was ordained. One of the four ministers chosen had been employed as a shopkeeper, and another was a trained mechanic. One had been ordained as a minister of the Countess of Huntington Connection, a church organisation for Anglicans sympathetic to Calvinistic Methodist teaching. This was done at short notice, only twelve months before the mission ship set sail for Tahiti. All of the 'chosen ones' belonged to a social class recognisably lower than the ministers and laymen who were Directors of the Missionary Society. Captain Wilson expressed 'mock' surprise that none of the prominent ministers in London had come forward as recruits.

After contributing £500 to the enterprise, Thomas Haweis preached the opening sermon marking the foundation of the Missionary Society on September 21 st 1795. The event was attended by two hundred clergy, including Anglicans, Congregationalists, Methodists and Presbyterians. The preacher referred to the Solomon Islands and the New Hebrides where 'savage nature still feeds on the flesh of its prisoners, and appeases its gods with human sacrifices'. In the florid language of an 18th Century preacher, he made it clear that a rescue mission of heroic proportions was required to save the Islanders from such horrors.

The Duff

Searching for a source of inspiration to face great danger, Haweis wrote about the courage shown by outstanding Christians throughout history. The anthology included forty pages of adulation surrounding the life of Captain Wilson before his conversion, named by Haweis as 'God's Man' for the. Pacific enterprise. It seemed excessive praise. Strange too that attention was drawn to the privations endured by Wilson due to his status as a gentleman. Imprisoned in India he had been denied the company of fellow officers, being chained to a common soldier! It is difficult to avoid the suspicion that elitism existed among the Directors of the L.M.S. in their relationship with the worker- missionaries preparing to sail to the other side of the world.

During the weeks between purchasing 'The Duff',and setting sail for Tahiti, Wilson was asked by the Director to convene meetings of the missionary group to decide how to share responsibilities whilst living together in a confined space for seven months. At the same time consideration was given to the form in which they would express their Christian faith, both on board ship, and on arrival in Tahiti. They were opposed to monolithic church organisations, believing that taking that road led inevitably to Rome and nominal Christianity. Confederations of the soundly converted were preferred.

Differences emerged about the heart of the gospel to be preached, and two of the group were excommunicated. Reverend John Jefferson and William P Crook believed that personal choice was needed in the acceptance of God's election for service, whilst the majority view was that if God wanted someone for a chosen task,it happened. 'Man proposes, God disposes'. A recent convert to undiluted Calvinism, and upholder of the majority view, Captain Wilson had immediate access to the Directors. He was supported by the Board of Directions in the action taken, and Wilson's authority was strengthened. One result was a letter written by Haweis to all the missionaries on behalf of the Board of Directors. It recommended that a council of four, including Captain Wilson and the ship's surgeon, was to act as a surrogate Board Meeting.

Social demarcation lines drawn up for the missionaries by elitist Directors caused disquiet among Congregational Church supporters of the overseas venture, particularly among those educated in Academies connected with Independent churches. A former student of Dr. Bogue at Gosport Academy was John Angel James (1785-1859),an influential supporter of the London Missionary Society for twenty five years. For 20 years he was the minister at Carrs Lane Church, Birmingham, otherwise known as England's

'Congregational Cathedral'. James wrote 'Directors regard missionaries as menial servants governed at their sovereign pleasure'. Others said that Captain Wilson had a disposition similar to that of Bligh of the Bounty, 'whose interpersonal ineptitude undermined his undoubted nautical skill, flair and courage'.

18th century Mission Society documents and correspondence reveal disputes that cause the reader to marvel that sufficient agreement could be reached to create an overseas missionary organisation. Providence ? Humanly speaking there must have been enormous goodwill present in gatherings, which never found a way into the written minutes. A mixture of motives, attitudes and expectations was at the heart of the creative tension that brought about the inauguration of The Missionary Society, later known as The London Missionary Society. Was London's growing financial and business acumen in a potentially global economy responsible for the change of name?

Supporters of missionary enterprise were convinced that skilled manual workers would demonstrate to South Pacific people the material advantages of a Christian civilisation. It was thought that in the unsophisticated environment of Tahiti, a largely artisan commune, sustained by the ministry of four ordained ministers,would make a considerable impact. Haweis, Sir Joseph Banks, and Captain Bligh, had different reasons for seeing the possible benefits of closer ties between Britain and Tahiti. A base in the Pacific raised the possibility of a centre for evangelistic,commercial and scientific outreach. Made secure, these interests might stretch out like the tentacles of an octopus to include other island communities.

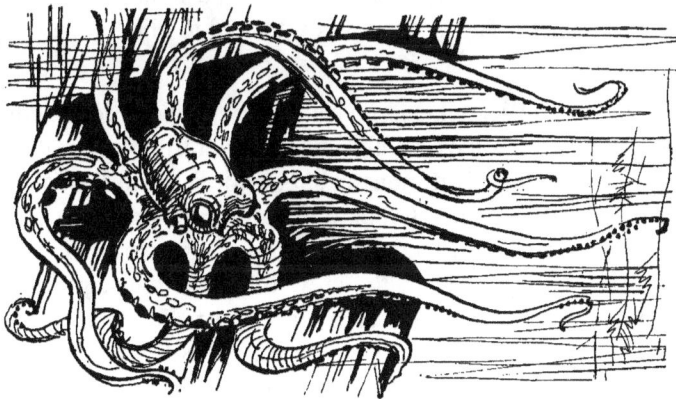

Chapter Four

Fourth Wave - Rough diamonds

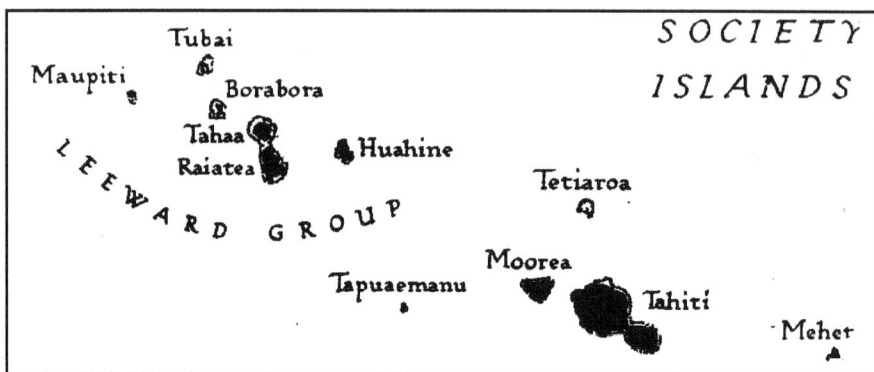

After seven months at sea, 'The Duff' arrived off the island of Tahiti in the Society Islands in March 1797. Captain Wilson, the recognised leader of the enterprise,was honoured as such by Tahitian high chiefs. One of them, Mane Marie from the nearby island of Mo'orea, welcomed Wilson effusively. As an esteemed navigator, he was compared to a high chief. Later gifts were exchanged with the Captain at dinner on board the Missionary Ship. Young women wearing garments made from several layers of tapa cloth, removed and presented them one by one to the honoured guests until they were left naked. Often misunderstood by sailors and other visitors as an invitation to sexual relationships, the individual gifts of tapa indicated a village chief's welcome and respect. The gesture was intended to elicit a material response from the guests.

John Davies, Henry Bicknel, John Eyre, Henry Nott and John Jefferson, their wives and children settled in Tahiti,whist others moved on to the nearby island of Mo'orea. The Duff then set sail, with William Pascoe and another unmarried missionary named Crook on board in the direction of the isolated Marquesas Islands, the last land-fall for ships sailing to Peru, 4,000 miles to the east. Nearly one year later, the crew of a ship registered in New York, named Betsy, was attempting to catch seals near to Tahuata in the Marquesas group. They were surprised to see two white men rowing out towards their ship. Coming alongside they begged to be taken aboard..

Single, and therefore without chiefly status, the two men had been subject

24

to constant sexual harassment from unmarried women, who claimed that marital union would enable the strangers to be accepted into the local social system. The missionaries were unwilling to accept sexual favours in order to be accepted into a social system, about which they had much to learn. Their decision brought hostility and isolation. The experiment of involving unmarried men in similar situations was not repeated.

Back on the islands of Mo'orea, and nearby Tahiti, (the artisan missionary's first port of call), the following years were heavy with disappointment, as well as tragedy. The islanders regarded them with a mixture of curiosity, suspicion and indifference. Trying to understand local customs and cultural norms, such as staying within the clearly defined limits for each level in social hierarchy, led to friction. In daily life the difference between borrowing and stealing goods was unclear. Bargaining involved methods foreign to those involved, and consequently were fraught with dangerous misunderstanding. The apparent freedom with which the Polynesians shared one another's belongings did not mean that they were simply held in common. For example there were definite privileges associated with particular tools, and rights over their use, that were confined to certain individuals with the necessary skills. Borrowing between kinsmen was allowed and such loans could not be refused, but the article or equivalent had to be returned. If a gift was made, it was matched by a counter gift. Reciprocation was a fine art in a closely knit community.

A few pioneers separated themselves from those who had been their companions on 'The Duff', and went to live with native mistresses. Three of them met horrible deaths through beatings and mutilation. Mercy was not shown in frequent tribal squabbles, and the use of firearms that were inaccurate,cumbersome and unreliable in damp weather added to everyday hazards for anyone caught in crossfire. After brutal encounters, five of the missionaries shrank from all contact with the islanders, and eventually escaped on passing vessels to Australia to begin a new life. The territory's Governor Phillips said that they became the first 'respectable settlers' of Parramatta, Sydney. Stories of narrow escapes, starvation, murder and infanticide in the South Seas circulated in the colony, and eventually reached Britain. They satisfied a need of the reading public for colourful adventure stories from all corners of an expanding Empire.

It was a different story for the pioneers who were prepared to tough it out. They tried to make sense of different social customs and unpredictable behaviour. They came to see that in general terms Tahitian society was divided into three castes. Firstly, there was the nobility (ari' i or ali'i) chiefs, and paramount chiefs (rahi ari i), who were selected for high office from old noble families. Secondly,there were the craftsmen, boat and house builders, innovators, navigators and artists /tattoo experts who made a recognisable grouping. Thirdly, the labourers were those who provided the muscle in any enterprise, be it warfare, tending plants or gathering crops, and fishing. Twenty years were to pass before the original voyagers on the Duff from England, living in Mission Stations, began to sense that toleration among the few had moved on to formal acceptance by the majority.

A separate enclosed community,the Arioi, were the guardians of traditions and rituals designed to ensure social stability, and to secure economic wealth. The Polynesian calendar recognised propitious and unfavourable days. Their religious rites included dramatic performances,dance, singing, poetic sagas, designed to maintain social cohesion in the face of a bewildering array of supernatural forces, some disruptive and others protective. Able to change guise according to the needs of the moment,(swimming as a shark before becoming a howl in the tree tops), particular 'aitu', or spirits, needed to be placated when crops failed. Tribal groups had their own particular aitu said to inhabit a tree, fish, reptile or animal, a belief which served to emphasise the inter-connectedness of all creation, and its sacral nature.

The Guardians(Arioi) were priests,judges,magicians,healers,bards,seers and diplomats-all rolled into one. Down to earth tasks included the control of the production of food through systems of irrigation taming the mountain torrents. The supervision of seasonal planting and pruning of fruit bearing trees, or producing timber for building work, were under their jurisdiction. Despite the efforts made by the Guardians, working together with the nobility, to maintain harmony between the constituent parts of Polynesian society, the environment in which local people lived their everyday lives was a capricious one. Different deities gained or lost their position in the divine Premier League, due to the success or failure of their supporters in securing a good harvest, or success in battle. Tension grew between social hierarchies as they sought to maintain or extend their power.

These were serious concerns,but they did not overcome the natural exuberance of Polynesians, who wanted to express themselves through distinctive art, sculpture and tattoo. Travelling minstrels, strolling players, dancers and jesters provided a cultural wealth that flowed through the veins of successive generations. Rhyming couplets performed in village or larger assemblies were spontaneously invented to be applauded by others present, who were expected to make an immediate response. Chanted back and forth, spun like a spider's web these word games were delivered in a competitive, playful spirit. Some legends took the form of a mimed dance whereas other narratives were delivered as a recited poem, all of which were presented to the sound of stringed instruments and drum. When the young men danced, attention of onlookers was drawn to knee and ankle joints moving in unison, inwards then outwards,followed by great leaps. In the case of female dancers it was the graceful hip movement synchronised to work with snake-like gyrations of both of her hands and arms, that gave pleasure to spectators.

Heart rending laments such as the Auega (Lamentation) of Sanalala, and royal songs (fa'aali'i) accompanied by the sharp shrill sound of a wooden instrument of the same name, displayed another artistic talent of Old Polynesia. It was a harmonious yet contradictory world, in which cultural diversity existed alongside the horror of infanticide as a form of birth control. Human sacrifice was thought to appease the gods who were expected to bring deliverance when economic disaster threatened. It was a world where grace and beauty in dance co-existed with the hula dance. This obscene equivalent to pole dancing was performed in response to the lustful cries of sailors on shore leave who asked for the Hivinau, meaning 'heave now'.

Roughly thirty years before the arrival of the missionaries in 1797, Polynesian religious beliefs had begun to be focused on a single all powerful deity who came to dominate the lives of the people of Tahiti, and the entire archipelago. In a domain accustomed to being torn apart by power seeking factions.'Oro' was seen as a warrior god (atua),who overwhelmed all comers, whose influence grew quickly as devotion to three previously powerful divinities declined. His sanctuaries, or Marai, placed in dominant positions were built to house 'Oro's threat. Built with geometrical precision these sanctuaries were constructed in a similar shape to a pyramid. The 'platforms' built on top of each other served to demonstrate the social cohesion brought about by rival tribes (levels) submitting to Oro's superior power.

Tahitians believed that Mana,or immanent spiritual energy,was concentrated in certain objects or chiefs, which was given to them by 'atua' (gods). Birds were thought to be intermediaries between gods and men, so that their feathers were frequently used in wrappings for sacred objects and people. Tapa cloth, material made from the compressed bark of the mulberry tree, was decorated with artistic patterns designed to neutralise the highly charged spiritual power surrounding a person, or a feathered wooden carving regarded as set apart (tapu). Rituals performed by an assigned elite person were designed to placate or satisfy what was 'holy' and untouchable, so that everybody else could get on with their lives.

Gradually the wrappings absorbed some of the Oro's mana, and became sacred in themselves, in the same way as the Shroud of Turin and other Christian relics are believed by some to possess sanctity. Beneath the protecting cover, the venerated object was studded with pearl shell reflecting the friendly light and vitality of the sea. The weaving of vegetable fibres to create fine matting was edged with blood-red feathers of the Tolai ula bird, (presently an endangered species), suggesting an image of Nafanua, the awesome goddess of war, who was found throughout Polynesia. The same aura of sanctity surrounded the 'Oro-maro'ura' (The red girdle of the warrior), which was a feather waistband, five yards long and fifteen inches broad, seen during a visit to Tahiti by Captain Cook in 1777. During the following years registering the rise of the cult of Oro, both the red or yellow girdle were symbols of supremacy worn only by paramount chiefs.

For more than thirty years battles were fought over the possession of Oro's waistbands,ordinary articles of clothing impregnated with highly charged sanctity. Victorious in battle a paramount chief,Tu (1779-1821),otherwise known as Pomare 1, and tribal chiefs allied through marriage, extended their group's power base. Rituals, including human sacrifice,directed towards 'Oro, could not go ahead until Pomare 1, Oro's earthly representative, was present. Tu, and next in line, Pomare II, strengthened their hold on supreme power by inheriting two more feather girdles or maro'ura, and other ritual objects. (These were equivalent to Britain's Crown Jewels). Morrison, one of the Bounty mutineers, present at the investiture of Pomare 11, wrote that 'the Royal Sash (maro'ura) worn by one king only, one day only, was later put into the Sacred Box'.

In the year 1800 Pomare I seemed to be secure as Paramount Chief in both sacred and secular spheres. The recently arrived missionaries such as Henry Nott and John Jefferson were not so sure. Increasingly uncertain about the mission's future, they were aware of mounting discontent with Pomare's rule. In their journals of 1800,one wrote 'commotions among the lower class of natives against Pomare I, chiefly on account of his tyrannical conduct in repeatedly plundering them of their little property'. Another entry referred to 'The depredations and wantonness practised by 'Oro's people are said to be among the causes for a desire of a change of government'. Excluded at that time from the circles of political power, and social control surrounding a ruling elite, the missionaries thought that a showdown between Pomare and his rivals was imminent.

Since their arrival in Tahiti the pioneers had experienced living with exclusive social divisions,which they thought they had left behind in England. The manual skills of islanders,with whom they readily identified, and the use they made of local materials provided a common interest. Artisan missionaries could impress skilled local builders regarding the usefulness of metal tools in precision work. Henry Bicknel (1766-1820) an articled wheelwright added another dimension to the Islander's mobility. It was however their ability to procure desirable goods such as iron, knives and axes brought from Sydney, that made them useful associates of ambitious local chiefs. The business instincts of former missionary colleagues, who set up in trade in the Australian penal colony, provided an economic lifeline for the isolated remnant in Tahiti, and a passport into local acceptance.

The lines of communication with the Directors of the Society in London were not working, and a sense of abandonment was experienced by missionaries living on the other side of the world. News from Sydney businessmen revealed that the blocking of sea lanes during the Napoleonic Wars had not prevented commercial interests continuing their operations. They were further disheartened when they heard that the Mission Stations in Tonga,and the Marquesas Islands, had been closed down. In 1803 the pulse of Christian mission in Tahiti was beating faintly. The settlers had left behind them in Britain an inherited class system beginning to crumble slightly at the edges. In Tahiti a highly stratified social system,where rank, and the right to rule was determined by selective breeding,seemed to be as impenetrable as volcanic rock,unyielding to an appeal dependent on individual conversion. It was about this time that Pomare II succeeded his father as a paramount chief.

The recognition of failure called for a change in mission strategy and decisions had to be made without consultation with London. At first Jefferson, Nott, Bicknel, Davies and their families thought that their primary task was to hold on believing that Providence would show them the next step. Following on from that conviction, they knew that Calvin's Institutes affirmed another possible course of action in circumstances similar to their own. 'If a Protestant did not enjoy the benefits of living under a 'godly prince', he had to make the best arrangement he could in unfavourable circumstances'. Brought up in a Calvinist Chapel environment of bread riots, and making the most of limited resources, they already knew the Reformer's words 'by heart'.

Two of the pioneer missionaries had been witnesses to violence as Parliamentary Enclosure Acts drove labourers off the land causing great hardship among rural communities in Britain. Nott, a hardy blacksmith from Bromsgrove, near Birmingham, and his colleague Davies, an unemployed schoolteacher from Pontrobert in mid Wales, knew poverty. Living in Tahiti Nott and Davies experienced deprivations of a different kind through isolation and ignorance of Polynesian culture and social mores. Recognising that the Mission was on its last legs, they decided to give their support to a warrior chief who they thought might, with patient nurturing, become a champion of the Christian cause. Whilst Pomare with the help of Davies, was learning to read and write in the Tahitian language, the Paramount Chief remained ambivalent about his involvement in human sacrifice. He maintained that being present on sacral occasions gave legitimacy to his claim to be royalty. Nott's attitude was that 'beggars could not be choosers', and persevered in a 15 year long effort to get inside the Tahitian Prince's mind and heart to discover grounds for Christian faith .

Warrior

Pioneer missionary journals written between 1800 and 1807 indicate that the losses sustained by Pomare II in local skirmishes cast doubt on his continuing supremacy. In 1804 Pomare was forced by rival warrior groups to leave Tahiti for the island of Mo'orea, Letters written to Nott in the Tahitian language, show that the chief was disillusioned with the ability of the war god Oro to achieve success on his behalf. He wavered in what had been a long allegiance begun by his father. It is also known from Nott's correspondence that Pomare II had by this time received material goods through the missionaries to pursue his war aims. This was in addition to the help received in becoming literate. In 1806 it was obvious that Pomare II and Nott had created an alliance to ensure supremacy for what had been two separate causes.

When Nott and Jefferson accompanied the Tahitian warrior chief into exile on the island of Moorea, they continued to help the chief in his studies, whilst attempting to persuade him to accept Christian teaching about loving one's enemies. He quickly became an accomplished student in book knowledge, but in a warrior culture in which the honour of a tribe was satisfied through acts of revenge, Pomare continued to struggle with the second requirement. 'Taui ma sui'(revenge) was written large in Polynesian genes. Facing this challenge was the first step on a long journey towards baptism fifteen years later. Nott was also engaged in a lengthy learning curve, but in his case it was with regard to Tahitian culture and language.

Through conversations with Pomare, Nott acquired a sound grasp of the intricate patterns of rhetorical oratory used by the Tahitian elite. This was an ideal preparation for the missionary who would later translate Luke's Gospel into the language of aristocrats (reo Tahiti). Pomare also introduced the pioneers to the intricate protocols and courtesies used when approaching men or women of distinction in Tahitian society. While this rarified initiation was taking place, a series of inconclusive wars questioned the missionaries earlier judgement that Pomare II was destined to gain supreme power.

Pomare finally proved to be the victor in the Battle of Feipi in 1816, and became the standard bearer for what had been a precarious missionary cause. Baptised in 1819, his previous savagery in war overlooked, his teachers were heartened by a rejection of revenge, which made possible a peaceful transition to a new dispensation. This did not prevent the destruction of many shrines devoted to 'Oro. The followers of Pomare rampaged through the island removing the possibility of future resistance arising from former enemies. The numerous idols, some of which encouraged worshippers to care and respect the physical environment of Tahiti were obliterated, alongside those intended to instil fear, and sanction violence.

The conversion of tribal chiefs from both sides in the conflict prepared the way for the rank and file to show their allegiance to Pomare, and to what became the national religion. Hundreds of them took part in mass Christian conversion celebrations. Candidates for baptism later formed village congregations with teachers and deacons, who were also men of rank in the social system. Endorsed by a traditional hierarchy, the Lotu Tahiti organisation was to be reproduced throughout the Pacific Islands.

Chief Paofa'i a Manu'a, an early convert, had been one of the leading Arioi, or guardian of tradition. Paofa'i was aware that the new religion could also become the standard bearer of Tahitian language and custom. Together with other Tahitian leaders he was aware of the corrosive effect of the white man's gods of trade and money, and the threat they posed to a cherished Tahitian culture. These leaders became active among the 'praying people'(bura atua) enabling them to grow in numbers to form the Tahitian Missionary Society (Lotu Tahiti) in 1818. The first task of the nascent missionary organisation was to share the new found faith with the chiefs and people of Ra'iatea, Borabora, Uporu and similar sized Society Islands in a geographical area as large as Western Europe. Good tribal, linguistic and sea links allowed the speedy communication of a New Dispensation.

Tahiti and her people, provided the spearhead of the enterprise in its initial stages, that is before the contribution of the island people of Ra'iatea took over in size and importance. As one form of social control broke down, British missionaries helped to create a monarchical system tied to the Pomare family. A new code of morality confirmed respect for chiefs, strengthened family networks, and tribal loyalty. Sunday became a day of legally enforced rest, and land sales were prohibited, unless Pomare and missionary representatives gave their approval. Wood carvings thought to display crude sensuality were destroyed, and some kinds of dancing were forbidden if they were associated with sexual abandonment.

From the outset the strength of the Tahitian Mission owed much to its claim to comprehensiveness. 'Pule lava le Atua', (God rules) had undergirded the belief systems of the Polynesians since ancient times. In the New Dispensation no area of island life was outside God's sovereign rule. Elements of biblical thought entered into the Polynesian bloodstream to confirm and enrich such attitudes. Not only Shakespeare's Hamlet understood 'There's a divinity that shapes our ends. Rough-hew them as we will'. The words capture an attitude found among Polynesian forbears who were great navigators. Later as emissaries of the Christian Faith traversing the Pacific Ocean they were sustained by a similar conviction .

A stern commitment, it was by no means the whole story. Supportive tribal and family ties were confirmed as the Polynesians enjoyed listening to recitals of epic journeys by skilled poets and orators. Singing and restricted dancing, communal feasting at the 'get together' (to'ona'i) meal after worship, such regular happenings expressed the Pacific Islander's way of exuberant bonding. The presentation and receipt of gifts, lively repartee and other welcome features of Tahitian life were always breaking through expressions of Calvinistic Christianity often associated with rigidity.

What more can be said about the first missionaries who arrived on the 'Duff' in 1797? Seen as rough diamonds, they were unprepared by the circumstances of their social background in Britain to 'fit in' with elite structures and formal etiquette. Providence had set them down in a country where everyone knew their place in a long established pecking order, where nonconformity was not an option. Coarse in expressing opinions about sexual behaviour, relaxed about possessing firearms,they were dismissive of those who arrived 20 years later advocating abstinence from alcohol.

The pioneers were a breed on their own. Accustomed to 'working the system' if the opportunity arose, they were said to have turned a blind eye to lechery and drunken behaviour among 'elite' members of Tahitian society. With many mouths to feed the 'matter of fact attitude to infanticide among the islanders shocked the new arrivals. They said that rudimentary medical care provided in missionary homes was an inadequate response. Equally contentious was the missionary newcomer's assertion that the nominal conversion of the warrior chief, later King Pomare II had been accepted too easily.

Greatly reduced in numbers by sickness, death and desertion, the band of missionary stalwarts remained constant in their loyalty to Pomare, and his occasional dissolute behaviour. Fifty years after his arrival on the mission ship,'Duff', the doggedly determined Henry Nott had to swallow a bitter pill. Living in Sydney he heard that the Pomare dynasty had been crushed by the French Navy in 1847. Roman Catholicism replaced the locally grown Tahitian Church. Had a life time's work been in vain? Taking the longer view it was increasingly clear that a sound basis for further expansion had been prepared.

The fourth tidal wave had run its course as the people of Tahiti and the other Society Islands such as Moorea had became more than nominally Christian. Many of her people became ambassadors for their newfound faith in faraway Samoa, Tonga, and the Cook Islands. A combined Polynesian /European missionary campaign was to become the fifth tidal wave. Rough diamonds such as Henry Nott, Pomare, Bicknel and Paofa' made way for others to ride its crest, to be known as the Lotu Tahiti (Tahitian Mission) among many Pacific Island races .

Henry Knott

Chapter Five

Fifth Wave - Book-Eaters

E to matou Metua i te
raira, ia ra a to oe ioa; ia
tae to oe ra hau; ia haapao
hia to oe hinaaro i te fenua
nei, mai te i te rai atoa ra
Ho mai i te i ma'a e au ia
matou i teienei mahana; e
fa'aore mai i ta matou hara,
mai ia matou atoa e faaore
i tei hara ia matou nei; e
eiaha e faarue ia matou
ia roohia noa hia e te ati;
e faaora ra ia matou
te ino . Amene.

The Lord's Prayer

Tahitian Bible

A mutiny led by Fletcher Christian and the crew of the Royal Navy's ship Bounty against Captain Bligh on April 28 1789, followed 5 months of free and easy living in Tahiti. Their sojourn in the tropical sun followed a particularly unpleasant passage from England. Mountainous seas round the southernmost tip of South America had been a severe test for Captain and crew alike. Arriving in Tahiti they had received generous hospitality, including casual sex, alcohol to encourage drunken revelry, and little work to do, all of which gave them an opportunity to enjoy warm sultry days in carefree indolence. It was an unlikely scenario for the creation of the Lord's Prayer written in the Tahitian language.

Captain Bligh wrote 'The women have too great an intercourse with different men but not so among those who are not related to them. If a man finds his wife with a Tahitian outside his tribe, he'll kill him'. As for white whalers and sailors, they were temporary playthings of Island men and women. They provided amusement to fill an idle hour, alongside the pleasure of display involved in bargaining over the relative value of material goods belonging to rival families, or foreigners.

34

Bligh saw beneath the blandishments of Tahitian women and their sexual romps to recognise that the ties and loyalties binding them to other members of their extended family, or clan, were of far greater significance. Inherited land conferred the all important benefit of security,which could be enlarged or reduced through marriage and death. Before the White Man arrived there had been a long period of occupation, during which every hill valley and stream came to be saturated with historical associations. The final resting places of adventurous voyagers and warriors were set apart for regular solemn assemblies,and sacred observance. Memorial stones marked the emergence of clans who were said to possess distinctive gifts of divination. Sites of crucial battles defined boundaries. Details of these were preserved through genealogies and stories. It was the ownership of land jealously safeguarded that mattered to Tahitians rather than the superficial sideshows guaranteed to deceive foreign visitors looking for an easygoing lifestyle after deprivation on long sea voyages.

The same size as the Isle of Wight, Tahiti in the Society group has rugged mountains of three thousand feet,with sharp peaks, deep valleys and precipitous cliffs. Many streams are large enough to be known as rivers, and the soil, especially on the narrow belt of low land round the coast, is fertile. Moving inland away from the luxuriant vegetation near the coastline, large forest trees and a variety of jungle plants grow in rich profusion. In the past six major kinship groups existing alongside each other, or widely scattered throughout the island, created a patchwork of communally held land. What would be a nightmare for a modern surveyor, was etched in minute detail on the memory of the guardians of Tahitian family history.

Each block connected to a major clan was divided into a number of smaller sections, also dispersed in an apparently haphazard manner, one or more of which would be owned by a lesser clan. These smaller portions of land were further split up, and families owning them, handed them on to their descendents. Each family,or larger group had exclusive rights, but these rights were subject in each case to the wider control exercised by the corporate body or clan. The head of the clan,or kinship group, acted as a trustee of the total amount of communal land belonging to the clan. He was accountable to tribal members.

Captain Bligh on what was his second prolonged visit to Tahiti appreciated the complicated nature of kinship groups and land ownership. He had seen Europeans make the mistake of regarding the chief of a clan as the sole owner of land, whose consent alone was needed to purchase or secure occupation. In fact consultation all down the line was necessary. Acting in ignorance meant that visiting seamen and traders often asked for trouble. In April 1789 it was time for the Bounty to leave. The world of British Admiralty orders, and the accountability of Ships Officers required that the South Seas idyll must end. Under duress the crew set sail for England, Bligh failing to anticipate the rebellion created by the contrast between the harsh rules and regulations of life at sea and life in balmy Tahiti.

Bligh and 18 loyal crew members were ordered into the Bounty's 23 foot long launch to begin a hazardous voyage of 3,600 miles to Indonesia,which was followed by a journey on regular transport to England. One of the junior officers prevented from journeying with Bligh was to become a very important contributor to the spread of literacy in the Pacific, the 5th wave of this book. Peter Heywood, a well educated man born into a well-to-do family in England, was restrained below decks by the crew during the mutiny. He spent the next 2 years identifying himself with the Tahitian way of life by learning to speak their language,and undergoing the painful initiation rite of tattooing. In 1791 he was arrested in Tahiti and taken to England by Royal Navy officers to face a Court Marshall. Convicted, and later pardoned by the King, he wrote a book in prison providing the first vocabulary and grammar in the Tahitian language. This book was to be a lifeline for the pioneer missionaries,who landed in Tahiti from the Duff in 1797.

Lewis, one of the pioneers who arrived in 1797 understood wooden letterpress printing but did not live long enough to use his skill. When he announced his intention to marry a Tahitian, he was excommunicated by his missionary colleagues. Two years later he was murdered by his wife's relatives. John Davies continued work on the spelling book,700 copies of which were printed in Australia in 1811. Papetoa'i School founded in 1813 attracted students of all ages requiring Tessier and Davies 'to sit up every night and copy lessons for them'. This led to a request being sent to London for a press and printing materials.

An increasing number of Islanders saw the advantages of entering the wider world represented by the missionaries. Written material was a curiosity, and possessing a book symbolised belonging to the New World. The School produced many literate Islanders from an archipelago that included Tahiti, who besides receiving a basic education, learned a variety of skills involved in printing. The wave of literacy swept all before it.

Before the arrival of the written word, Polynesians relied on oral tradition.

Events in history were not incised on clay tablets nor written in ink on scrolls. Nothing lasted in the hot humid climate of Pacific islands. Carefully structured timber dwellings and palatial meeting houses returned to dust, decorative cloth and basketry disintegrated, carefully worked murals lost colour and delicacy, artistic patterns were erased by time, shell ornaments lost to stormy weather. In their place were the memorised details of epic voyages and gradual settlement in far flung island groups. Memory banks including the 200 names for stars and constellations, essential knowledge for ancient mariners,were replaced by printer's ink. The wisdom of the past became distilled in the spoken word, especially in proverbs

As they sat down with European missionaries to translate stories from the Old Testament, the Tahitians recognised a familiar pattern in the recollected history of events that had taken place in Asia and the Near East. The myths of creation, together with journeys into the unknown recounted in Genesis carried echoes of ancient Polynesian poems. The interest of Judges and Joshua in land and genealogy, the laws of the Covenant in Leviticus and Deuteronomy echoed their experience of Polynesian codes of behaviour. Pacific Islanders felt that they were entering familiar territory. They read about successful war leaders who were regarded as agents of their gods, and were given semi-divine status. Reading about Hebrew leaders such as David being anointed by God, the Tahitian readers felt 'at home' with Old Testament characters who had been set apart in the same way as their own chiefs.

Several British missionaries in the contingent who arrived in Tahiti in 1817, had received both a classical and theological education at Gosport Academy. Courses in 'Writing and Publishing Books' and 'Civil Government' had been included in their studies. Despite the critical attitude of the newly - arrived towards Henry Nott, he finished in that year, a translation of the Gospel of Luke in the royal Tahitian language, revealed to him by Pomare. Nott went on to complete the entire Bible in 1835, by which time Polynesian readers had become ardent 'Kai Parau' (Book Eaters). This was the name given to them by fellow Islanders as if to declare that they had become a separate tribe. Their discovery of reading labelled them 'People who were captivated by the new order of things'. Translating, composing type, sewing sheets, curing skins or beating tapa for covers, using plant juices to make glue, organising transport, Islanders and Europeans worked together at every stage of the printing process

William Ellis, one of the 1817 contingent had an extensive knowledge of printing and bookbinding,and brought with him the necessary equipment and supplies to begin work. He supervised Pomare's interest in the printed word and prompted the king as he composed the letters in the right order,including the insertion of spacers, in the production of a small spelling book. It was painstaking work, because one loose bit of type would cause the composition to fall out of the composing stick,requiring every piece to be put together again. Pomare inked the type, pulled the handle and lifted the first sheet from the press, all within the space of 20 days. Ellis wrote that 'Pomare rendered very important aid to the missionaries in the translation of the scriptures, and copied out many portions before they were printed. I rate printing fourth in Pomare's remarkable acts – after abolishing idolatry, showing clemency after his final victorious battle, and visiting and corresponding with leaders throughout the archipelago in an attempt to convert them to Christianity'.

With Edward Threlkeld, a companion on voyage from England and fellow student at Gosport Academy, Ellis helped to document the encounter between evangelical Protestantism and Tahitian culture. Ellis possessed an intellectual curiosity, shown by a love of horticulture and ethnology, which made him an invaluable guide to colonial administrators trying to evaluate the impact made by the British Empire on other cultures. He wrote several text books in Tahitian, and a standard book on Old Tahiti, its customs and traditions before returning to England to became a Government advisor, and later a diplomat in Madagascar.

Ellis was an outstanding example of the upward mobility of men of humble origins in the Victorian Era as they served some of the nobler aims of the British Empire. Among such a talented group in Tahiti, disagreements arose about an agreed spelling, of sharing expertise and equipment. Despite several 'fall outs' and breakdowns in communication, an irreversible chain of events ensured that oral tradition began to give way to literacy. Islanders became a 'People of the Book'.

John Williams and Lancelot Threlkeld who were included in the second Missionary Society contingent from London, were appointed to accompany converts loyal to Pomare on a mission to the Polynesian heartland on the island of Raiatea. Following the conversion of High Chief Tamatoa, a steady growth of the Tahitian Missionary Society took place in Ra'iatua, and a Code of Conduct was drawn up on similar lines to the one in Tahiti. Pepehia was a student of Williams, and together they sailed a distance of 350 miles to Aitutaki, where Pepehia encouraged the first of the Cook Islands to become

Christian. After a brief, near fatal visit to Mangaia in the same group, Pepehia moved to nearby Raratonga, where he was joined by a fellow Tahitian,who became a teacher and pastor throughout the Cook Islands.

John Williams had been apprenticed as an ironmonger in London. Highly desirable 4 sided 'rosebud' nails or hinges were the ironmongers stock in trade but the sturdy housing of a printing press also needed their specialist skills. The wide-ranging abilities of Williams included accountancy and a practical ability to build sturdy sea-going vessels with limited resources. Converted at the age of eighteen, he sailed for Tahiti aged twenty to be responsible for training Tahitians as fellow missionaries. Young himself, he prepared Island fellow workers to be self sufficient exponents of a demanding faith. Provided with a sea-going vessel,by courtesy of High Chief Tama-toa of Ra'iatua, it just about survived one journey. During a brief sojourn in the Cook Islands, Williams helped to form a working group of Islanders, who built in three months, a sixty-foot brigantine named 'The Messenger of Peace'. Williams wrote in his journal of 1830, that they used corroded, cast-off anchor chain, wooden bellows and a stone forge, and native timber. Rats caused delays by eating the tallow used in making the bellows.

Lotu Tahiti Printing Press

Restless to be at sea again, Williams and a team of eight Tahitian and Cook Island teachers sailed on the Mission Ship to Tonga. He described in his journal the method of navigation used by his Polynesian companions. Williams commented on the apparent waywardness of their initial projections regarding direction, which were at variance with those of his own. The Islanders proved however to be unerringly accurate arriving at the intended destination,and on time. Impressed by their navigation Williams observed that 'Polynesians must be allowed to communicate in their own way'. He questioned a 'pot plant' view of European Christianity that was to be transplanted in Oceania. The wider application of this attitude was heeded by some early missionaries such as Hardie, Stair, and Samuel Wilson, son of Charles who voyaged on 'The Duff', but not accepted by other colleagues.

In Tonga, Williams met a Samoan chief named Fau'ea, who had fled from his native Savai'i because his life had been threatened by a paramount chief named Tamafaiga, said to be 'a bloodthirsty savage'. Fau'ea, had become a Christian after he had heard the message of several Tahitian missionaries, who had arrival in Tonga in 1823. He wanted to accompany Williams and the Tahitians on a voyage to Samoa to introduce the people of Savai'i to the Christian faith.

When a crowd of Samoan canoes came out to greet the ship with Fau'ea on board as it was anchored outside the village of Sapapali'i, the exile hoped to be told that the dreaded Tamafaiga was dead. As his death had happened only a few days before, a successor had yet to be appointed. The resulting power vacuum provided a golden opportunity for those entrusted with promoting the Lotu Tahiti. John Williams and company took it thankfully. Later in the 19th century the Samoan Islands experienced seventeen major wars as paramount district chiefs formed alliances to outwit each other in a struggle for supremacy. During a later visit to the small island of Manono nearby, Williams found that the people had kept a record of these internecine wars by means of stone memorial mounds. He counted 192.

When in 1830 Malietoa Vai'inupo, the victorious Samoan paramount chief returned to his stronghold at Sapapali'i, he discovered that the arrival of the missionary ship, appropriately named 'The Messenger of Peace', had coincided with his victory over Tamafaiga. As a result Malietoa expressed a willingness to give attention to the stranger's message ,especially when he saw that the Samoan companion of Williams, Chief Fau'ea, had been his ally until forced to leave his native land. Following the victors acceptance of the bearer of Good News, which confirmed his good fortune in warfare, the mass conversion of his people to the Christian Faith began in 1830.

Looking across the strait towards the island of Upolu ,Williams wrote later that 'he saw the mountains enveloped in flames and smoke. On enquiring the cause, he was told that a battle had been fought that very morning, and that the flames he saw were consuming the houses, the plantations and the bodies of women, children and infirm people, who had fallen into the hands of the conquerors'. After Williams had received assurances from the paramount chief, Malietoa, that the Tahitian teachers would be accepted and supported, he sailed back to the Cook Islands.

Attempting to evaluate the growth of the Tahitian Mission, there are clues to their success in the 'on the spot' appraisal of local political realities, next a broad strategy of involving Pacific Islanders, and thirdly a focus on island groups where early indicators suggested that a power vacuum was waiting to be filled. The hierarchical structure of Directors in London who provided oversight for workers at the cutting edge of overseas mission, was the pattern followed by the equivalent Tahitian organisation (Lotu Tahiti). Initially a few European missionaries were the overseers and the bulk of the spade work was done by Islanders including Samoans. They in turn recognised different levels of chieftainship within the Worker Missionaries (Aufaigaluega) organisation. The effective organising of both human and material resources goes a long way to explain the steady expansion of the 'Lotu Tahiti'. The printed and spoken word complemented each other.

Pragmatism with regard to organisation was matched by an open-ness to the possibility of a surprise beyond the next reef. Missionaries trained as commercial entrepreneurs understood that unpredictable benefits could come to those who were prepared to take a chance, and push the boat out. (Williams set up a sugar mill or some form of trade, in the islands he visited). Polynesian missionaries also showed the same opportunism, as was shown in the meeting between the exiled Chief Fau'ea and Williams in Tonga.

Another example of an adventurous spirit producing unexpected results was a sea journey in the 1820's, when a small flotilla of Tahitian canoes set out towards the Marquesas Islands. A sudden storm blew them off course, and three months later the survivors landed on the island of Ta'u, Samoa, a distance of nearly 400 miles to the east. Among them was a Christian named Hura, a follower of Pomare II, the converted paramount chief of Tahiti, who salvaged a recently translated part of a Tahitian Bible from the wreck. Recovering from his experience, Hura began to share his knowledge with the people of Ta'u. A 'Book Eater', speaking a variant of their own language, would have had a captive audience. Following such fortuitous events it wasn't long before the speeches of most Samoan orators depended on the use of a biblical proverb to express a welcome to visitors. 'The hope arrived is a tree of life' (Proverbs 13:12).There is no end to the benefits lying in wait for a daring spirit.

Williams returned to Samoa in 1832, and called first at Ta 'u, in Manu'a. He was astonished to meet Hura, now an established teacher using the treasured section of the Tahitian Bible retrieved from his shipwrecked boat 10 years earlier. When Williams moved on to Tutuila, the 'Messenger of Peace' cautiously entered Leone Bay. Those on board were aware that A'asu was nearby where the massacre of the French explorers under La Perouse had taken place in 1787. Williams was relieved when a chief of Leone, the Amoamo, came alongside to assure the voyagers that they were in safe hands. He went on to explain that the Tahitian teachers left at Sapapali'i, Savai'i by Viliamu in 1830, had taught Leone villagers about the Christian Faith in the intervening two years (Map of Samoan Islands p64). Williams then identified himself as Viliamu.

The apparent 'hit or miss' element in the history of the Tahitian Mission was vividly brought home to me when I regularly passed a mangrove swamp near the village of Leone. It was full of rotting coconuts, which happened to come ashore in a waterlogged area. Nearby, coconuts had taken root in sand deficient in nutrients which nevertheless grew into tall productive trees. Having overcome saturation hazards and barren landfalls, they provided health giving food and drink. Given time to take root and grow, the coconut is a survival kit for stranded humans. It provides sturdy poles for house building, fronds to be plaited into mats, screens and baskets. The husks provide the material to be made into string, rope and fire-lighting tinder.

A proverbial expression of the Samoans people refers to the falling of a ripe coconut from a tree, taking root and growing. 'O le pa' u a le popo uli' refers to a person who never gives up despite being unsuccessful on many previous occasions. The growth and spread of the Lotu Tahiti in the Pacific in the 19th Century depended on careful calculation, taking chances, but above all on perseverance. For Islanders and Calvinistic missionaries alike, a belief in the Providence of God provided the confidence to launch out into the deep.

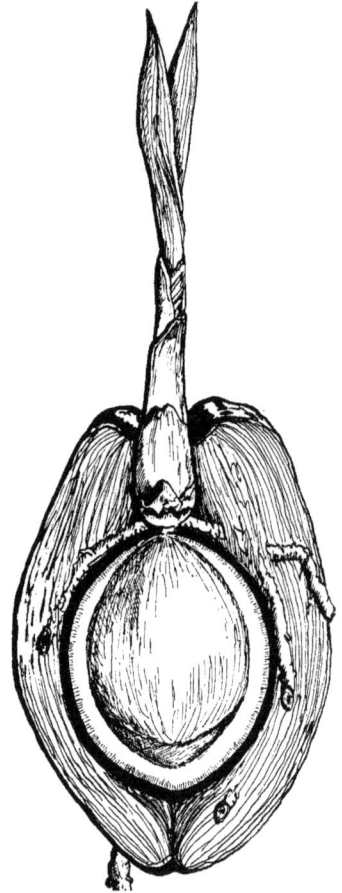

Cross-section of germinated seed nut

Chapter Six:

Sixth Wave - Do or die

Rainforest above Poloa village, Tutuila Island

Archie Murray was one in a group of five Scottish L. M. S. Missionaries who boarded the Dunottar Castle, that set sail from Tilbury Docks, London in November 1836. The sailing ship arrived in Fagasa Bay on the island of Tutuila, E. Samoa in June 1836 when Murray said goodbye to his colleagues before they continued their journeys to other islands. Murray was about to begin a lifetime of service, which ended in his burial in Samoa 35 years later. The dry bones of such men testified to their commitment. His first action after planting his feet on the soil of his new homeland was to seek out the High Chief of the district, who was named Maunga (mountain). Murray set off immediately on the mountain track through the rainforest towards Pago Pago Bay, a natural harbour formed by the rim of a submerged volcano, long extinct.

The trail across the mountain zigzags up to a height of a thousand feet before descending by a circuitous route to the head of the bay where Murray was told that Maunga was already a Christian. The High Chief's son Pomare, named after the Tahitian king, had learned a little English from a white man named Salemi (Salem), a former sailor on a whaling ship from Massachusetts. Pomare volunteered to accompany Murray and act as his interpreter. Soon afterwards Murray set off in a westerly direction along the coastal path towards the village of Leone. There he met Teava, a teacher born in the Cook Islands in 1807, who was able to brief him on the situation facing the mission in the coastal villages of both Upolu and Tutuila.

Stationed on the neighbouring island of Upolu, Teava had journeyed many times in his paopao (outrigger canoe), along that island's northern shoreline from near Apia to Fanuatapu in Aleipata. This was followed by an open sea voyage of 40 miles to Amanave, before crossing Fagalele Bay to Leone, on the island of Tutuila, Teava regularly covered this trip of a hundred miles or more. Living on the headland overlooking Leone village, I often admired the view looking towards Amanave, and marvelled at the fortitude of those early stalwarts, Teava and Archie Murray (Map p64).

In the years from 1836-1839 Murray encouraged revivalist gatherings in Pagopago.'The awakening' had sensational results at the time, but eventually subsided with disappointing long term results. A fellow Scottish Presbyterian named Lundie recorded that High Chief Maunga appeared to be regularly 'possessed by the spirit', and on one occasion was carried out unconscious from a highly charged gathering. Murray's intention was to challenge converts to remain ardent in their Christian allegiance. Outward conformity was not enough in his reckoning. Re-creating the situation of Samoan wrongdoers called to account for their misdemeanours in a village environment, he reminded them that punishment was to be expected. In the heightened emotional atmosphere of a evangelistic rally, release instead of punishment was on offer.

Deliverance was often greeted with the release of excessive pent -up emotion, similar to the screams and crying associated nowadays with the response of crowds at a 'Pop Concert' or 'Rave'. A comparable situation arose in 'Old Samoa' when a Samoan chief's marriage took place. Social controls were lifted temporarily, and sexual activity would often take over as groups from a bridal party's village descended on another for the marriage. On such occasions lewd dancing (sa'e) and fornication often followed the ceremony. Revivalist rallies in Britain and America were also well known for arousing similar physical responses, including rolling on the ground before jumping up and down uncontrollably. Sexual excitement was present, but denied.

Evangelical preachers were dissatisfied with nominal faith, and looking for a genuine life changing response to the Christian Message, and witnessing instead crowd behaviour bordering on hysteria, knew that they were building on shifting sand. Converts were inclined to be 'hot then cold' in their new found allegiance, and many relied on a regular 'fix' rather than the acceptance of the long haul and steady growth in the Christian life. Persistence with a personal discipline was a tall order among people living in close proximity to each other. Households open to the four winds in which everybody knew each other's business encouraged conformity to group behaviour, one way or another. Available evidence from an account written by an evangelist named Lundie suggests that Murray moved on from his early preoccupation with emotional fireworks, followed by backsliding.

The need for an informed and sensitised Christian conscience remained. An incident recorded by Lundie, his Scottish missionary colleague on the Donottar Castle voyage, suggests that quick results based on a heart-rending appeal had lost their early attraction. Murray was accorded the rare privilege of being an eyewitness at the disclosure of an ancient Samoan shrine, which he insisted should remain undisturbed after it had been unearthed. In Sailele, near Masausi on the north east coast of Tutuila, Murray strongly rebuked one of the onlookers who vandalized one of the stone idols. Sensitivity towards other people's beliefs was uncommon among most Europeans who thought that such dependence belonged to the Polynesian Dark Ages. In many cases time-honoured religious practices were swept aside, and stone images (idols) related to former beliefs were either destroyed, or sent back to London to be displayed in museums as lifeless artefacts.

Matthew Hunkin was another thoughtful colleague of Archie Murray. Hunkin had arrived in Pago Pago, Samoa on an American whaler, having jumped ship in 1834. Wishing to share his Christian Faith ,he was Murray's companion when they lived in Pago under the patronage of High Chief Maunga. Together they went on to visit villages at the eastern end of the island of Tutuila to further a shared enterprise. Eventually Murray moved to Leone in the west to prepare the ground for the founding of the Mission Institute for Pacific Islanders to be located at Fagalele ,on the outskirts of the village. This was to be the next stage in the Forward Movement of the Tahitian Mission.

The murder in 1839 of the renowned ' Apostle to the South Seas', John Williams, and his partner Harris in the New Hebrides sent shock waves throughout the Tahitian Mission. Soon afterwards Archie Murray began to organize further missionary campaigns to Melanesia. He did this from my old home named Fagalele, situated close to Leone village in Eastern Samoa.

Fagalele provided basic training for Islanders who were willing to serve at the 'sharp end' of missionary enterprise. Frequently the cost was an early death, through violence or malaria. Exploratory work having taken place in the New Hebrides and New Caledonia, the ongoing task of consolidation required dedicated trained teachers, mostly from islands within Polynesia. Discovering 'on the ground' what was required in terms of character and necessary learning, those involved in leading the Mission made plans for battling on with ignorance and superstition. Sustenance was to be provided through institutions founded for that purpose.

Malua Theological College in Western Samoa was founded in 1845 by former Scottish missionary colleagues serving in Melanesia, George Turner, John Stair and Nisbett. It was to be their crowning achievement after returning from the New Hebrides following the murder of several fellow workers. Malua Theological College was established to provide training for overseas missionary work. In addition it was intended to equip men and their wives for pastoral ministry in villages throughout the eastern and western islands of Samoa. Sturdy missionary homes together with classrooms were built with walls of stone. Stone was the word used in missionary correspondence with London, when reference was made to the construction of eighteen-inch thick walls. Coral boulders from the reef were bonded with a cement made from burnt coral, reduced to a powder in massive kilns.. Fagalele Institution in Eastern Samoa was founded in 1851,

During the time when these solid English farmhouse style homes were being built, work was begun on the translation of the Bible into Samoan. Va'aelua Petaia and Mala'ita'i, students at Malua in 1845 made an important contribution to the translation of the Bible into the Samoan language. Dr. Pratt, relying on their help, later compiled a comprehensive Samoan Dictionary, which was also printed on the Malua compound. A printing press had arrived in 1838, and under the supervision of Mr. Stair, it was soon turning out the four Gospels with associated commentaries. Catechisms and elementary school textbooks on the three R's were also produced. In 1846, a translation of the New Testament had been completed and printed in Samoan, and the whole Bible by 1855. O Le Tusi Paia (The Holy Book) became the standard for correct Samoan spelling and pronunciation. In addition to their teaching duties L. M. S. missionaries Turner, Nisbet and Frazer recorded Samoan folklore, beliefs and customs. At the same time they gave an account of local plant and animal life. Their work was recognised by Edinburgh University when they each received the accolade, Doctor of Literature.

At the same time as Malua College in W Samoa and Fagalele Bible Institute in E. Samoa was preparing students for overseas work in Melanesia, Aaron Buzacott founded Takamoa College in the Cook Islands. As a former colleague of John Williams, and a former student of Dr David Bogue of Gosport Academy, Buzacott considered schools to be one of the most important departments of missionary labour'. Gifted as an architect and builder, a linguist, printer, and horticulturist, he gave special attention to the selection and education of those undertaking missionary work in the malarial infested territories of the New Hebrides. Cannibalism was an ever present peril. Buzzacote often travelled to mission outposts with his students to ensure that suitable placements were made and that back-up was provided for them. Archie Murray, embarking on the Mission Ship, The Camden, when it anchored near the Fagalele headland in Samoa, also exercised the same pastoral care towards his students.

In 1840 the 'Au Matatua' (Mission Directors) in London received a glowing report from Buzacott about an Cook Island student named Ta'unga, whose practical skills, linguistic ability, and grasp of biblical teaching had impressed his mentors. During an extended visit to Eastern Samoa in 1841-2, working alongside Murray in Pago Pago and Leone, Ta'unga renewed friendship with Teava, a fellow Rarotogan teacher. Based on the island of Upolu, Teava provided pastoral care for Leone village from 1838-1855, after which he retired to his Cook Island home.

A significant feature of the Tahitian Mission's work in Melanesia was the cooperation of pastors and teachers born in widely scattered Polynesian islands. Samoans served the people of faraway Cook Islands and vice versa. Tahitians worked and died in Samoa. Following this brief survey of a slowly developing back up system (Malua, Takamoa and Fagalele) for a dangerous enterprise, the clock is turned back to 1842. This is done in order to appreciate the hazards faced by many Polynesian martyrs. Three years have passed since the murder of John Williams on the island of Erromanga.

In March 1842 Ta'unga, and Pao'o, another protege of Buzzacott, accompanied the missionaries from Scotland Murray, Turner ,Nisbet, together with a number of Samoan missionaries, on a journey to consolidate the Tahitian Mission's work in Melanesia. Boarding the mission ship, The Camden, at different locations in Polynesia, the mixed racial group was bound for the New Hebrides (known today as Vanuatu), and New Caledonia. Both island groups had been named by Captain Cook, in memory of his Scottish father.

The Mission Ship, Camden, set off from the Cook Islands early in 1842 to make several landfalls in Polynesia en route to life in Melanesia. Polynesian and European missionaries disembarked at different locations after a long sea voyage to begin their dangerous task. The Mission Ship reached Rotuma on the 14th of June, where John Williams had placed two Samoans, Leiataua and Sao in 1839, shortly before his murder on Erromanga Island. Rotuma was the crossroads of an island world, where Samoan and Tongan traders lived alongside Fijian (Melanesian) settlers. It was also a haven for runaway sailors and whalers, being an obvious port of call for British Naval officers searching for mutineers from The Bounty. Williams had hoped to meet someone from Erromanga, or a nearby island. He wanted someone to act as an intermediary with people known to be unpredictable in the reception they gave to strangers. It was not to be. John Williams was hacked to pieces soon after his arrival. Three years later The Camden had returned.

The South Pacific Islands showing the route of Ta'unga's voyage on the 'Camden'

Mountainous Erromanga appeared on the horizon June 22nd 1842. The abundance of sandalwood attracted unscrupulous traders,who knew that this hard wood was highly valued for its fragrance in Hindu and Buddhist temples throughout Asia. Used also as incense to heighten alertness in worship, and an integral part of religious observance, sandalwood provided the aromatic base for subtle blends of perfume, regarded as an aphrodisiac. An insatiable demand led to devastating attacks on the forests, and the enslavement of the Melanesians living beneath their canopy.

The curse of the Blackbirder came next. Their ships were often disguised as the vessels used by missionaries. Such stratagems meant that kanakas', (a dismissive term for Islanders),spent two months in an overcrowded hold as a search continued throughout nearby islands. Barbaric conditions on sugar plantations in Queensland was their fate. Inevitably the attitude of the remaining islanders towards the white man was one of murderous intent. The introduction of firearms by returning workers increased the number of victims. Cannibalism added to the sense of horror at the approach of death. Reinforcements for those who were starved out, or who died from malaria and dysentery, were Polynesian and European. Few survived. Five years later four local Erromangans, trained as teachers, began to convince their own people that the Mission was there to stay. Their inbuilt resistance to yellow fever helped them to survive. Progress remained desperately slow.

Tanna was the next stop for those on board The Camden, who had spent five nights being tossed about in heavy seas. Nisbet,Turner and two Samoans, one named Vaoofanga,went ashore to begin their work. Mose, a Samoan and Kapao, a Cook Islander both left there two years earlier,came on board ship preparing to return on leave to their native lands. Turner later recorded that during 'their time' they saw many instances of a man's wife, or wives being strangled after he had died. 'They do not know why they do it, but say that such has been the custom of their forefathers'. Efforts to stop the strangling were not appreciated by the wives, as they would be ashamed, for it is an essential mark of affection'. Turner added the comment 'It is similar to Suttee, a custom of a Hindu widow sacrificing herself on her husbands funeral pyre.' Turner returned to Samoa in 1845.

John Paton, a Presbyterian missionary born in Dumfries and educated at Glasgow University, began his labours on Tanna in 1858. In 1859 his wife died in childbirth, and her infant son born in Scotland died six weeks later. Local people were merciless in their opposition to the strangers in their midst. Paton was driven away by savage physical attacks four years later. His memoirs became a best seller in Britain during the 1890's. Other people's heroic suffering found a ready market.

Aniwa Island, next on the Camden's itinerary in June 1840, was the challenge awaiting Iona and Fale'ese who had been converted at a Murray's Revivalist Meeting in PagoPago in 1837. They were accustomed to living under the authority of chiefs who ensured order in village life, but now they had to learn quickly that an hierarchical social order was absent in Aniwa. Social rank depended on an individual's ferocity in war, and a man stood out as superior through the number of wives he possessed, or human skulls collected. Bush dwellers and coastal people segregated by geography, and different languages further complicated efforts to build the trust necessary for growth.

Fortuna Island was sighted two days later and Samuela, a Samoan missionary came aboard and spoke of working among a mixed population with rivalries including descendents of early Polynesian voyagers. Samuela was murdered in 1843. Later entries in Ta'unga's diary refer to a narrow escape from cannibals, and witnessing the eating of cooked bodies, killed in skirmishes on Yate, one of the Loyalty Islands. When malaria and dysentery occurred, locals blamed neighbouring tribes, and interfering missionaries. Writing specifically about New Caledonia, Ta'unga saw women taking part in war, fetching and carrying dead bodies and chopping them up. He wrote 'Their craving for human flesh is irrepressible. Vengeance was the main cause, and quickness to anger'.

Aneityum, the southernmost island of the group, with a dense rainforest at its heart, was next on the Mission Ship's itinerary. Two teachers left there on a previous voyage, had disappeared without trace. After six years the Tahitian Mission had lost staff and momentum. In 1848 the Presbyterian Mission, in cooperation with the London Missionary Society, took over a new advance with the appointment of John Geddie. Learning to speak Samoan, and receiving in-service training from Archie Murray whilst living at Fagalele in Tutuila, Geddie was to work with Samoan missionaries, as well as his fellow countrymen, Gordon, Paton, Copel Matheson, and Inglis. Other Scottish colleagues Turner, Nisbet, Mills and Hardie, who had recently returned to establish and staff Malua College in Samoa, continued to visit Geddie in Aneityum to provide back-up for the 'aufai galuega'; the 'Team of Workers' at the cutting edge of mission.

Geddie's policy was to delegate responsibility to Melanesian converts, and in 1855 ordained deacons began to take over 'practical matters' given to them by elders and missionaries. Presbyterian order and discipline brought results, so that by 1860 most of Aneityum's population had an allegiance to a home grown church, rather than loyalty to a Mission Station. Nicknamed 'blue nose'(frosty), by his critics, others noted his warmth, Geddie proved to be ahead of his time in devolving to local Church Councils the task of managing finance, and overseeing the general maintenance of Mission Stations.

Thomas Powell, a L. M. S. Missionary born in Wales, arrived at Aneityum in 1845, after a short time spent in Fagalele Tutuila, E. Samoa. In 1849,

Powell had a disagreement with his newly arrived colleague,Geddie. Correspondence suggests that there was a disagreement about the most suitable location for new arrivals. It didn't help that Powell was not a Scot. He came from a denomination called in Welsh, Hen Gorff (Old Body), a mixture of Presbyterianism and Congregationalism. Local autonomy, and flexibility in organising its life and work was given to separate village churches in Wales. The Scottish Presbyterian model followed in New Caledonia relied on District Councils for overall planning and decision making.

Transplanting a system of church government (Presbyterianism) overseas appeared to deny the Fundamental Principal of the London Missionary Society, which valued 'home grown' (indigenous) churches more than imported patterns of church organisation. Clearly Powell, a Welshman, was the 'odd one out' in Aneityum, a Scottish Presbyterian enclave. The difference of opinion unresolved, Powell returned to Tutuila, Samoa, to be District Missionary.

Aneityum disappearing behind the stern, The Isle of Pines was next on the itinerary of the Mission Ship during June 1840. Agreement had been reached among the European missionaries, that Ta'unga should disembark at 'Pines', but an outbreak of inter tribal warfare brought about a change of plan. He remained on board and was taken instead to Yate in New Caledonia. Afterwards on the first of many visits to 'Pines',Ta'unga learned that all members of the crew of the brigantine 'Star' had been massacred, and eaten during the Camden's earlier visit. During several visits in the next 6 years Ta'unga wrote that he was constantly aware of cannibals stalking him. After sailing between Yate and 'Pines',spears were frequently thrown at him as he went ashore. Walking through clearings he smelt the ovens smouldering and human flesh burning.

Moving to the Loyalty Islands, an archipelago of six inhabited islands including Mare, Lifou and Ouvea,which together made one of the three provinces of New Caledonia, Ta'unga brought part Polynesian –Melanesian chiefs together, The son of Mare's headman became a Christian. An adopted hierarchical tribal system (Polynesian) was more receptive to the Tahitian Mission's message than a fragmented (Melanesian) organisation. Ta'unga was one of 25 Polynesian missionaries who served in New Caledonia before any Europeans arrived. Pao'o (1810-1859) was another. He prepared the way for Macfarlane, a Scottish Presbyterian as he began work on Lifou,the largest and most populous of the Loyalty Islands,120 miles N.E. of New Caledonia. The Mission Ship Camden, having delivered the cargo of missionaries and their belongings on the outward journey, prepared to retrace the same route and ports of call back to Samoa. New Guinea now beckoned as a further opportunity. One of the largest islands in the world, with a coastline 5,000 miles in length, Europeans had little commercial interest in the territory until the late 1860's. Latter day exploration was begun by the Tahitian Mission in 1871. They had voyaged from the Loyalty Islands to land first in the Torres straits region. In the following year Macfarlane, Archie Murray and Puo'o carried out a reconnaissance on the southern coast of the large New Guinea mainland. Their aim was to gauge the likely response of local tribes to strangers attempting to make a home among them. Later an experienced Cook Island missionary named Ruatoka, and a group of his compatriots, went ashore west of Port Moresby. They prepared the way for two London Missionary Society hero figures, Chalmers and Lawes, the latter being the first white man to reside on the mainland of New Guinea, in what was a small settlement in 1874. It later became the bustling city of Port Moresby.

Between 1871 and 1890 over 190 South Sea Island teachers served with the Tahitian Mission (L. M. S.) in Papua /New Guinea They contributed positively to a major cultural change experienced by indigenous people living on the coastal fringe of a largely unexplored land mass. For many on the expedition it meant enduring isolation, disease or violent death. Samoan Faifeau (Pastors),such as Pita and Simeona, to name two, brought with them the distinctive feel of an easygoing lifestyle, the structure of family prayers, hymn singing, and a requirement to be self supporting. John Garrett wrote 'Cook Islanders tended to be the shock troops of the Christian warfare, Samoans the occupiers and stabilizers'. The East End District in New Guinea was the home of many Samoans from 1883 until 1917 when the last of them departed. The tidal wave,which began in Tahiti, had run its course.

Today when Samoans are asked to name their religious affiliation the majority of them answer 'Lotu Tahiti'. It is an affectionate reminder of what they owe to the Mother Church in distant Tahiti. Similarly, Loyalty Islanders in Melanesia respect the memory of Pao'o born in faraway Aitutaki (Cook Islands). They call him 'The Apostle of Lifou', because he became one of them. Having served on a whaling ship before his conversion, Pao'o had trained alongside Ta'unga in Aitutaki's Takamoa College with Aaron Buzzacote (L.M.S.) as the Principal.

Buzzacote in the early 1820's had been a student of the Scottish academic Dr. Bogue in Gosport Academy. Being prepared to die in the service of others had been central to Bogue's message. 'Let us do or dee' is a line from a poem written by his contemporary living in Edinburgh, Robert Burns (1759-1756), a poem that would have been meat and drink to Bogue. 'Scots wha hae' (Where were you?) are the opening words of his famous poem. Ending this chapter it seems fitting to apply them to the Scottish and Pacific Island missionaries who died in the service of the Melanesian people.

Head hunter

Ruatoka, Cook Island missionary

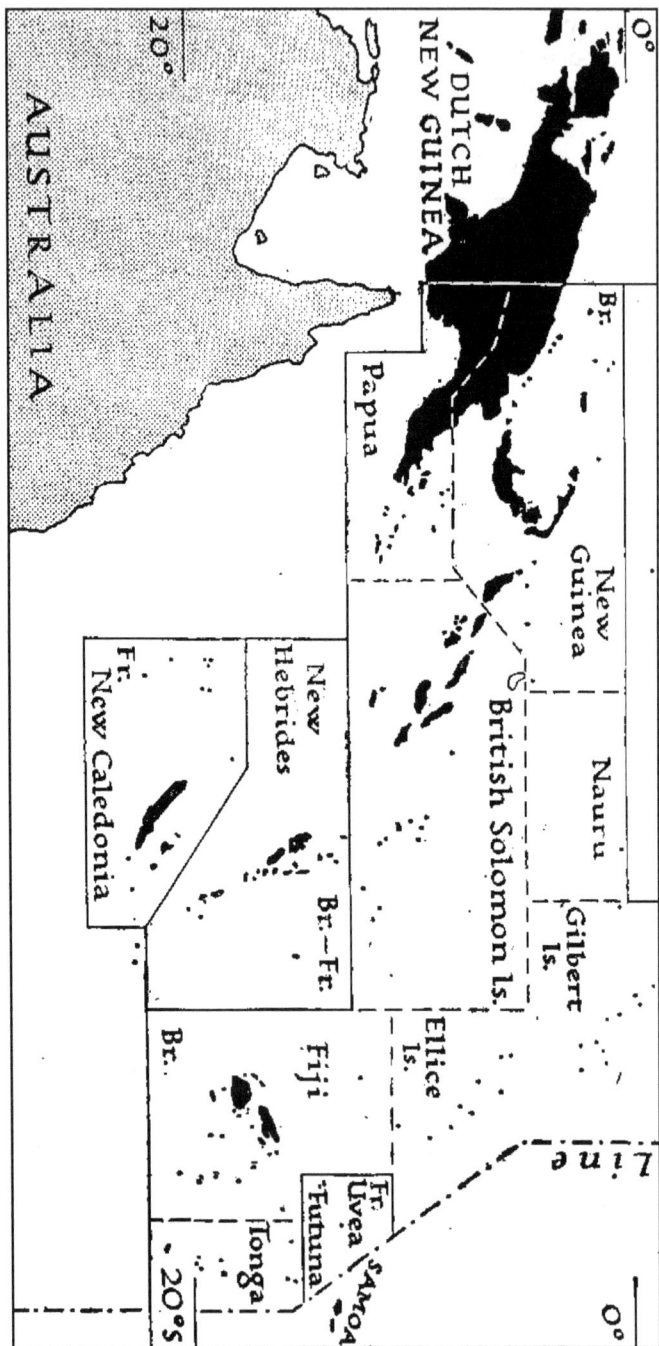

Colonial Possessions in SW Pacific 1900 - British, French, American Samoa

Chapter Seven

Seventh Wave - Commerce, Gunboats, Self-rule

Removing coconut 'meat' from a shell to make copra

After working among cannibals in New Caledonia, Ta'unga the Cook Islander teacher was transferred to Samoa to face a very different task. This included collecting coconut oil throughout the islands of Manu'a, Eastern Samoa, as part of a trading operation designed to raise revenue for local church schools. Money gained through this business operation also supported the missionary cause in Melanesia, where Ta'unga had served with distinction from 1842-48. His main task in E. Samoa was to supervise the work of local teachers and 10 village churches.

He wrote in his journal that the larger villages in Tutuila and Manu/a produced most coconut oil, and consequently attracted pastors who had family connection with the higher echelons of Samoan society. To be able to stand on your own feet, and then to be prepared to share your created wealth with others, was the characteristic response of Samoans to the message of 'self-made' European missionaries, nurtured in London trade and commerce.

The Samoans had stone lamps using coconut oil long before the white man came to their shores. As early as 1818 the L. M. S. had begun to collect oil from their converts as a contribution to missionary work elsewhere in the Pacific. In Manu' a the flesh of the nuts was placed in the sun, the liquid formed drained, and stored in unused canoes, before being transferred in barrels to a mission-trading vessel. It was a wasteful method, but after 1840, when pressing machinery had been imported to crush solid fractions of the coconut fat, there was an increase in the volume of oil extracted.

Production began with the sun evaporating the water content of the nut, and shrinking the flesh from the shell. These solid halves or quarters of ripe nuts were put into sacks for easy transport to the oil extractor. Ta'unga, who remained in charge of the Manu'a Mission's trade for several years, ensured that the bits of dried coconut meat, known as copra, were collected by a mission vessel, and taken to a central collection point. Rancid copra became the distinctive smell of the Pacific. Mission traders haggled for the best prices on their sour smelling product, because the extension of mission work depended on their astuteness.

John Williams, Junior, son of the 'Apostle to the South Seas', was involved in the copra trade from 1842 onwards, a year in which he exported six tons to Sydney. From the proceeds of the sale, he was able to establish a general store in Apia, which sold goods manufactured in Britain, and then shipped to Samoa via Auckland and Tonga. A jibe aimed at several missionary families was that they had gone to the South Seas 'to do good, and had done very well!'

By 1860, a hundred Europeans in the Apia bay area, in addition to a similar number scattered among the islands of Eastern and Western Samoa, were running general stores, boarding houses, and grog shops. A few of them used local land to grow fresh vegetables and fruit for ships crews and passengers visiting Pago Pago and Apia. Others practiced a variety of trades, including boat building and wrought iron work. The manual labour required in harvesting, handling and shipping copra was at the heart of Samoa's growing overseas trade.

Healthy independence and generosity were aspects of Lotu Tahiti's progress reported by Ta'unga in his written summary of the fledgling missionary society. In the same journal, he reveals his uneasiness about the village council of chiefs being the sole arbiter in matters of morality. He instanced the punishment for sexual offenders, which was determined first by the council of chiefs. Gathered as a Church Deacons Meeting, they usually doubled the punishable offence by expelling backsliders from Holy Communion for a specified period. Being named and shamed in an enclosed community was a powerful deterrent.

Exclusion by order of the Manu'a Council of Chiefs also included Roman Catholic priests. Expelled from Tahiti and sent to Samoa at the behest of the Roman Catholic priests, the L. M. S. Missionary, George Pritchard, thought that R. C.' s should be given some of their own medicine. He was probably thinking of the sadness of one of the pioneer missionaries who had given long and sacrificial service in Tahiti. Fifty years after his arrival on the mission ship Duff, Henry Nott learned in 1847 that the Pomare dynasty had been crushed by the French Navy, and Roman Catholicism had largely replaced the indigenous Tahitian Church. .

On balance, life within the Lotu Tahiti in Manu'a gave Ta'unga grounds for optimism, according to his journal written in 1870. This mood was replaced by despair in 1872, when reprisals for an alleged slight resulted in tribal warfare between the people living on the neighbouring islands of Olosenga and Ta'u. Heads began to roll as hatchets were wielded in fresh outbreaks of communal violence, which continued for four to five years. Despite set-backs, the people of Manu'a regularly expressed in formal welcome rites, their gratitude for the Tahitian Mission's opposition to the spirit of revenge shown by individuals, and rival families.

Whenever Samoan chiefs met in council they began proceedings with reciting the historic 'days' in their history. Finally he leading orator would intone that 'The greatest day' was when the Good News of Jesus Christ was first proclaimed in Samoa'. The corporate response was the word 'malie' meaning 'Well said'. Deeply embedded in the Samoan culture,particularly when village chiefs drank kava together in their most binding ritual, the thankful remembrance of a drawing back of a curtain to reveal a New Day. ('Se'ia tafa mai ata') was an important part of the proceedings. A better life had been revealed, and genuine progress had been made in its light. Revenge was recognised as destructive, whereas good relationships were honoured and respected. The drawing back of another curtain to reveal an awe inspiring event that took place near Ofu Island, Manu'a marked Ta'unga's closing years. He wrote in his journal about an enormous explosion from the depths of the ocean floor.

This happened just before he retired to his birthplace in the Cook Islands in 1878. An exceptionally large tidal wave (tsunami) lowered the sea level in Pago Pago Bay to such an extent that it was compared to a plug being removed from a full basin of water. Crowds rushed forward to gather the floundering fish and were drowned as the sea returned. It left a lasting imprint on the collective memory, recalled when in September 2009 a tsunami struck again. Ta'unga's account is a reminder of powerful natural forces, such as earthquakes and hurricanes, which disturb Pacific island life.

Final entries in Ta'unga's diary noted the rumblings of discontent surrounding mission trade in coconut oil, which provided the wherewithal for the work of Lotu Tahiti at home and overseas. With the price of coconut oil low in the European market, local traders resented missionary involvement in copra sales. The 'noises off', became louder when Big Business became involved in local production. Large merchants in Sydney started to enlarge their business interest in Western Samoa. Apia, the capital became the centre of a trading system, with stores and plantations in many outlying islands.

Ta'unga's description of the tensions and difficulties between small traders and Mission agents amounted to nothing, compared with what followed. An agent of Godeffrey of Hamburg, a company with large capital resources, capable management, and bold plans for expansion, arrived in Samoa from Germany in 1854. Independent traders, and Mission agents attempting to raise money by transporting copra, were left squabbling with each other over the scraps falling from the rich man's table.

Godeffrey and Son established a depot in Apia in 1857. Through agents stationed in many islands, copra was purchased and collected by a fleet of small schooners and brigs. Transported to Sydney and Europe, copra was used in the manufacture of soap, candles and cattle cake. Starting out as dealers, the German firm branched out to own huge coconut plantations using imported Chinese and Melanesian labour, mainly Solomon Islanders. Supervised by German overseers, and despised by the Samoans, 'Tagata uli' (Black people), were indentured for a stated number of years,on the understanding that they would live in Samoa without the companionship of Melanesian women. Blackbirders promised a better life as they gave away cheap trinkets and beads to lure the Islanders on board ship. The end result was rapid depopulation in the New Hebrides and Solomon Isles.

Between 1869 and 1872, Godeffrey's company bought 25,000 acres for plantations. When the Samoans eventually realized the extent of various land sales, they reacted with anger towards both the British and Germans. Samoan leaders had always been anxious to restrict land sales, but a powerful trading firm such as the Hamburg giant, acting with German government support, appeared to have taken the first step in appropriating all the land, and owning the people. Through Godeffrey's contacts with Berlin, and his knowledge of the Western world's money markets, the merchant tycoon worked tirelessly to secure annexation by Germany.

Coercive international diplomacy threatened the survival of the Samoan way of sharing wealth, (tamaoaiga). This trusted method of distributing land and property, gathering and sharing the fruits of labour, be it food or money for the common good, was not be abandoned without a fight. An extended family depended on the wise rule (pule) of the elected chief, who was expected to deal with family conflicts, famine and disease. It was usual for the distribution and re-allocation of wealth in the form of fine mats, to take place during ceremonies of exchange following an initiation, marriage or death of a titular head of a family, or district. Fine mats were also presented and exchanged during the necessary political manoeuvres leading up to an election of chiefs.

A British Naval Officer on a visiting gunboat ' showing the flag', suggested to a gathering of chiefs, that coins and notes should replace fine mats, which was an outdated currency. He was listened to politely, but the suggestion was ignored as inappropriate in a society which valued good relationships more than acquisitiveness. Despite brave efforts to maintain a bartering system Samoans eventually incorporated money into their traditional system of sharing goods of value. The inherent strength of customary barter, reliant on local communities trading with each other existed alongside the demands of a modern economy dependent on world wide financial markets.

Samoan leaders also learned to move with the times as they tried to prevent the annexation of their islands by the colonial powers of Britain or Germany. They knew that the Americans were waiting in the wings to obtain long term rights over Pago Pago harbour. Long before Godeffrey bought coconut plantations in Samoa during the 1860's, Wilkes, the leader of a U. S. expedition to the South Pacific in 1839, had recommended PagoPago harbour as 'best adapted for the refitting of vessels'. This claim was endorsed by the U. S. Government in 1872. Steamships requiring coal were gradually replacing sailing ships, and when a service between San Francisco and Australia, by way of Honolulu, was at the planning stage, Pago Pago was seen to be a highly desirable coaling station. The U. S. Navy also saw the advantages of having a naval station in the South Pacific to link with a canal being constructed at Panama. Aware of the value of the harbour, and lack of interest in its hinterland, the Samoan leaders approached the American Government. It was an astute move.

Albert Steinberger, a 'special agent' of American State Department on a visit to Samoa in 1869, appeared to propose the creation of an American protectorate. Samoans would retain internal autonomy. A greater measure of self-determination was attractive to a politically aware Samoan leadership, as it was thought that it could provide some form of protection from the two colonial powers. Delivered from the colonial power of Britain through the War of Independence, the U .S. was uneasy about behaving as imperialists. Knowing also in 1870 that the combined business interests of Germany and Britain had created a powerful base in Apia, and a network of settlements throughout the region, the U. S. eventually backed away from involvement.

When Steinberger attempted to establish a stable native government, with himself as prime minister, he was denied the support of his own State Department, and forced to resign from office. It became obvious to a neutral observer that European business interests were too deeply entrenched, and the U.S. Navy's limited objective of a strategically important Coaling Station, rather than territorial oversight,was insufficient to stop the flow of events. The Samoan attempt to avoid annexation had come to nothing. The colonial powers seemed to have had their way.

Another plan had to be found to express the Samoan's deeply felt need to have a greater say in their own affairs. The desire for a louder voice in determining the shape of their economic and political future had not gone away. An alternative way of expressing the same resolve was being explored within an organised body of opinion,which had a power base in every Samoan village in Western and Eastern Samoa. This was the Samoan Church (L. M . S). To understand how this organisation became deeply rooted in Samoan life, it is necessary to go back to the year 1797 when the London Missionary Society was founded. Its stated aim was to share the Good News of Jesus Christ, and not to establish institutions overseas, which mirrored English Nonconformity or Anglicanism.

In the 1860's, British missionaries claiming what looked like Episcopal authority,wanted to refuse ordination to local Samoan pastors, or permit them to administer the sacraments. During the 1870's, indigenous ministers decided that they would not defer to their British 'superiors' on what was a crucial matter for them. At an annual Church Assembly, missionaries were faced with a 'walk-out'. The Reverend Dr. George Pratt, a long serving translator and lexicographer, wrote despairingly in 1876 to the Mission Directors in London. 'We bought off their opposition with ordination - not intentionally but really. What other bribe can we offer at the next meeting ?' Samoans were deeply suspicious that the Directors of the Missionary Society in London wanted their missionaries to retain control of an emerging Church. Whereas gun boat diplomacy was used in the world of trade and international rivalry, Samoan leaders in the Church knew that they had real power 'on the ground'.

One of the reservations expressed by L. M. S. personnel, was that an hierarchical Samoan society had already determined the way in which the Church was organised ; that the Samoans had absorbed the Christian Faith into their own culture, and overlooked the need to change their culture to express a distinctive Christian way of life. Further it was said by Foreign (Palagi) missionaries, that the addition of an educated elite to an existing social structure of orators (Tulafale) and chiefs (Ali'i),had added another layer to what was in effect a caste system.

It was too late for challenging views to make an impression. Beginning with the 'Fathers in London', who were Directors of the L. M. S., (known to Samoans as the 'Au Matatua'), through to local pastors demanding ordination, hierarchies already ruled the roost. Just as orators through their diplomatic and bargaining skills could gain credit and influence on behalf of a chief with similar political aims, so pastors could use their 'top table' oratorical and political skills to advance the interests of a new aristocracy. A new and old elite had joined forces. Preferably educated in Malua Theological College, or in Leulumoega High School on the same compound, these leaders provided a powerful thrust to those searching for an informed strategy in furthering the desire for self determination.

Eventually Samoan leaders emerged to find ways of circumventing those Europeans who thought that Samoans were not ready for self-government. Writing on the 13th of October 1881, the British Consul named Churchward, was critical of missionary policy.'The aim of the L. M. S. to educate the natives to conduct their own affairs, affording them every assistance to do so. This, in my humble opinion has been let go just a little too far.' Many Samoans thought that missionaries hadn't gone far enough.

In village and district meetings Samoans had long experience of the inner machinations of councils. Without using the nomenclature of committee procedures, they knew how to achieve unity of purpose through complicated alliances of labyrinthine complexity. At a deeper level they accepted that their religious beliefs, and the ordering of social life (politics) were inseparable. Providing a framework for everyday life, the changes that some thought were necessary, took place very slowly. Invariably, the leaders edging the way forward to self government were financially capable, knowing the subtleties of negotiation, and the time to strike bargains. A church organisation rooted in village communities throughout Samoa became a good training ground for political self determination. It provided the drum beat and rallying cry.

Domination by the Colonial Powers still applied in other areas of Samoan life. Twenty years of unstable civil government was the unhappy consequence of a scheme of joint supervision that had been agreed between the International Powers. Germany, Britain and the USA in 1878. Each of them assumed the right to a naval station in the Samoan group. Prolonged periods of civil unrest, lapsing into violent conflict between supporters of paramount chiefs seeking precedence, and the persistent pressure exerted by commercial groups for greater local autonomy solved nothing. In 1898 sailors from a German warship supported one side against the other in an inter tribal conflict. Two British destroyers and an American vessel arrived on the scene, and an 'International Incident' seemed imminent.

At the same time as Samoans became aware of armoured might supporting diplomacy, France was advancing her claim to be a major colonial power in the Pacific. In 1835, French Roman Catholic missionaries became established in Tahiti after challenging the London Missionary Society's religious monopoly. Knowing Britain's preoccupation with securing New Zealand as a dominion, and that her economic interest in Tahiti had subsided, the French forced the repeal of the anti-Catholic law by using naval gunfire and troops. In 1843, Tahiti became a French protectorate, and a valuable trading post. Surprised by its colonial rival, the British decided to accept the fait accompli.

A similar pattern of gunboat diplomacy occurred in New Caledonia,which became a place of exile for political enemies of the French government, and a penitentiary for criminals. New Hebrides (Vanuatu) became a source of labour to unearth New Caledonia's mineral riches in the 1870's. Unquestionable French in sympathy, but tied to Australia (Britain) economically, Germany further exploited this area of Melanesia. Godeffrey, the copra producing giant and his successors, enticed local men to leave their families, to work in the Samoan plantations. (Map of Colonial Possessions p64)

In Samoa there was still talk of war when in March 1898 a hurricane struck Apia harbour. Seven warships were there at the time, three American, three German and one British. The only one not driven onto the reef was H. M. S. Calliope, a new ship with more powerful engines than the others. Her captain was able to force her through the storm to safety. Germany's warship 'Eber'

The German battleship "Adler" on the reef at Apia

disappeared under the reef's overhang. 'Adler' became a wreck on the reef.

The disaster led to a conference in Berlin in June 1898. Major colonial powers decided that the only means of providing stable government was to divide the islands. Tutuila and Manu'a became possessions of the USA, while Upolu and Savai'i were divided between Britain and Germany. Later these two powers came to a separate agreement, in which Britain withdrew entirely from Samoa in exchange for adjustments to boundaries in W. Africa, and the surrender of rights in Tonga. The Solomon group, including the island of Guadacanal, also became a British Protectorate. Germany formerly annexed Western Samoa in 1899.

Although the Seventh Wave of this story of Pacific people has been taken up with the description of big business, international rivalries and struggles for independence, most Samoans and the foreigners who had settled amongst them got on with their everyday lives. Tribal warfare interrupted cultivation, it cut across the work of missions, and interfered with trade, but these factors never dominated the Samoan scene. Unpretentious Protestant chapels, and more elaborate Roman Catholic churches gave promise of security and calm. Attendance at the Pastors School or Sunday Worship remained steady, and the voice of prayer was never silent. Copra was exchanged for cheap prints, and hardware was sold at the local store. Fishermen got on with mending their nets.

A Vision Shared - Part Two

Beyond Colonialism

Introduction

The group of islands previously known as Eastern Samoa became known as American Samoa in 1900. Responsible for the government of the islands of Tutuila, Aunu'u and Manu'a, the main task of the US Navy was to protect and service the Naval Station located in the Pago Pago Bay Area. It was a highly desirable site for a growing World Power making its presence known in the South Pacific. Life in the villages outside the Bay Area continued much as it had throughout the previous century.

The previous seven chapters describe seven powerful waves of human exploration and settlement throughout the Pacific Ocean. The remaining chapters focus attention on one Island Group known as Samoa during the 20th Century.

The author lived in both Western and Eastern Samoa during the years 1955 - 1968,and returned to American Samoa for six months in 1993,and again in 2005. The proverbs and sayings used as headings of chapters 8-12, are intended to convey the wisdom found in the Samoan Way of Life.

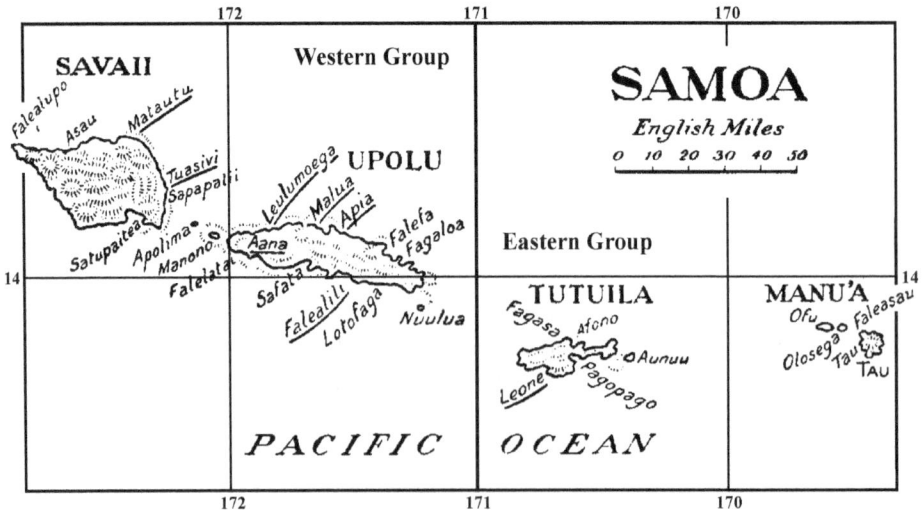

Samoan Islands 1900

Pacific War 1941-1946

The following five chapters are concerned with the fortunes of the Samoan people as they came to terms with the huge wave associated with the Pacific War 1941-1946, and its aftermath. Further upheavals came with the attainment of Independence in Western Samoa in 1962, and President J .F. Kennedy's New Frontier Programme for American Samoa begun in the same year.

U.S. Marines come ashore. Landing craft opposite the village of Fagaitua in the Eastern District of American Samoa in early 1942,

Part Two - Beyond Colonialism
Chapter Outlines

Chapter Eight   **Green bananas**   **p66**

The main thrust of the chapter is about raw recruits discovering, with Samoan colleagues, what was to be the nature of their work. Being 'green' is first applied to the U. S. Navy Administration after 1900, and then to the arrival in Samoa of U. S. Marines (Greenhorns) in early 1942, soon after Pearl Harbour. In 1955, the transfer of power, a place to live, vagueness about a Englishman's place in a rapidly changing Samoa, acclimatisation, and gradual progress in language learning are recalled as inexperienced foreigners began their given task. Trekking through mountain terrain, accepting village hospitality, appreciating the leisurely pace in 'Old Samoa', learning from culture shock, living with compromise, British aliens tried to get their bearings living under an American administration

Chapter Nine   **Falling apart**   **p98**

Samoan floor mats flying in all directions provide the image to describe a sequence of events that shattered preconceptions. At the same time they opened my eyes to the shapes and patterns of a different culture. The significance of protocols and welcome ceremonies, honour satisfied,adventurous longboat journeys, village exams,Polynesian dancing contributed to a jumbled scene. A large youth population challenged social cohesion, as did the tension between E/W Samoa due to the former's sense of inferiority. 'Near enough' business methods threatened the progress of the newly opened Bookshop. Domestic issues surrounding schoolboys, pigs,neighbours and ghosts,an earthquake, a Sputnik appearance, coping with tropical humidity kept the head - and the mats -spinning.

Chapter Ten   **Well done the rowers**   **p130**

The connecting theme of partnership runs through this chapter. Science and religion, biscuit tin rhythm, and roller coaster rides across barrier reefs provide examples. W. Samoa Independence expected in 1962, and an expensive face-lift promised for American Samoa in the same year, exposed uneasy relationships between the two groups of islands. Working alongside a maverick Elder Pastor proved to be a headache, and political cohesion was threatened as one tribal network displayed Big Brother attitudes towards another. A Pacific Unity movement, and local educational initiatives with trusted colleagues restored faith in cooperation. Youth Work boosted my confidence in crossing a cultural divide, although improved economic ties with the USA questioned traditional links with Independent Western Samoa. Consequently experienced both satisfaction and frustration in developing partnerships.

Chapter Eleven   Proceed with caution   p159

'Proceed with caution', the theme of W. Samoa's Independence Day Cele-brations is reflected in the subjects covered. A New Frontier promised by President Kennedy in E. Samoa 1962 threw caution to the winds. The resemblance and difference of two Government systems reacting to the speed of change was a preoccupation. Worms, mosquitoes and bush medicine depict daily concerns. Nuclear tests and a missile crisis increased dependence on the BBC. This section leads to the question 'Who do you believe?' being asked of newspaper censorship,medicine,and the reliability of informants. The embarrassment of hidden rocks,and the perils of a 'Colonial trap' underlined the tension between the two Samoan groups. One consequence was my dismissal from The Bookshop's activities and becoming a 'backroom boy' in the service of the church in Samoa for the next three years.

Chapter Twelve   A Durable Network   p190

The chapter begins with the practical task of mending a fishing net for an unfinished task. Beginning with the language of Lake Galilee, and Samoan fishing traps, ' A Durable Network' takes us into the Internet world. 'Out of the loop', explores the common experience of rejection, which leads to the next section about 'connections' made with the outside world through tourism.. The Island's educational television's failure to deliver, and its return to a 'default' position is examined. Attitudes to sexual behaviour, and suicide rates among Samoan adolescents raises a question about Islanders being 'programmed'. A review of positive and negative features of world wide 'systems' is followed by the final section giving a brief survey of one world wide network which provides mutual support to its members.

Chapter Eight

1955 - 1956 - Green bananas

Samoan Proverb. 'E valavala a tumanu.' refers to a young bunch of bananas. 'Spindly and lacking substance' is the literal translation of the Samoan words. An inexperienced person lacking credibility in the eyes of others is called either a green banana or a greenhorn.

Greenhorns

Hordes of U.S. Marine 'greenhorns', (originally a name given to cattle with young horns), landed on the shores of Samoa early in 1942. World War Two had begun with the Japanese in control east of a line drawn from Hawai'i to Samoa, and north of a line from Samoa, through Fiji to New Guinea. Through a League of Nations mandate of 1936,the Japanese already possessed airfields and harbours in the Marshall Islands, north west of Samoa, In December 1941 the Japanese immediately invaded Tarawa, one of the Gilbert Islands protected by the British, and began to build a defensive ring around their conquests, reaching Guadalcanal in the Solomons during May 1942. Airfields were constructed posing a threat to Queensland, Australia, with the intention of cutting the supply line to the USA.

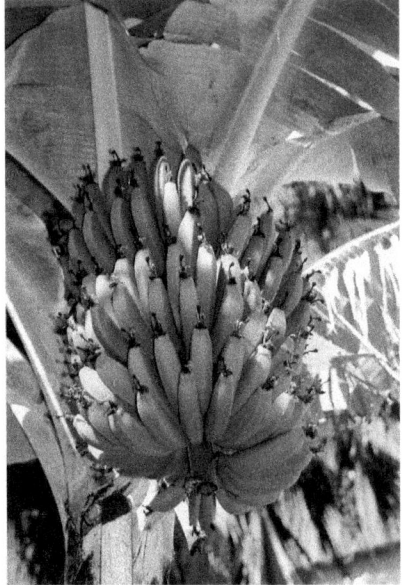

American Samoa stood exactly on the front line between opposing forces, when shells from a Japanese submarine fell on the Pago Pago bay area in January 1942. The rising sun emblem was soon seen on reconnaissance aircraft flying over Tutuila Island, but then the theatre of war moved on rapidly to Tarawa and the Solomons. Marines previously stationed in Tutuila took part in the gruesome Battle of Guadalcanal, and seriously injured men began their recovery in the Naval Hospital built at Mapusaga in American Samoa. Midway Atoll, halfway between Tokyo and Pearl Harbour, was the scene of a critical sea battle won by the U.S. Navy in June 1942, after which the American forces fought an offensive, rather than a defensive war. Briefly on the front line of the Pacific War, the people of Tutuila lived in an armed camp, outnumbered by U.S. Marines training for combat. They were greenhorns, without experience of combat. 8,000 marines and 20,000 Samoan men, women and children shared the living space on a small island. A wartime pill box and gun emplacement in the Fagalele School grounds are reminders of the defences that were constructed. When troops were billeted in the Missionary's home, a grenade exploded wrecking part of the building. With Marines everywhere, from one end of the island to the other, relationships between American servicemen and Samoans became close. This was in complete contrast to pre-war American Samoa, when U. S .Navy personnel lived on 'The Station', in the Pago Pago Bay Area, which became an enclave separated from village communities..

Before the war the Naval Administration, acting on behalf of the U.S. Government, aimed to govern the island's life in such a manner as to facilitate the maintenance of a Naval Station. Interference in the island's life outside the Bay Area was minimal. Bay Area land had been bought by the Navy, and ahead of traders and speculators, its officers had ensured that land ownership was in the hands of the Samoans. Overseas service for Naval Officers was never longer than two years, so that the exercise of Government executive power meant keeping things ticking over.

During the war years, 1914-18, Annual Reports to United States Navy maintained that the increase of extra marital relationships between naval personnel and Samoan women was not a major issue. Later in the 1920's, reference was made to local people appreciating the respect shown by the naval administration towards their culture and customs. It is clear from the record that vigorous sanitary inspections were maintained by naval medical officers, as was the strict enforcement of legal regulations regarding the sale of land. Education was left to the Missions.

A Commission proposed in 1930 to settle land boundary disputes, had a membership of American Samoans only, but it was unable to function satisfactorily. The Justice Department Annual Reports on Samoan Court Cases reveal that interested parties preferred the 'Palagi' (White man's) High Court. A U.S. Navy Report also concluded that 'Samoans felt considerable pressure to consider their own family first, and justice as a concept applying to other family groups, was of little concern to them. The Justice Department therefore worked on the assumption that Samoans did not trust their own people when it came to property rights, or chiefly title'.

American Samoa's political and economic development, the subject of U. S. Navy Reports, one in 1931, another in 1932, mentioned attempts made through the U. S. House of Representatives, to grant citizenship to the Samoans. Clinging to the system of land tenure being vested in different chiefs created a major problem. It came up against the hard truth that becoming U.S. citizen required the acceptance of an alien voting system ; that is one man, one vote. Although a Bill of Rights to Samoans was granted, apathy replaced the desire of the negotiating teams to reach a settlement on the main issue of citizenship and voting rights. The resumption of talks was prevented by the outbreak of war.

In the inter-war period Naval personnel had a way of life centred on the 'The Station' in the Pago Bay area. In the early 20th century their task included replenishing coal stocks, maintaining loading equipment, and providing the ancillary services needed for old-time steamships. During the years between the two World Wars the main reason for the U.S. Navy's continued presence was to provide the facilities for refuelling oil burning vessels. In order to discharge mainly tedious responsibilities, the U. S. Naval community, and their friends attempted to overcome their self imposed isolation through the leisure activities of the Goat Island Club.

The 'Club' operated unwritten rules of membership along similar lines to those adopted by British Army Officer Clubs in their colonial pomp. A Commissary was available where stateside food and other goods could be bought to make life more like home. Samoan and Stateside members living in this 'comfort zone' for Naval men with their wives, enjoyed privileges that often led them to adopt a superior attitude towards those outside their social set. It was not unlike the attitude of Samoans of chiefly status, towards their inferiors. For many servicemen life in the PagoPago Station became an agreeable cocoon leading to retirement with a good pension in the States.

In 1942 a large contingent of new recruits arrived to ruin the 'old salts' sunset experience. Hordes of marines took over the whole island, including the Naval Station,which had been a distinct Bay Area. Such a concentration of men and materials on a small island for more than three years, made a considerable impact on the Islander's daily life. When the Pacific War ended in 1946, the U. S. Navy continued to govern until 1951, whereupon a Civil Administration, responsible to the Congress in Washington, came into being to cause further upheaval.

Raw recruits 1955

Green bananas were carried below decks as the Motor Vessel Tofua drew alongside the wharf in Pago Pago Harbour on June 2nd 1955. We had seen the fruit being loaded into the ship's hold in Tonga, ready to be sold in New Zealand. Having heard ourselves described as green bananas by the crew of the Mission Ship, John Williams VII ship in Suva, Fiji, we knew ourselves to be two raw missionary recruits as we stood nervously at the top of the gangway waiting to go ashore.

Both my wife Eileen and I were apprehensive about meeting the Elders of the Church, as well as being introduced to Edith Maxfield, the joint head teacher of the Girls Boarding School at Atauloma, for she was to be our British colleague and mentor. Arrangements had been made for us to stay at the school for several months to become acclimatized, and hopefully learn the rudiments of the Samoan language. Edith was to be our supervisor, sharing meal times and her experience of working in the District, whilst at the same time continuing to perform her school duties.

As the vessel drew alongside the wharf, a group of women could be seen in overflowing white dresses and large straw hats. Standing beside them were men in starched white suits and black ties holding aloft their umbrellas as a shield from the midday sun; at the same time fanning themselves to keep cool in the sweltering humidity. Their standard black and white uniform showed that they were Samoan ministers of religion with their wives waiting to welcome us. The picture of a penguin parade crossed my mind..

Awake before dawn, and on deck by morning light, there had been ample time to reflect upon the irregular outline of Tutuila Island, only nineteen miles long, seven miles at its greatest width and reduced to two where Pago Pago Bay nearly cuts the island in half. The island seemed so small and isolated in the vast expanse of ocean, that had been our home for nearly two months. Volcanic mountains between one and three thousand feet high formed the islands backbone, which was covered with dense vegetation cleared in places to make plantations. Below them there appeared to be a low-lying rock barrier at sea level.

A closer look revealed sea spray breaking on the edge of a reef about a mile seaward of a few small villages spread along the shoreline. The inter island Banana Boat slowly eased its way along the eastern coastline, with the villages of Aunu'u and Fagaitua clearly visible. Pago Pago harbour and the wharf drew nearer. Tilbury Docks, London, was seven weeks away, thirty

71

four days on the M.V. Rangitiki, five days in New Zealand and ten days on the M.V.Tofua. It was journey's end and the beginning of a clearly remembered first year of two young people on a tropical island, said by a ship's steward to have had 263 inches of rain that year. To cheer us up he added that the island had a stifling, steamy atmosphere.

Fuluiole Meleisea, the Samoan head teacher of Atauloma School was one of the first of the waiting Samoans to rush up the gangplank. She went past the 'green bananas' at speed, and threw her arms around her brother Peseta, a member of the Legislative Council in Western Samoa ,accompanied by the Chairman of the Church, Elder Pastor Tupe, her uncle. Both of them were returning from New Guinea after the Diamond Jubilee Anniversary celebrating Samoan missionary service in Melanesia. After the welcome formalities, including the traditional kava ceremony,the raw recruits travelled by taxi through the western district of the island towards their temporary home. A few carefully prepared words of greeting, spoken in Samoan, had not been needed.

First impressions

Rough road between Fagalele and Atauloma 70

For the first 5 miles the road hugged the coastline, which meant negotiating a succession of hairpin bends at the ocean's edge. Little space was available on the other side of the road for the few Samoan homes cut out of the volcanic rock face, and sloping upwards at a steep angle. After the village of Nu'uli the road went inland to reveal a succession of clearings ; the vivid scarlet and yellow colours of hibiscus flowers giving promise of a tropical world to be explored. Driving through Pava'ia'i we arrived at Leone, a name easier to pronounce. The gleaming white spire of the large Roman Catholic Church and the equally imposing Samoan Church (L. M. S.), both dominated the bay where, in 1832, John Williams waited for a signal from a Tahitian teacher in order to proceed ashore.

Looking eastwards from Leone village a volcanic headland could be seen jutting out into the bay like a jet black finger. Upon it was a large white English farmhouse building, incongruous yet strangely majestic with its huge canopy of rusty red corrugated roofing iron. The edifice was named Fagalele. Well named, 'flying over bay', its situation gave a spectacular view of Leone Bay, opening out into the vast South Pacific Ocean, and on to New Zealand. Beyond was the South Pole. Looking towards Atauloma School, three miles away, the bold, irregular coastline was surmounted by the rough outline of the central mountain chain. Gradually the ridge descended to meet the reef at the village of Amanave two miles beyond Atauloma Girls School. Built on a platform dug out of one of the lower slopes of the mountain massif, with breathtaking views across the ever-changing colours of the reef, Atauloma was to be our residence for the next four months.

After language study on our first morning in Samoa, the turquoise coloured lagoon beckoned invitingly . In the late afternoon, we decided to investigate the shallows of the reef beyond the shore line. It was a mistake. The sharp shards of coral easily penetrated the thin soles of 'flip flop' sandals, to inflict poisonous and painful cuts. Buds which develop on minute sea coral creatures form new colonies attached to the parent coral. When the coral dies, a stony skeleton is left behind ,and these build up into a solid lime coral rock to resemble a jagged wall of concrete. The reef becomes home to spiky looking fish, sting rays, sea anemones and jelly fish, - not a hospitable environment for humans with soft white skin.

As an easily embarrassed young man living in a teenage Girls School, I was often caught unawares when taking a shower, because my underwear would be taken for laundering as soon as it was discarded. The room service was much appreciated, and the intrusiveness accepted as a source of amusement all round. After sweating profusely on Sunday in the hot humid atmosphere of a crowded church, a used white suit would be whisked away to be washed, then starched and ironed by midday on Monday.

Every Sunday there were three services in the Samoan language, each of them one and a half hours long, beginning at 8am, 3pm and 7pm, during which mosquitoes nipped any exposed skin. An infected female delivered minute worms from one person,who had filariasis, to a neighbour's bloodstream, and caused damage to their lymphatic glands. In 1955 it was not unusual to see Samoans who suffered from elephantiasis, the consequence of adult parasitic worms taking control of the body's lymphatic system, to create large and painful swellings on the legs and genital area of the sufferer. A quick swipe on hearing the characteristic whine of this elusive creature, became part of everyday life.

Wearing the obligatory white suit and black tie, and sitting on the front row, in church an attempt was made to join the rest of the congregation reading alternate verses from the Bible. After the preacher had read the first verse, he invited us to follow him as he used the words 'O le a tatou faitau fe'au'au'a'i' i'ai'. Reading responsively in unison was a great help in pronouncing Samoan words with its clear and distinct vowel sounds The word meaning 'alternatively' (fe'au'aua'i.), required 3 glottal stops.

One particular hymn was sung frequently, so that the words stuck in the memory. 'Sasa'e, sisifo, Toga po'o matu, ua i ai le silafia po'o le fea itu'.' East, West, Tonga (South), Matu (North), whichever direction you take', is an adequate translation. The use of the word Tonga was a powerful reminder of the Polynesian's nautical heritage. The islands of Tonga provided a fixed navigational aid meaning towards the south. We heartily sang that Jesus was our compass.

Three days after our arrival I was told that the District Treasurer, Fiti Sunia, had arranged a meeting between myself and the American Governor. Together with his officials, it was to take place in Fagatogo, the town at the heart of Pago Pago Bay. At 6 a m. the next day I waited at the roadside, listening for the bus to sound its horn as it passed through the villages along the winding coastal track from Amanave Bay in the far west. I was to learn that it was futile to ask 'Has the bus gone?' Even if the bus was known to have departed much earlier, I was told what they thought I wanted to hear. 'It will be here soon'. A young man in a hurry, I thought that being polite had its limits.

In later years,I learned that the long hours I had stood fretting waiting for

Lava's converted truck, would have been better spent if I had investigated the stream flowing down to the sea very close to the Atauloma bus stop. Two - three thousand years earlier this locality on the volcanic island of Tutuila was well known among the islands of the South Pacific for its industrial scale production of Stone Age tools, such as basalt adzes. In the black lava flow, several hand-worn depressions in the shape of bowls, showed that on this site basalt adzes went through the process of sharpening and finishing. To think that this was the spot where stone age artisans sat at high tide, putting the finishing touches to products that would find their way to distant archipelagos, using prehistoric trade networks. Looking beyond the reef, it was possible to imagine long distance canoes tugging at their stone anchors. Instead I listened for the screeching of brakes as Lava's bus came to a halt.

Lava the bus driver was built like a large wedge of volcanic rock, often arrived with a sore head as the result of heavy drinking the night before. He insisted that I should sit beside him at the wheel as an honoured guest. I had heard that the brakes on the buses had been known to fail on the switchback road. Subsequently I twice experienced of the bus careering out of control over humps in the coastal road going downwards towards Leone, the bus groaning and the gears grinding before stopping in the well-populated village. Despite knowing that there had been a recent incident in Masefau, E. District, of a bus plunging down the hillside towards the sea causing fatalities, a youthful belief in indestructibility led me to accept the doubtful privilege of sitting next to the driver. The bumpy dusty ride over potholes was to be the first of many journeys into 'town' during the next few months. Gradually I was demoted to a position behind the driver's seat, thankfully sitting on the benches on the sides of the bus. A space was created in the middle of the bus for family belongings of all kinds, fruit, vegetables and chickens, mostly intended for sale in the 'town' market.

Lava was a chief and a member of the Lotu Tahiti (L. M. S.) in Amanave. A huge, jovial rogue he gave 'free' rides to family members, who by my reckoning formed a large part of the population living west of Leone village. Amusing the passengers with his constant flow of village gossip, I gathered from the nods in my direction that some of his stories were at my expense. Gradually picking out words such as 'moe' (sleep), and 'to'alua', (wife), I was aware of the carnal nature of the exchanges, but bored by my lack of response he soon switched his playful ribaldry to others. Later on that first day in 'town', my linguistic limitations were exposed again when a young man asked me where he could obtain a bible, except that I thought he was asking me for a 'Piebald'. Why did he want to buy a horse from me? I could not make head or tail of what he was saying.

A reporter of the Chicago Daily News on September 8th 1948 referred to two of Samoa's most powerful chiefs and rivals for political power, Mariota Tuiasosopo of Tutuila, and Toufeli from Manu'a. 'Both want the U.S. Navy to stay boss in Samoa,' he wrote. 'Their intention was to keep the money coming from Washington, and not to be supplanted by the Department of the Interior. Both chiefs want to keep seats on the gravy train of income tax immunity,and anti -white trader legislation, which protects their special privileges. Governor Vernon Huber, in line with Navy policy of staying out of Samoan affairs, tries to steer as equally between the rivals as possible'. In the same newspaper article George Weller mentioned that Chief Toufeli managed to obtain $27,000 from the U. S. Government to repair Manu'a 's inter island boat, and Chief Tuiasosopo got a generous grant for his business enterprise selling Samoan arts and crafts in return for switching allegiance. Their lips were sealed until the transition to civil government was a done deal'. Weller concluded his report with the observation. 'In only 50 years under the American flag, where do you suppose the Samoans learned politics?'

On the 17th of April 1950 Tutuila celebrated the fiftieth anniversary of its cession to the United States with the raising of the American flag on the Malae (sacred ground) in Fagatogo. Nearby, on the waters of Pago Bay, racing longboats with twenty four rowers in each, provided the main attraction. Intended as a day of day of thanksgiving for fifty years of government under U. S. Navy control, there was unease among many Samoans as they watched the celebrations,which included the spectacle of three hundred men in unison performing a 'savage' knife dance. Anxious spectators knew that a civilian administration,with limited financial resources, was about to replace a generous benefactor. Fifty years of Naval stewardship was to come to an end.

After Senator P. Phelps was appointed the first civilian governor in 1951, he discovered to his consternation that the Dept. of Interior had underestimated the loss of income, which would follow the departure of the U.S. Navy. The economic situation became so desperate in 1952, that one thousand Samoans migrated en masse to Hawai'i, transported by the U. S. Navy, their Uncle Sam with his large pockets. Between 1951 and 1953 four governors and four acting governors were appointed in quick succession. The territory's Naval

Base economy had collapsed with nothing to take its place.

By the time the Navy pulled out, the Samoans, many of whom were dependent on monthly paychecks, had almost given up growing enough food to feed themselves. Moreover the population had increased from 5,600 in 1900, to 20,000 in 1951. Although a civilian government had taken over, most of their local employees had been trained in naval establishments, and preferred the old regime's way of doing everyday business. If I had known this background information about the colonial rule of the USA in Eastern Samoa, I would have been better prepared for the meeting with Governor Lowe soon after my arrival in early June 1955.

Governor Richard Barrett Lowe, appointed in 1953, made it clear at the beginning of our conversation that territorial appointments, such as his own, were made on the basis of political patronage from either an elected Republican, or Democrat administration. This meant that the American Department of the Interior did not have an independent career structure similar to the British Colonial Service. Their system of budgeting allowed a Senate sub committee to throw out carefully drawn up plans intended to restore an ailing island economy. This despite the fact that estimates had been approved previously by a major Government review group. Governor Lowe claimed that long term planning was nearly impossible. In Samoa he was glad the relationship between his administration and the L. M. S. Church was in good shape, especially in matters concerning Health and Education.

During the two years before our arrival in June 1955, Lowe had brought some stability to the islands economy by giving permission to the Van Camp tuna-canning factory to build a plant in the Pago Bay area. The creation of new jobs was the direct result of the Japanese and Koreans using a method of long line fishing. Huge amounts of fish caught in a relatively short time, whilst discarding smaller varieties, proved a winner for a company concerned only with improving profit margins. The havoc unleashed on the maritime environment was another matter, and not appreciated at the time. In 1954 the creation of new jobs seemed all-important, and the plundering of an abundant, but now rapidly diminishing supply of fish, only began to be recognised in the 1990's. Pollution and stench increased in those forty years.

In answering a question Governor Lowe said that America Samoa's economic weakness made political self-government unlikely. In his opinion if independence become an important issue, then a closer union with Western Samoa was the only way forward.

Governor Lowe stayed three years and during that time the island's economic outlook improved to pave the way for the more dramatic changes associated with the name of Rex Lee, the Governor from 1961- 66. Six years earlier the relationships between an 'alien' Englishman living in an American territory, and officials directly responsible to the Governor were often less than cordial. In the 1950's I had a cool reception from ex navy government heads of departments, who dealt with 'bread and butter' requests requiring their stamp of approval. The Office of the Attorney General dealing with questions of land and property, was particularly unhelpful, and the Department of Public Supplies, which at that time controlled freight, building materials and equipment gave me the 'run around' as two school construction projects went ahead.

Being a foreigner

Whilst trying to speak Samoan, an unexpected challenge was the need to learn the language of Americans. Meeting them occasionally in their 'South Seas Bubble' it was necessary for an alien in an American territory to understand their distinctive attitudes and lifestyle. Friendships made with churchgoers from a variety of denominational backgrounds, Methodist, Episcopalian and Baptist, became one way into their world. On our first day in Samoa we had been driven in comfort by taxi along the pot-holed road a distance of 12 miles to our 'home in the west'. For 3 years journeys made in comfortable limousines were paid for by the U. S. citizens belonging to the English -speaking Church who met on Sundays in the Goat Island Club.

News came back to me through a some local friends, that club members had a critical view of missionaries in general. Somerset Maughan's story 'Rain' did not help it was said. In what became a box office success at the cinema, the author's book was about an English missionary named Davidson, who attempted to convert a prostitute while he was in Pago Pago. He finished up in her bed. The missionary was portrayed as a bigot who succumbed to the warm sensuality of Sadie Thompson, portrayed by the actress, Rita Hayworth. The hypocrisy of the white missionary in a story, who happened to be a 'limey'(English), fed local prejudice.

An English alien's leaning towards paranoia was given another nudge by a persistent rumour circulating among the Club's clientele, that money was regularly collected from Samoan L. M. S. Churches, and shipped off to London on their Mission Ship. This rumour was encouraged by an article in the Chicago Daily News, mentioned above, which included the paragraph,

'Tuiasosopo has also won silent honour in Navy quarters by establishing a new religious sect, the Congregational Church of Jesus in Samoa. The aim of Tuiasosopo's church is to halt the leakage of American funds to British Samoa through the London Missionary Society. The Navy has longed to plug this leak, but never quite dared to take the step.' With difficulty I learned to 'absorb' the distortions and the prejudice, but it wasn't easy.

The new civilian administration relied on the infrastructure of a former naval base, which for fifty years had thrived on signed dockets made out in triplicate. These were then countersigned by junior clerks secreted in offices awaiting discovery in adjacent buildings or further afield. (Kafka wrote in 'The Trial' about Joseph K being told to go somewhere, when it was always the wrong time ; that he was made to feel absurd, guilty or stupid, sometimes all three!'). Questions about the registration of land ownership and building permits took up a lot of time and energy in the years 1955 - 57. What was an Englishman doing in American territory dealing with Samoan land issues? The frustrations should have been an early warning signal of a controversy,which finally came out in the open in 1961. The underlying issue was to divide leaders in both church and government in Eastern and Western Samoa. The consequences of that disturbance were still being felt, when I returned to the Islands after twenty five years, in 1993.

An urgent decision was needed in June 1955 about the location of the raw recruit's home, and it necessarily involved exploring rights over Samoan land. Was the home-base of our work to be close to the commercial and Government administrative centre in the Bay Area, or 12 miles away in Leone on the Fagalele School compound? The choice would shape the nature of my work. Surveyed and registered in accordance with the Native Lands Ordinance of 1900, the Pago land dossier included a description of the property and a map. An assistant from the Justice Department, John Cole, joined me in the steamy heat to thrash about with stout walking sticks clearing rope like bind weed as we looked for markers. A dense undergrowth of prickly Honolulu Rose, and wild hibiscus clumps, hid what we were looking for on the steep hillside above Pago Harbour.

Below us good and bad housing stretched along the valley bottom to climb the steep mountain sides. The sun shone, and the cloudless sky was beautiful. It was in complete contrast to Pago on a bad day in January described in Maughan's story 'Rain'. There it is described as 'a seedy shanty town where it never stopped raining. 'It did not pour', he wrote ' it flowed and rattled on the roof of corrugated iron with a steady persistence that was maddening'.

Trying to re-establish the position of the original boundary on a pleasant June afternoon, I thought about the Reverend Archie Murray and his attempt in 1834 to erect the first missionary home in Pago, that is before he moved out to Fagalele at Leone, his second option. Murray also had to decide on the best location for a mission station long before the Samoan Church existed. The foundation of the ancient home in Pago was now covered with bushes, and there was evidence of long term encroachment by neighbours. It became painfully obvious that prolonged legal battles made a 'town' settlement out of the question. Why hadn't Samoan leaders and colleagues spelt out the problem before I arrived? The green banana had much to learn about double speak, that deliberately disguises or reverses the meaning of words.

Twelve miles to the west a similar survey was carried out on the registered Church land at Fagalele School near the village of Leone on July 2nd 1955. In the records of the High Court, detailed reference points were included, and these showed that the leased L. M. S. land extended 70 feet beyond an old wire fence, put in place at a later date by persons unknown claiming it for themselves. In the U. S. Navy Report on American Samoa, 1926, reference was made to the 1910 regulation regarding the alienation of native lands, which stated that 'in line with government policy, the London Missionary Society had made no attempt to buy native land.'(Good old Ebenezer Cooper!). Cooper negotiated a lease for the establishment of a Church School at Fagalele before 1901, and soon afterwards a lease made on land at nearby Atauloma School was granted .

As the lease on the Fagalele land reached expiration, the L. M. S. missionary, W. Hough, then stationed in American Samoa, and afterwards his successor, C. J. Kinnersley, approached the descendents of the original lessors with a view to acquiring the land permanently for the Samoan Church. For some years funds needed for all new property required for church work, had been raised by the people of American Samoa. When therefore the first transaction was negotiated in 1915 between the Samoan Church and Atofau, the chief at the head of a family owning part of the Fagalele land, the Secretary of Native Affairs registered the title of the church as 'The Congregational Church of American Samoa', not including Western Samoa. Future discord between leading chiefs of American and Western Samoan was assured!

The transaction included a statement that similar plots of land would be recognised by the High Court. Later still, in 1919, a further transfer of land at

Fagalele was made, Talking Chief Maiava being the recognised owner of the piece of land released for educational purposes. At the same time, Molio'o (Lutu) offered a small piece of land in Utulei to the Church District, and this was registered in the Court Records under the same title. The inclusion of the word 'American' in the four land purchases mentioned here drew attention to the political separation of Western Samoa from American Samoa. The Samoan Church, embracing the islands both east and west, demonstrated a linguistic and cultural unity. Land registrations on the other hand confirmed the political and economic division between American Samoa and Independent Western Samoa.

Anyone who dared to sort out matters of land ownership in Samoa could expect trouble and strife. Quoting again from the U.S. Navy Report, 'The owner of the last section of the Fagalele land for transfer, Talking Chief Vaotu'ua put his signature to the sale of his land to the church in 1921'. The missionary living next to the Fagalele School Leone at the time, the Reverend Kinnersley, took an active part in the negotiations on behalf of the Congregational Church of American Samoa.

The Secretary of Native Affairs raised objections and questioned the sincerity of Mr. Kinnersley's motives. He asserted that the L. M. S. was seeking to acquire these lands by subterfuge, despite the fact that neither did the name of the London Missionary Society, or that of Mr. Kinnersley, appear in the agreement. The Samoan Church was entirely self-supporting at this time. Discussions continued until 1924, when on the 15th July of that year, the Governor signed a legal document confirming the transfer of what had been the property of Vaotuua to the Samoan Church (L. M. S), but only American Samoans could be its trustees.

Two months after our arrival in 1955, it was obvious that the only legally secure site for a place to live was Fagalele. The ancient structure at the heart of a Church School campus near Leone village was a wreck. A 'town' site in Pago was unavailable. Why had we travelled half way around the world to discover that an agreement on land for a home was insecure? In addition we were about to learn that a decision made two years earlier about the nature of our future work was about to be reversed. How green can you be?

Reality check

Two years earlier in April 1953 an Assembly of American Samoan chiefs and church leaders told a representative of the London Missionary Society Board that they would welcome the appointment of a Youth Worker from Britain.

Particular concern was expressed for the well-being of young adults and children, who had moved into the overcrowded Pago Bay area. They had left behind a structured village community life in exchange for the greater freedom, better schooling and employment associated with 'town' life. Many of them had become disaffected with traditional institutions, and were

Fagalele

turning to alcohol abuse, disruptive behaviour and the neglect of parental responsibility. Many had settled for an individualistic urban lifestyle, having left behind them an allegiance to village chiefs. Now urbanised they tried to avoid paying the annual Church tax (taulaga) that maintained two outmoded Boarding Schools, one for boys, and the other for girls..

Most of these urban dwellers had made it clear that they had no intention of sending their own children to independent Boarding Schools, which they felt lacked the financial resources required to provide teachers, buildings and equipment to match the satisfactory alternative of Government Schools. Parents were prepared to pay for bus passes etc., along with the majority of the village children who received a Government Education, but the Church Tax for lack lustre Boarding Schools was a burden grudgingly accepted. This negative attitude towards Church Schools was supported by the Government census. It showed that the population of American Samoa was 20,154, with 60 % of that total being children below 19 years of age. (16 % of those 12,000 children were in the school age group 5-9 years, (3,227) and 11% (2,149) were in the school age group 15-19 years). 70% of these children came from Samoan Church (L. M. S.) families.

Discussion in the 1953 District Assembly showed that Youth and Children's Work had come to be regarded as a high priority, mainly because the government schools were using the American system of education based on a secular agenda. Nearly all of the students expected to move along the educational escalator to Honolulu and California, and afterwards take advantage of educational and job opportunities in either State. Many church members had begun to recognise that the separation of Church and State in the USA, their 'land of opportunity', was being copied in the curriculum of American Samoan schools. Opinion had become increasingly divided about the best response to the challenge of secularism. Some felt strongly that the 'Samoan Way' was rooted in restoring the teaching of traditional values through two relatively small Church Schools exerting their influence.

A different view maintained that American education recognised a separation between the secular state and organised religion. An opportunity was being given to emulate American Churches with their all-age programme of Christian learning, which depended on well-trained teachers supplementing what was available through normal Sunday Worship. A revitalised Pastors School in each village, with pastor and people discovering together a contemporary means of nurturing the Samoans love of learning expressed 120 years earlier,should be encouraged to perform a similar function. Modern educational aids and an interesting presentation, allied to a Youth Club programme could help young Samoans meet the challenge of modern life. That had been the vision in the 1953 Assembly in American Samoa, and the majority had been attracted to it . Appointed to serve in Samoa at a London Assembly in May 1954, this had been my understanding of the assignment.

Two years later in August 1955, that is two months after our arrival as green bananas, a specially convened meeting of representatives of all sixty five villages in American Samoa took place. Listening to the debate through an interpreter it became clear that the goalposts had been moved. Contributions concentrated on the need to raise standards in the Church Boys School.

Others said that the teachers should ensure that obedience to their elders was understood to be as important as academic ability. A proposition that a teacher in a Government School named Tagata'ese be appointed was accepted with acclamation. It was anticipated that Eileen,a trained teacher, would agree to being appointed a member of staff, and I was to be the nominal Principal.

At a loss to understand how a 'new look' at the Church's educational policy had ended in rejection, and that a corporate, binding decision had been made to stay with an old and familiar system, 'muddling through' became our only option. Bowing to the inevitable, an agreement was made to renovate the Fagalele Mission House on the edge of the School Campus. Our hearts sank when we looked again at a ramshackle, English farmhouse with twelve large unfurnished rooms with sixteen foot high ceilings, eighteen inch thick walls rising from a massive foundation made from coral cement, and six feet above ground level. Our spirits rose again as we enjoyed the marvellous view. It was to be our home for thirteen years.

An enormous area of rusty corrugated iron roofing needed to be replaced in several places, protective paint applied, supporting joists and other timber struts to be put in place. All of this had to done before work could begin on doors, windows and plumbing to make the place habitable. Recovering this broken monument to past endeavour to make it serviceable again would be a huge task. The tank for catching rainwater needed attention ; a link with the Leone village reservoir was still in the pipe-line ; house plumbing would have to wait.

District ministers, both those in pastoral charge and an equal number of surplus or 'resting' pastors looking for a vacancy, set up camp from Monday to Friday for several weeks. A strong community spirit (mafutaga) was created, and the exchange of banter was uplifting. Singing, card playing, engagement in church politics,sharing local experiences of success and failure, taking part in worship, all of these things contributed to a 'camping out' holiday experience enjoyed whilst doing hard manual work. Throughout the structural work I made frequent bus journeys to the Government Supplies Department in Pago to order cement and timber. Making arrangements for the transport of building materials from Government stocks to the Fagalele site required much form filling and unnecessary delays.

The Samoan Way of tackling a big project was to have an intense burst of group activity involving twenty or more strong men, when progress was remarkably rapid. This was followed by a lull when card playing and 'joshing' took over. As a result many tasks requiring an individual's effort in joinery or plumbing dragged on for several months. Some essential carpentry jobs had not been done two years later. No doubt an 'old time' missionary would have brought out his tool box, and organised the considerable individual building skills available, to get the job finished efficiently and well. Samoan colleagues liked to take part in conversations in which their broken English was given a sympathetic hearing. Their humorous asides often had an edge to them. How was it that the friends of Jesus learned to speak so easily in other languages ? 'Had Pentecost passed me by?' During the Fagalele Mission House renovation, Atauloma School continued to be our temporary home.

Elite language / manners

The Reverend E. V. Cooper, living at Fagalele, died from a severe bout of malaria while supervising the building of Atauloma in 1902. Previously he had served as a missionary in a swampy area of New Guinea , which claimed the lives of many colleagues His burial place can be seen in the thickly overgrown school plantation alongside the graves of several children, all of whom died in the world wide influenza epidemic of 1918.

Before his death he had succeeded in an appeal to the competitive spirit of the people of newly constituted territory of American Samoa to build Atauloma School. It was to be the younger sister of the London Missionary Society Boarding School at Papauta in Apia, Western Samoa. Cooper persuaded pastors and chiefs to take part in a joint construction exercise of heroic proportions. Papauta, the older school,was founded in 1892 two years before the death of Robert Louis Stevenson at nearby Vailima, and eight years before American Samoa came into being in 1900. Papauta students, born and raised in what was now a U. S. Territory, were transferred to the Atauloma Boarding School, along with the Principal, Elizabeth Moore, and other Papauta teachers in 1902.

Atauloma

Ebenenezer Cooper had begun missionary work in 1892 at a time when there was growing concern about the moral fibre of church members in Tutuila. Replacements for Ta'unga and Thomas Powell were thought to be less important than the needs of W. Samoa experiencing serious political turmoil. The people of Eastern Samoa would have to wait for quieter times. This attitude became a habit of mind in the Missionary Meeting, and the Council of Samoan Elders gathered in Malua, Western Samoa..

Sadly, the truth was that the number of Tutuila backsliders more than equalled the number of new members, according to the 1890 church attendance rolls. A tangible sign of a new commitment, possibly associated with the arrival of Cooper,was the raising of sufficient money to buy materials, including Californian redwood and fir for the peaked roof, class rooms and dormitory on a site 60 feet by 106 feet at Atauloma. It is significant that it was American Samoans, in the first years of U.S. Navy Administration, who financed this ambitious project. The land was registered in their name, and would become an issue in church and government relationships in the 1960's.

Building work began on the school in 1900 above the village of Afao, where cup shaped indents in volcanic rock on the sea shore, provided archeological evidence for the sharpening and finishing of stone adzes. A two story building in 1900 was also of historical significance in that the foundation and the supporting pillars were made of coral cement. The first story walls were 20 inches thick, and those on the second floor were slightly less at 18 inches. Coral boulders were reduced to powder by huge bonfires on the beach, and carried on backs to the emerging colonial style edifice recessed into the hillside, forty feet above the sea shore.

A 1910 report of the U. S. Navy stated 'Atauloma girls made excellent nurses, for they had already received instruction in physiology and hygiene, but they had one serious handicap-they have no English.' From the age of five or six, Atauloma students would have attended village primary schools where a pride in spoken and written Samoan was the bedrock of a basic primary education. English, Writing, Arithmetic, Geography, and Scripture were taught at every grade after the girls had entered Atauloma at the age of fourteen years.

To help provide their own food, they were required to do plantation work one day a week, and were given the opportunity to find out about nutritious food, and how to prepare it. Graduates of the school were received annually into the Nurses Training Class at the Hospital in Utulei, Tutuila. The teaching staff, (two English teachers, Miss R. G. Holder and Miss J. N. Barker acting as co-principals). Together with the three Samoan teachers, all would have been disappointed with the U. S. Navy's assessment of their students English language skills. They maintained that the value of speaking correctly in their own language, and receiving a 'rounded' education closely related to Samoan village life, was more important.

Working in parallel with Papauta, sewing, embroidery, arts and crafts were included in Atauloma's curriculum, with the intention of developing the girls' appreciation of their own culture. When they returned to their own villages for the school holidays, it was hoped that an understanding of the needs of their fellow villagers would motivate them further in a desire to be of service. A mother's ignorance of childcare, the neglect and cruelty to animals, the dullness and boredom of life through lack of interests, all the wasted opportunities to learn new skills, these were the challenges that they faced.

For seventy years the sister schools of Atauloma and Papauta had tried to encourage the importance of sound hearts and bodies, matched by an appreciation of those spiritual values, which can enrich a nation's life. In the school nursery the girls learned about child care and developing children's inherent qualities. Long before environmental studies became a world wide concern, Atauloma encouraged respect towards the natural world, an attitude, which had been at the heart of Pacific Island life in earlier centuries. Another aim was to encourage students to use their critical faculties to avoid the indiscriminate acceptance of all things foreign. They were to cherish the qualities found in their own culture.

In 1955, whilst staying in the school, it was odd to see students reading a book on English etiquette as they attempted to lay the table for breakfast. At first sight it seemed to contradict the school's emphasis on preserving Samoan traditions. Edith Maxfield, an English teacher from Bridport in Dorset was a stickler for such proprieties, which sometimes led to rather stilted conversations at meal times. The daily task of the girl on duty was to ensure that a slice of papaya, a bowl of corn flakes followed by toast and marmalade were made ready. Along with the students, we learned that good manners and decorum were essential attributes if we were going to move comfortably among the elite in Samoan society. At the end of each lesson the schoolgirls would say to their teacher, 'Thank you for teaching us.' Edith had kindly agreed that we could share her small flat during the day, whilst we had the use of one of the teacher's rooms in the main school for sleeping. 'Mosquitoes a real menace today' was a frequent entry in the diary.

Every day stories were told to help newcomers from the suburbs of London to piece together the background to the lives of Samoan people, both high and low. On one occasion, after an evening meal two junior teacher named Pogisa and Vanilla talked about the ghost 'aitu', who looked after the boys school compound at Fagalele, our future home. The aitu was said to sit on the stone chair, 'le ma'a o Tuiatua', near the blowholes. It seems that at Atauloma the students tried to scare each other by talking about an 'aitu' with the same name, who lived in the surrounding plantation. This behaviour had occasionally led to mass hysteria, and teachers acted as guardians in this respect.

One of the girls of a previous generation, Savali Sunia, wrote in Samoan later in life about two women missionaries,Misi Paka (Barker) and Misi Olita (Holder). They often read and studied late,and were disturbed by strange apparitions. 'La molimau mai ai, e alu atu lava le tagata ma tautala atu e pei o se tagata ola. Ae sa to'ilalo uma ia temoni i le fa'atuatua o nei tama'ita'i). 'One of the spirits spoke like a human being, but the faith of the two European teachers was able to overcome their fear'. Strange 'goings on' in later years in and around our home at Fagalele, which I was unable to explain, were shrugged off as pranks by persons unknown. We were told that if we did not deliberately give offence to such spirits, then our peace was respected. However the mere mention of Le Telesa, a goddess, could still produce a genuine shudder among some Samoans in 1956.

Fuluiole Meleisea, who had been a teacher at Papauta, would have none of it. She was 55 years old when I knew her in 1955 as the teacher who shared the leadership of Atauloma with Edith Maxfield. Her manner denied any attempt at familiarity, and it was obvious that the deference she received from visitors, was more than her due as an authority figure within a Boarding School. Fuluiole was the granddaughter of a Paramount Chief in Western Samoa. Something I said must have suggested that a person's bearing,and a sense of decorum were not high on my list of priorities regarding a person's worth. She made a point of stressing the importance of outward show in Samoan society.

I gathered that the word 'feagaiga' (covenant), referred to the special bond that existed between sister and brother. This had been dramatically demonstrated when she pushed past us as she rushed up the gangway of the M.V. Tofua to greet High Chief Peseta, her brother, after the ship berthed in Pago 'A sister is the inner corner (ioimata) of her brother's eye' is a Samoan saying indicating that men are emotionally dependent on their sisters at a deeply unconscious level. I remembered her words many times in the following years when alliances defied explanation.

Six months later during a discussion with a friend George Milner, I was reminded of the conversation with Fuluiole. George, who stayed in our home at Fagalele in 1956, mentioned that in recent times 'feagaiga 'had moved on to mean an agreement in a more general sense than previously. (George had been commissioned by the two Governments, and Oxford University Press to compile a new dictionary). He commented that in the past the primary meaning had been a cordial lasting relationship between a sister and brother, whereas its secondary use referred to a legal bond regarding land or a covenant made between village chiefs and a prospective pastor. Nowadays the order of precedence given to the word's meaning has been reversed.

In the past 'feagaiga' (Covenant) meant that the respect attributed to one side of an agreement honoured the dignity and legitimacy of the other person, or group. It summed up an ideal of order and stability running through all levels of Samoan society, where everybody knew their place. Honour and dignity (mamalu) was what groups and individuals craved more than anything else. The responses most earnestly desired from others were acceptance and deference (fa'aaloalo). These attitudes, it seemed, were the essential ingredient in Samoan social life. In practical terms, Fuluiole had been at pains to tell me that unhurried dignity (mamalu), in a teacher, or other authority figure, was a prerequisite for anyone wanting to be accepted in Samoan society.

In modern Samoa 'feagaiga' applies to a lasting covenant, 'to have and to hold' in a mainly legalistic sense. However the thinking behind the earlier usage is still influential in understanding the concept. A sacred contract (feagaiga), upheld the Samoan political system, kept the upper class in power, confirmed alliances between influential families, and allowed serial marriages among the aristocracy. Sex and marriage for the upper classes was about begetting a child to link up with other lineages of superior social rank. (Sexual morality among 'the other ranks' in the olden days had been more relaxed.) When monogamous, faithful marriage was expected of Christians, the resulting conflict of interest among some of the highly born accustomed to serial marriage, the issue was not resolved conclusively. Appearances did not provide the whole story. Aristocrats had their own morals.

In this regard, Fuluioli said that as a daughter of a pastor she was not allowed to marry an important chief because of the traditional obligations associated with honour being satisfied in the marriage bond. Public defloration was no longer required, but underlying attitudes turned a blind eye to easy 'break-ups'. To promote faithful, monogamous marriage the church had long since decided that a top priority was to emphasise the importance of family life. This was to done through the example of fidelity shown by the village pastor and his wife.

Attendance at Malua College for male ministers in training, and a few chiefs seeking political office, meeting girls from the sister Boarding Schools of Papauta, and Atauloma, prepared them for the ideal Christian marriage. It was hoped that their life long feagaiga would be copied by couples in their congregation. Just as the daughters of high rank were protected from sexual intrusion to uphold the honour of the family, Papauta and Atauloma students were also a protected species who would hopefully embody sound marriage principles as an example to their contemporaries..

Class and quality was also to the fore when the Samoan language was spoken, because two distinct pronunciation of words existed alongside each other. The one was used on formal occasions by chiefs, and the other in everyday conversation by chiefs and commoners alike. The letter 'k' seems to be easier to use than the letter 't' and I quickly learned that village children called their island 'kukuila', and when they said 'hello' it was 'kalofa' not 'talofa'. Expected to speak in the chiefly language at all times, because I was normally 'on parade' taking part in public worship, or present at ceremonies, when a convoluted, respectful form of address was used, it seemed that I was destined to live life on a pedestal. Even when I reached the point when I tried to listen attentively when others spoke in the 'k' language, I always held back from using the same form. Trying to speak the 'posh' version of the language had become ingrained

A potential stumbling block, the glottal stop sound did not present a problem, for as a boy my parents reminded me that milk came in a bottle and not a bo' le. However 'o', without the glottal stop meaning 'of'', had to be distinguished from 'o' meaning 'the'. Samoan was also a language full of idioms, and the meaning of many words could only be worked out by knowing the context in which they were used. At that stage of formal learning I found that there were three different ways of addressing wives, each according to their rank. For example, a commoner's wife, or one's own was called a to'alua or 'ava', that of the head of the family, 'faletua', whereas a high chief's wife was known as 'tama'i ta'i'. I became bogged down in details addressing wives each according to their rank.

Preoccupied with fine distinctions, looking out through palm trees on energy sapping views of the reef, the lagoon and the wide Pacific beyond, the intermittent whine and nip of the mosquitoes did not aid concentration.. Trying to understand the Samoan language through studying Pratt's Dictionary and Grammar using dry as dust methods was not a good idea. The language spoken by the Samoan people,soft, musical and flowing eluded me. Because of its pure vowel sounds, some linguists have called it the Italian of the Pacific.

Struggling to speak a few words in a recognizable sequence I was informed that Amperosa, one of the five Senior Ministers, (Toeaina) had announced in Leone Church, the largest congregation in the Western District (300 people), that Nimese, my Samoan name, was leading worship on the following Sunday.

This led to panic stations because I still found it difficult to get my tongue around the correct pronunciation of the first words inviting the congregation to join in worship. Edith Maxfield, our tutor, was able to convince the messenger that it was too early for me to do so, but Amperosa came on the following day to make a personal request. Standing in the pulpit I proceeded to make a fool of myself, -but it was a start to public speaking. .

As if to reinforce the message that I should be making greater progress in language study, the flickering lights of the monthly banana boat, M. V .Tofua appeared to wink mockingly in the night sky as it leisurely made its way across Leone Bay on the way to the port of Apia in Western Samoa. After three months I had made little progress in speaking Samoan. Whereas I knew that a commoner had eyes, 'mata', and a chief's were known as 'fofoga', that a chief's food was 'taumafa', and a commoner's meal was 'mea 'ai', I still could not begin to string simple sentences together. I had made the mistake of first trying to get the grammar right, instead of plunging into badly spoken Samoan in a village situation, and sorting out the mistakes afterwards. I had also spent too much time on land and property issues.

Living with compromise

Nearly four months after our arrival in Samoa we moved into the bare Mission House at Fagalele in late September to sleep in the comfortable bed bought in London in February. Three flat wick kerosene lamps placed in different rooms provided a poor light while we waited for the delivery of two Tilley storm lanterns. For the next three years these pressure lamps gave a brighter light, but unwelcome heat on steamy hot nights. Two bulky homemade chairs made from wooden boxes painted bottle green added to this picture of an isolated colonial outpost. Open to sea breezes on balmy nights, the solid structure provided a beautiful view across Leone Bay. We imagined the attractive location of Fagalele house and school compound being transformed into a luxury hotel, with all modern conveniences. The dream was to be shattered as its exposed position felt the full force of regular storms and occasional hurricanes.

Living on a school compound, and contrary to our expectations required to work within an outmoded Boarding School system, I continued to meet with Samoan colleagues to explore ways of working among young people in nearby villages after school hours. The Elder Pastors asked both of us to give palliative care to a school, which was struggling to justify its existence. We agreed to do our best to carry out the wishes of the Church District Council, but we knew in our hearts that the financial resources were not available to do an adequate job. It did not help the morale of Church teachers to know that the Government school system was the preferred option of most Church people.

A disturbing picture of the school's life emerged when we eventually got round to examine the Fagalele entry rolls compiled in July 1955. They revealed that many of the students were late teenagers waiting for the monthly cheque from family members in the Armed Services to pay for their passage to Hawai'i and California. Several students were hefty young men, whose ages ranged from 17-18 years. They were 'filling in time' before leaving for the USA. With little to occupy them in their own villages, the main reason for them being sent to Fagalele, was to keep them out of mischief. Two or three of them showed some interest in taking the entrance examination to Leulumoega, the Church High School in Western Samoa.

Soon after Eileen began teaching, a colleague named Malaki, a former marine who had taught English, left for California to be followed in quick succession by Talamoni, Simati and other short-term appointments. American nationals, they were marking time in whatever paid work came along, as they waited for their entry permits to arrive. With Tagata'ese as the newly appointed Samoan Headmaster, and Eileen respected as a U. K. qualified teacher, the numbers of students remained constant. The older boys in particular benefited from their supervision over a two-year period. In particular their parents welcomed Tagata'ese's dedication to the cause of preserving the Samoan culture and language.

An early visitor, as we settled down in our Fagalele, was the Senior Pastor Luavasa, aged 74. I already knew him as a friendly counsellor, who was particularly helpful on the first occasion I was called upon to lead an Assembly Communion Service with over 300 people present. Over the last 55 years I have often recalled his gentle prompting at key moments in the celebration, when he whispered in Samoan what needed to be said or done. He gave me confidence in leading sacred rites with large numbers of people present, which proved invaluable on subsequent occasions.

During a visit to our home Luavasa suggested that instead of considering work in the Pago suburban sprawl, I should try to find out more about life in the villages outside the Bay Area, that is in 56 of the 64 villages in the District. He would make the necessary arrangements with village chiefs. Luavasa also gave me to understand that, unlike people living in the Bay Area, where villages had begun to merge, there were many others in which time honoured social discipline still applied. He thought that it was important for me to experience such villages at close quarters, to be present at village meetings as chiefs conducted their normal business,to observe the Pastors Schools, and to take part in the preparations for the annual District examinations. Luavasa suggested that I should get to know Samoan life at the grass roots through the educational work long practised by village churches.

Pastors Schools and cricket

In 1901, Commander Tilley the first U. S. Navy Governor reported to his superiors in the Navy Department that 'the missionaries working in Tutuila and Manu'a have given me much help, especially those of the London Missionary Society'. He told them that when Wilkes visited in 1839, the American explorer found that many of them could read and write well. 'Their books are constantly before them, grey men puzzling over the alphabet, and taught by some of the youngest of the family. As the books, mainly concerned with bible knowledge, came off the press (1836), they were in great demand for there was great interest in the magic of the printed word'. Tillley was also impressed when he wrote 60 years later,'The Pastor's Schools are held 2 hours a day, 4 days a week, where attendance was voluntary. Classes are conducted in the home of the Pastor or Faife'au'.

Naval officers noted in their reports that the Faife'au were unwilling to teach in English, but appreciated that the first duty of a minister was to preach and teach in Samoan, to visit the sick and help, to preserve peace and good order. The same naval personnel reported that the factors that kept Pastors up to the mark included a healthy respect for the annual examinations, (Faiga Suega), which spurred an ambition to get high marks, and to avoid being thought ill informed by a rival village.

According to Commander Tilley the children were taught sewing, music, reading, writing, arithmetic, and a little geography in their own language. Among the Samoan books in my possession used in 1900 and the 1950's is one entitled 'Elementary Geography', and another reflects on 'The Journeys of the Apostle Paul'. 'A Guide for disciples of Jesus' (O le So'o o Iesu), 'Five short plays based on the Old Testament, Pilgrims Progress, and R L. Stevensons 'Bottle Imp' accompany a translation of 'The Black Tulip' by Dumas. Clearly the Pastors Schools provided a good basic education.

Parrot learning, where youngsters gave set answers to questions from a book by Moffat (1900), prepared the way for a more thoughtful approach for the older children. 'Sa faatuina le Faamanatuga anafea?' was answered 'Sa faatuina e Iesu i le po ua faalataina ai e Iuta'. (When was Holy Communion established? Answer. Jesus established it on the night when Judas betrayed him.) A Christian Catechism of more than 70 questions and answers were learned by heart, which meant that children had a grasp of the basic facts about the Christian Faith. They could be regarded as memory tests, but they could also form a basis for growth in the Christian life. It all sounded rather heavy going, but team games, sports and dancing helped to create what became a worthwhile, even enjoyable experience for many village children, especially when cricket matches were arranged at short notice.

From the concrete pitch at the centre of the village could be heard the whoops of enjoyment accompanying successful strikes. Matches between rival teams resembled a jamboree. Beginning with a procession headed by a group of umpires, they paraded first to the accompaniment of a pipe and drum band. Brightly coloured banners were made especially for the occasion. Parade ground drill followed with the players armed with baseball bats, which from a distance appeared to be war clubs. Marching as if on combat duty, their orderly progression was constantly interrupted by the tomfoolery of several young men and women drawing attention to the physical attributes of particular individuals, powerful biceps etc. among the team players.

On the edge of the 'malae', a large open space shaded by coconut trees, the teams lined up to face each other to perform what in the old days would have been a war dance to frighten the living daylights out of the opposition. It was a pale imitation of the Maori rugby football team representing New Zealand doing the haka named 'kapo o pago'(eruption of a volcano). Bringing up the rear was a group charged with providing sufficient food and drink for everyone during the match, and to round off the event with a feast.

Although the game played on the concrete strip had a single stump at each end, and a bat and ball were at the centre of proceedings, the fact that it was called 'kirikiti' had little to do with the rules laid down by the Marylebone Cricket Club. The ball used in baseball was thrown full toss at the stump, (or the batsmen), by a succession of bowlers hurling the missile with lethal ferocity. To create confusion in the batsman's mind the number of balls in an over varied considerably. A bowler on a 'winning streak' was kept on until he was exhausted.

Finesse with the club was impossible, but a 'big hitter' was much appreciated by the groups of singers and dancers, who maintained a barrage of sound throughout the proceedings. Their mimicry of unproductive strokes made by opposition players was merciless. I know because I was out first ball,-and

94

the squealing of many tin whistles revealed their unbounded delight at my discomfort. The general melee,which took place on and off the pitch when one of their players made a big hit meant that play on the pitch was interrupted for more than five minutes to allow time for adequate celebrations. It could be great fun, but when fights broke out at cricket and rugby matches between rival villages, onlookers were reminded of the Samoan people's warrior past, and disputes over hereditary rights.

House of learning

The scheduled trips arranged by the territory's Senior Elder, began at the western end of Tutuila with the villages of Amanave, Nua and Se'etaga. I was accompanied by a strapping 18 years old Fagalele student, named Feleti, when walking to these coastline settlements. Approached by a mountain track, followed by a rowboat journey across a narrow bay to Fagamalo, Poloa and Fagali 'i villages I was a fortunate young man . The last named village pointed towards Aleipata, 60 miles away on the island of Upolu in Western Samoa, the district from which warriors set out for Tutuila in 1787,to meet unexpectedly with the French navigator, La Perouse at A'asu, an encounter, which resulted in 50 deaths.

Spending days in these villages, I began to experience at first hand the strong grip of the culture and tradition on local churches, with the separate seating arrangements for the elite, and the respect given to middle rank chiefs and their families. It became clear that a niche had been found for the untitled in the church choir, and recognition was given to those engaged in welfare work, or maintaining cleanliness. The sensible division of labour in the service of the community was brought home to me. There was much to value in Old Samoa.

Approaching the village of Fagamalo, the most important house

Inside view of chief's house

95

(Fale Tele), stood out in front of all the other houses. It served as a meeting house for chief council meetings,family gatherings, funerals or investitures for newly appointed chiefs (maota o ali'i). Oval or circular in shape, the houses reminded me of the thatched cottages of rural England, except that they were open to the breeze on all sides. Venetian blinds of coconut fronds were suspended from the eaves to provide protection in stormy weather.

Not completely circular, the principle rafters, made from flexible coconut wood curved towards the beams at the centre of the House of Learning in a gradually lessening which was calculated with unerring accuracy. Intrigued by traditional Samoan architecture, I saw that the tall central pillars, plus the lower posts, were spaced four feet apart to provide the basic shape of the building. Five feet high above the floor of the house, the lower posts determined the height of the roof at its edge. All of the posts came from the breadfruit tree. Tube shaped lengths of pliable wood, four inches in diameter,encircled the skeleton structure to be lashed to the lower posts.

The use made of the humble 'afa (twine) to bind the integral parts of the building together, both bulky and small, made a deep impression on me. First soaking the coconut husks in salt water the fibres were pounded with mallets to separate them, before drying in the sun. The process of plaiting the fibres into twine was done by elderly matai (chiefs) as they discussed village business. A common sight was that of men performing a useful community task as they sat in the lotus position on the floor. Combining the fibre strands by rolling them with their hands against bare thighs, as if they were rolling loose tobacco, twine was produced possessing considerable tensile strength.

The use and function of the large meeting house (Fale tele),provided valuable information about Samoan social organisation,and the fa'a matai (chiefly) system. Divided into four quarters, the front side of the floor facing the village green (malai) was named 'Tala luma' (front part),the quarter at the back the 'Tala tua' (back part),and the two sides are simply 'Tala'. Only the leading chiefs could sit in front of the posts known as Matua tala, and the side posts (pou), to the left of them in the Tala luma (front) called Pou o le Pepe (small), are reserved for the Tulafale, or orators. Tala tua is the area where the stewards sat to mix and serve the 'ava, the ceremonial drink (Pole positions map p108). After the celebration a list of subjects for discussion was considered by the Village Council This was compared to a bunch of bananas picked in turn, the ripest from the top downwards. Some items from the agenda would be thrown away as not fit for the day's purpose.

Demarcation lines were invisible, but they were written indelibly on the hearts and minds of those sitting cross legged on mats in front of their correct pole position. The rank of an ali'i (chief) was immediately obvious, but when the orators (tulafale) began to vie with each other for the honour of making the welcome speech, it appeared to be a genuine contest, but it was showmanship. In fact a long established hierarchy existed among the orators, and they each knew their assigned role. Recognition was given to both high low as each spoke in turn to satisfy family honour. The place in the proceedings where they were expected to speak was predetermined, and a guest needed to know his place and time before making an appropriate response.

An important stage in my learning curve was when I began to appreciate the line drawn between the sacred and the secular. The feagaiga (covenant), between a pastor and a council of chiefs, meant that the pastor was owed respect and deference as the local representative of God, irrespective of his own family status. Pastors were not allowed to take chiefly titles or sit in the Village council,unless invited. Chiefs did not discuss church ('au lotu) matters in the village Council, but strongly influenced decisions in their parallel role as deacons when Church Meetings took place .

Working on hillside plantations, fishing over the reef or playing cricket, there was always a distinctive Samoan way of doing things. Staying in the home of Pastors during weekends it seemed that even the smoke that slowly lifted into the Sunday morning air from dozens of wood fires lit to cook the 'to'onai', (the meal eaten at the family gathering after worship), had an unmistakable Samoan fragrance. I had known in my head, that Samoan society was linked with the past by an intricate network of conventions indicating what was the 'done thing' in personal conversation or public meeting. I had seen examples of traditional behaviour considered to be in appropriate for every situation from the cradle to the grave. After a tour of six villages I had begun to appreciate its emotional power..

During conversations conducted in a mixture of Samoan and English, I gathered that the authority of the chiefs had become less respected. Clinging to past loyalties losing some appeal, allied to the dollar providing a passport into better world in Honolulu and beyond, it was obvious to these leaders that a well loved world was slipping away. The unsettling effect of change among an older generation bred a nostalgia for an idealized past. This was focused on well tried Church institutions, such as the District Schools at Fagalele and Atauloma. During those visits I grew to love and respect Old Samoa. At the same time it seemed right to encourage engagement rather than withdrawal from the task of fishing in what would become troubled waters.

Section headings

Greenhorns 1942 - Raw recruits - First impressions - Transfer of power - Being a foreigner - Reality check Elite language and etiquette - Living with compromise - Pastors Schools and cricket -House of learning.

Fishing in troubled waters

Chapter Nine

1957- 1958 - Falling apart

Samoan proverb. *Uu solo le falute.* The bundle unwraps. When a number of floor mats of different shapes and sizes need to be stored among the rafters,they are first gathered into a bundle. If other mats need to be included, the bundle is unrolled. At this point they can easily fall into a disorderly heap. The word 'falute' usually refers to mats, but it can also apply to a project falling apart, or an individual dropping to pieces.

Come in !

As guests in their homeland, Samoan people welcomed us with friendly restraint in June 1955. Allowance was made for our clumsy attempts to feel comfortable whilst sitting cross-legged, and they turned a deaf ear to frequent gaffes made in exchanging pleasantries. Eating chicken in Manu'a it was impolite to use the common Samoan name for that particular dish. 'Moa' was the name of a high chief, who was associated with sacred observance. Another word meaning creature was used instead. Mountains of American style food were placed before us at several 'welcome' ceremonies, when our hosts outdid each other in making us feel 'at home'. Porridge, corn flakes, plates of fried eggs and bacon, toast, potato salads, cooked meats and cakes appeared.

Samoan colleagues suggested that respect for their customs and conventions should inform our choice of clothes to be worn in public. Shorts and knee length skirts were to be avoided. Aware of local sensitivities, it became necessary to cover our extended legs with mats, when cramp crept up on us as speeches increased in length. It was considered offensive to point feet in the direction of others. We quickly learned the casual greetings expected of people passing each other walking along the road. Instead of commenting on the weather, or asking about their state of health, it was polite to ask where the person was going. An answer giving details about the other person's itinerary for the day was not expected! 'Inland' (i'uta) or 'seaward' (i tai) was enough. At a reception it soon became apparent that it was disrespectful to stand and eat in front of others. Walking through a village whilst eating was 'not done'.

Arriving at a chief's home without warning, broke a more important social convention. If I took a stroll into a nearby village to get some exercise, local people thought that I must want to see a chief on formal business. An informal visit was out of order. The role I had been given by Samoan leaders made me a 'special' visitor, requiring 'red carpet' treatment. I also learned that as typical homes (fale), did not have walls or privacy, visitors were not recognised by the inhabitants until welcome formalities had been observed. Invisible to a foreigner, the space in the home reserved for the family, and that which was the preserve of visitors, was clearly understood by 'locals'. This meant that certain protocols had to be observed, which I negotiated gradually by trial and error.

I remember now with acute embarrassment my mistake in approaching a fale without giving fair warning of my visit to members of a family inside, who I had spoken to two days earlier in more formal surroundings. As an unexpected caller, I could see the mother and daughters were taken aback, for they gave no outward sign that I had been noticed. Tentatively standing between two of the posts, at what I hoped was the front entrance, I stood motionless waiting for something to happen. Fortunately a girl came forward and a fresh mat from a rolled bundle was laid out. Spreading the mat was equivalent to answering the door in England, that is after first peeping out of a side window to see who was the visitor.

Relying on such an unforgettable experience, the structure of this chapter relies on the sight of a rolled bundle of mats collapsing into disarray. Each mat falling from the bundle represents a layer in the Samoan culture and tradition, which questioned my own limited experience of life in 1956-58.

Round trip (Malaga)

The first mat has 'malaga' or journey written on it because this activity helped me to understand a core value in the Samoan way of life. A journey could be mistaken for a pilgrimage. It seemed to confirm membership of an extended family with all its benefits,- and obligations. To a Samoan every village is an inn or hostelry, where it is possible to claim a relative by blood, marriage or adoption. At the very least a message can be passed on from a relative of one of the local villagers. It follows that a tab is kept of the state of a relationship in the same way that a Westerner knows what is in his bank account at any given time.

Chiefs and their wives receive generous hospitality, which includes feasting whist the men drink kava and share news from various regions about who's in, and who's out. Political ideas and changing alliances grip their attention, as well as the gossip going the rounds about people exercising power in other districts. A group on a malaga could be concerned with family business such as a marriage, funeral or the appointment of a chief. Others might be concerned with medical, school and church matters. Sometimes a malaga is a group presenting a play or concert to raise money for a new village building They descend on a host community, having given prior warning.

An opportunity to fraternise with members of the opposite sex was also provided by a malaga, particularly among young people who came from outside the immediate area of the host village. The behaviour of young men and women was normally circumscribed by family honour in village life, where everyone knew each other's business, and boundaries between stable relationships were safeguarded. Nevertheless a more relaxed atmosphere during an overnight stop-over allows dancing and entertainment. A sexual match leading to an elopement, and a later return as a young family to the host village, is discouraged, but eventually accepted.

Casual sexual liaisons between daughters of chiefs and men living in their home village were not permitted because they threatened family honour and stability. Yet arranged marriages between the daughters of high chiefs or pastors often relied on intermediaries who accompanied malaga,. In Old Samoa these developed into impressive processions. The ceremonial journey (malaga) of the elite in Samoan society led to marriage and the introduction of new blood into local communities. On top of everything else the malaga took the place of a newspaper,as it provided a political forum and an opportunity for a concert (fiafia).

In April 1956 I had responded positively to the suggestion of the Senior Ministers (Au Toeaina), that I should get out and about. The result was a visitation (malaga), to a small group of villages beyond Amanave, seven miles west of our home at Fagalele. Building on that experience I was given the honorary title of Leader (Ta'ita'i) of the Pastors School Examinations, which was to take place in July 1956. Beginning in the Manu'a Group, and returning to Tutuila and the island of Aunu'u, our team of examiners, made up of three ministers, their wives and numerous retainers were expected to test children from sixty-four village schools.

Our assignment was to visit sixteen venues on a journey which would take us close to all the villages in American Samoa. Children from several Pastors Schools in a designated area would come together for a day-long Event of examinations, cricket and dancing. An elaborate formal welcome and reception in the chosen villages would recognise the Visiting Team as representatives of a nation-wide (Establishment) Church. Congregations were present in every village in American Samoa. Protocol having been observed in each of the appointed venues, the Visiting Team began its work.

The Examination Event (Faiga Su'ega) in July 1956 began at midnight on board the Motor Vessel named Samoa, (the size of a North Sea fishing boat), as it left PagoPago harbour in Tutuila for Manu'a, a group of islands sixty miles to the east. In the light of dawn, around 4 o'clock, I saw the two volcanic islands of Ofu and Olosenga, in the rough shape of massive pyramids rising from the ocean floor. Both surrounded by a solid jagged reef, they had no harbours. However on the south side of the islet of Nu'u, near the village of Ofu, there was an anchorage reasonably protected from the trade wind and the mountainous Pacific swells.

The sea conditions on the morning of our arrival made the landing of cargo and passengers from small lighters difficult. Jumping at the right moment from a heaving deck towards slippery rock surfaces, was both exhilarating and demanding. Earlier from the ship's side I had admired the skill and daring of those who manned the lighters (tulula). They drew alongside in rough seas to load the goods for the island Store, before rowing ashore to discharge them. It was to be the last delivery for a month. The engine of M. V. Samoa broke down outside Pago Harbour on its next trip, preventing the delivery of 'pisupo' (corned beef), and other provisions.

Ofu, 3 miles long and 2 miles wide was a mountain with a narrow strip of cultivated land at sea level. An additional small plantation on a nearby ridge had soil composed of long decayed coconut trees, fronds and bird droppings. Ofu was separated from a neighbouring island, Olosenga, by a channel a quarter of a mile wide. This was sucked dry by receding currents at low tide. Children and young people who had already crossed over the temporary bridge between the islands had gathered to meet the examination party. After crossing over in an outrigger canoe (paopao), it was obvious that Olosenga, lived up to the meaning of its name, 'Fortress'.

Three miles long and in places only five hundred yards wide Olosenga was clearly the tip of a long- extinct volcano. Close to the water's edge a perpendicular rock face rose to a height of two thousand feet. On a narrow strip of land, the local community sheltered beneath the jagged edifice, proud of an impressive looking church building, and well furnished pastor's house, When Ta'unga, the Raratongan L. M. S. Missionary was stationed in Manu'a in 1870 he wrote in his journal that when the warning note of the conch shell indicated the approach of enemy warriors,the bulk of the population retreated up the path to the mountain top. Tauaga wrote about the feuding and warfare of kith and kin fighting each other for the control of elite titles, and the enhancement of sectional power and prestige.

Communities of two to five hundred people such as those who lived on the twin islands Ofu and Olosenga, considered themselves to be distinct from each other. They treasured the freedom to act as they had decided through Island Councils, whose rules and regulations had been handed down through many generations. Seven miles away across the water Ta'u Islanders in their distinctive village order also managed their own affairs through separate Councils of Chiefs.

For 100 years agreements made by Village Councils regarding the appointment of pastors, represented a Congregational style of church government that was at the same time genuinely Samoan. Encouragement was given to local Councils to join with others to form a District Council. High Chiefs depended on several villages for support through alliances built on relationships of blood or marriage. This affiliation was reflected in Church Assemblies. The islands of Manu'a plus western and eastern halves of Tutuila Island, American Samoa, was one district. The islands of Western Samoa had Six Districts and the total of seven Districts met annually in General Assembly on the island of Upolu in Western Samoa.

On board the M.V. Samoa again, the examination party left Olosenga and chugged across the six miles to the east, parting the huge Pacific rollers on the way to Ta'u, the principal island, which measures a hundred square miles. On the first of two visits to the Manu'a group I travelled east to the outermost island of Ta'u, before returning several days later in a westerly direction to the island of Olosenga by fautasi. This was a longboat built of small planks, or slabs, fitted together and sewn with coconut fibre, and manned by sixteen rowers. An account of what was a personal odyssey,of seven miles on the ocean wave appears in 'Well done the rowers', the title of Chapter Ten.

Importance of ceremony

The majority of the villages on the island of Ta'u such as Amouli, Fagamalo, and Faleasao are on the west side of the island, but three are on the northeast corner, including Fitiuta. Small and glittering jewels in a wide expanse of ocean, the people of Manu'a enjoyed enormous prestige throughout the Samoa Islands, both east and west, because of their lines of chiefly authority based on an oral genealogical record, (Fa'alupenga), going back though more than 50 generations to the earliest Polynesian navigators. Voyaging westwards more than a thousand years ago from the hub of the Polynesian universe, in what we know as Tahiti, Manu'a had been the first port of call for the ancestors of the Samoan people. Thereafter, the leaders of the three islands of Manu'a had been accorded particular veneration throughout E. and W. Samoa.

Whilst the examination malaga was in Manu'a, its members were given the 'The full works' of a ceremonial welcome. Genealogical details in welcome speeches varied from one political district to another, but the actual ritual contained four basic elements ; the speeches, the presentation of food and finely woven mats, drinking 'ava individually from a common cup, and finally a feast. Each chief of the village brought a gnarled root of the 'ava plant (botanical name, Piper methysticum) and gave the stick to a representative of the examination party. Acting as talking chief, he then lifted up each root, admired it, thanked the hosts, whereupon the roots were redistributed among those present, one being set aside to make the ceremonial 'ava drink'. A 'tongue in cheek' contest then took place between the talking chiefs of the host village, for the honour of making the welcome speech. The need for recognition satisfied, the leading orator performed his pre-determined role of reminding the assembly of significant events in Samoan history, making reference to long dead heroes of the locality, and ending the oration with a glowing testimony to the all-important Day when John Williams and Papu (a Tahitian missionary) arrived with the Good News of Jesus Christ. A saying from the biblical Book of Proverbs (Hope arrived is a tree of life), was incorporated into the speech at this point to further emphasize the importance of the reception given by the Samoan people to the first emissaries of the Christian Faith.

Sitting cross-legged I invariably became aware of cramp slowly moving down my legs as the orators speech continued. After whispering to someone nearby, 'Ua vela the fala.' (The mat is warm), allowance was made for long legs and undignified posture, by covering the offending limbs with one of the mats from an unrolled bundle. Next, a young man representing the untitled strength of the village ('aumaga), stirred a mixture of ground kava root and water with a handful of shredded fibre torn from the inner bark of the hibiscus plant. Three times the steward threw the pad of fibre (fau) over his shoulder to a waiting attendant, who shook it several times before tossing it back. The steward then called out that the 'ava was ready, and each of us sitting in front of an assigned post in the oval-shaped Ceremonial House, clapped our hands in a regular beat to show that we were ready to receive the kava of hospitality.

A cupbearer took a polished half-coconut shell, and gave it to the steward who held the saturated fibre over the cup to fill it. Representing the wider Church at examination time, I was considered to be the most prestigious person present, and therefore the first person to acknowledge their courtesy. Following few polite hand claps, the cupbearer brought the cup and presented it with a deep bow while the orator called out, 'Au mai the ipu o Misi Nimese' (Bring the cup to Neems), as the other participants continued to clap rhythmically. On receiving the cup it was necessary to lift up the corner of the mat, to pour a small libation on the floor surface made with white coral fragments, and then to wish the assembly good health and happiness, 'Ia

manuia, ma ia soifua'. The taste of the liquid was earthy, with a subtle tang of ginger and the appearance of pale tea. It was pleasant enough. Said to be a stimulant, I found its relaxing qualities hard to resist. At the same time the potion encouraged the body's inner juices to seek relief.

During the feast, which followed the kava ceremony, the participants remained in the same places observing the rules of precedence appropriate to a Council of Chiefs. The correct place and dignity of each chief (matai) of a family had been recognised earlier in the proceedings, and reference made to the relationship of these local names to the broader social structure of Samoan Society. This 'fa'alupega' was recited on all formal occasions. A sumptuous feast followed. Food was placed on two banana leaves used as a table cloth and included a portion of taro, a breadfruit, some pork, fish or fowl, and palu sami.

A great delicacy, the last was a thick cream made from pounded coconut meat seasoned with spices, then wrapped in tender taro leaves, cooked slowly on hot stones and served on slices of baked taro. My mouth waters as I recall the smooth, yet tingly sensation of the palu sami as it hit the taste buds, combining well with the bland chestnut taste of breadfruit, and ta'a mu, a taro with white flesh covered in coconut cream. It had been cooked gently at the centre of a pile of heated stones, covered by banana leaves. To cleanse the palate between courses, the pulp and juice of young coconuts was provided as the equivalent of a sorbet before bowls of water and towels were brought to wash our hands. I had enjoyed the best of Samoan culinary art and gracious presentation.

Honour satisfied

According to Samoan custom, a much-prized gift in the Ta'alolo (Presentation of treasure) was the 'Ie Toga, (Fine mat). This was a finely woven robe worn by chiefs on ceremonial occasions. A particularly ancient example was much admired. The fibre used in weaving was produced from the serrated edge of a pandanus plant or 'screw pine' from which the outer skin has been stripped.

Next it was pummelled into a silk like texture, and woven into a delicately fine material. Before being plaited the fibres were bleached in the sun, and then squeezed by the woman weaver between the thumb and a blunt to make them flexible. They were then slit to the required size, often as thin as e thirty second of an inch in width. The vegetable dyes used came from secret recipes of a village or island guilds, and produced a light golden honey tone of colour associated with lasting quality. Not surprisingly these fine mats were regarded as a family heirloom to be safeguarded by its members.

Food in various forms were presented next, including barrels of salt beef, five pound cans of corned beef or ham called 'pisupo' named after the first canned food to be sold by local traders, which happened to be pea soup. The flesh of pig and fish included in the presentation of food was cut up and distributed to different people according to their rank and status. Since a well-cooked pig was difficult to divide, the usual practice was to undercook the meat. From the Samoan point of view the table condition of the meat was of little consequence, because the essential factor in the share-out was not to provide a tasty cooked meal, but rather to pay proper respect to the participating families, by presenting them with the part of a communal sacrifice appropriate to their position in Samoan society.

Division of pig and fish

Having received the cut of meat intended for a prestigious family, for example the prime back section for a paramount chief, or the underbelly for a lesser chief, the partially cooked meat was toyed with before being passed back to family retainers to be taken home and made edible. At the same time finely woven hibiscus fibre mats and strips of tapa cloth were presented to important guests. These cherished expressions of Polynesian art and craft continued to circulate at weddings, funerals, ceremonies of initiation for appointed chiefs,and the dedication of important public buildings and events in the Church's Calendar, such as the collection of tithes (Faiga Taulaga). The Ta'alolo served to confirm the validity of an economic system based on mutual exchange, through which heads of families maintained their position in a settled Samoan hierarchy. Great care and consummate tact was required in the distribution of gifts, to avoid injuring a family's pride. Rolls of fat covering the pork meat did not look appetising,but fortunately colleagues in the examination party acted as my 'minders'.

They made it clear that it was discourteous, and reflected badly on their mamalu (dignity), if we did not press for our rightful share in the distribution

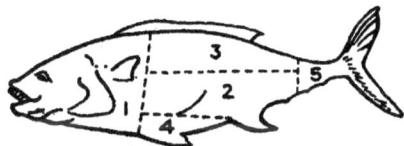

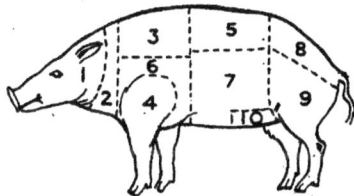

of gifts and food. Fulsome expressions of gratitude were given in accepting the meat, followed by appreciation for the gift of a fine robe which was admired for its valued longevity. Another esteemed gift was tapa cloth made from 'lau'ua', the bark of the paper mulberry tree, worn by chiefs in former times. Thin white strips scraped from the bark were then pasted together with the juice from a cassava root.

Oven baked fish was a much desired gift at a Samoan banquet. Cooked immediately after being caught in the sea inside the reef, the blue crevally (malauli) was a special treat. Tightly plaited coconut leaves adhering to the shape of the fish provided a tasty wrapping, which was then broken off leaving delicious flesh. Better by far than the gift of cartons of tuna fish from Van Camp's factory, packed on the shore of Pago Bay.

Pole position

Aware that we had received generous benefits on these ceremonial visits, without being expected to return the compliment, I gathered from those present that as the leader of the malaga I was included in the concept of Feagaiga. This was an agreement between the chiefs and the spiritual leader (Minister or Faifeau), in which physical needs were satisfied in return for spiritual benefits associated with his priestly role in Samoan society, In the Anglican Church it is customary to speak of the Parson's 'living' and the Samoan tradition is much the same. The mutually agreed link between Samoan parties to a Feagaiga was firm and lasting, and among their chiefs there was a reluctance to change a cultural and religious bond, which included a link with honoured European missionaries. Often on the receiving end of generosity, I appreciated the privilege granted by the Feagaiga.

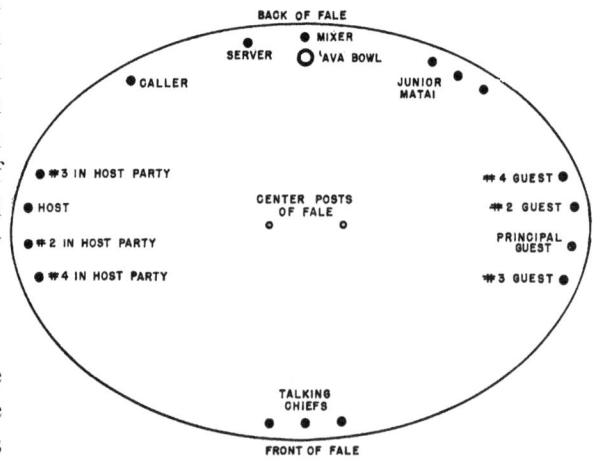

Diagram labels: BACK OF FALE; MIXER; SERVER; 'AVA BOWL; CALLER; JUNIOR MATAI; #3 IN HOST PARTY; #4 GUEST; HOST; CENTER POSTS OF FALE; #2 GUEST; #2 IN HOST PARTY; PRINCIPAL GUEST; #4 IN HOST PARTY; #3 GUEST; TALKING CHIEFS; FRONT OF FALE

Challenge of youth

Depending on the length of the welcome ceremony the aim was to start the examination before 9 a.m., and the students would be through their verbal or written tests by 2 p.m. As the exams took place towards the end of the 3 months long Summer Holiday for the Government Schools, it was possible for all children associated with the Samoan Church (L. M. S.) to take part. The 1956 census figures revealed that the total population was just over 20,000. They also showed that if all of these L. M. S. children throughout American Samoa attended Pastors Schools, the total attendance would have been 6,408 young people. In 1956 the number who actually took part in the exams was 4,250, and over 400 of them were young people living in the islands of Manu'a.

Our group was aware of a responsibility towards teachers and children who spent long hours trying to stimulate minds and hearts through a long established educational system. Over 50 years earlier the U.S. Navy had subsidised a Pastor's School in Manu'a, and in 1911 the Governor appointed a board of education, standardised a curriculum, and made attendance compulsory for children between six and thirteen years of age, four days a week. Church and state operated separately, but with mutual respect. Reciprocity found at the heart of ceremonial Samoa was similarly applied to education..

Figures gathered by the Examination Malaga in Manu'a indicated that 80 - 85 % of the under 5's and 70-75% of children aged 6-9 were encouraged by their families to take part. Slightly less than 50% of the total number of children, aged 10-17, attended the school run by the Pastor, his wife and helpers. Those who took part went in the examination seemed to enjoy the excitement and challenge of the day. Others turned up anyway in order to gain the necessary attendance mark. All who took part received a small prize, and approval from parents and guardians. Pride in their village meant that students wanted to do their best and the top grades were highlighted.

Marking papers of the older children went on throughout the afternoon, and often the results were given out after darkness had fallen at 6.30. Waiting for the bell to ring created an electric atmosphere. After results had been declared,young people who had failed to bring distinction to their village through the examination, had their chance to shine. They did this through a display of fun and dance known as a 'fiafia', or happiness time.

Fiafia. (Happy hour)
For two hours, groups of young people took over the evening with dance routines absorbed from birth. They were performed to the sound of loud and enthusiastic singing. Maidens (taupo), from each village would take

it in turns to take centre stage in directing proceedings, to act as cheer leader for the wild applause,which greeted individual village items on the programme. Usually two or more young men whooped loudly during athletic leaps alternating with grotesque gyrations around the teen age girl dancer Everyone joined in the singing, often clapping in time to the sound of young men strumming on a tightly rolled mat as they supported a tune played on a ukulele, or makeshift guitar. The feet of the dancers provided an underlying rhythm as they were turned in and out, whilst the body swayed in time to the music, the head held high. The fingers of the hands traced delicate lines in the air, aided by snake-like arm movements. Face, hands, arms, hips, and feet created a coordinated, balanced whole .

Different to the Tahitian and Hawai'ian style of dance, which focuses attention on the pelvic region rotating as in belly dancing. Samoan dancing on the other hand relies on the female leader providing only a hint of sexuality, with the main impression being one of dignity and grace. The buffoonery performed with contorted faces, and extravagant gestures by the young men, provides a striking contrast. All taking part are expected to perform a clearly defined role within a 'custom built' format. Guardians of morality watched edgily for variations being made on the approved routine,which might encourage sexual attraction among the teenagers. I was reminded of the thoughts of a world famous anthropologist Margaret Mead..

Coming of Age in Samoa, a book written by Margaret Mead was based upon her study of adolescent girls during a 6 months stay on the island of Ta'u as a 23 years old research student in 1924. 30 years later, interrupted by the 2nd World War and a U. S. military occupation, I was a 27 year old male staying for one week in the same village. I knew that her seminal text in the 'nature versus nurture' debate had created world wide interest. Mead asked the question, 'Are the disturbances that affect adolescents in Europe and America found everywhere, or do the Samoans show that growing up does not need to be a time of stress and strain. She spent 6 months living almost exclusively with a group of girls aged between 10 and 20, and documented their responses to questions about life in Ta'u, drawing particular attention to their sexual experience.

This aspect of her work was seized upon by Westerners who wanted to believe her message that Samoans lacked inhibitions, and enjoyed the benefits of sexual freedom. Other observers found that sexuality in Samoa was far from being indiscriminate, but relied instead on formal arrangements usually found in interlocking families sharing a common life. Communal well-being dependent on the enforced acceptance of restriction, rather than the pursuit of a personal sexual freedom, was nearer the mark according to Freeman and others researching Samoan adolescent behaviour.

Certainly surreptitious rape (moetotolo) was not uncommon, and young women committing suicide as a consequence of losing the honour of the family was a growing problem in the 1970's. Unlike Mead in 1923, sexuality was not a suitable subject for discussion for a young missionary in the 1950's who represented a restrictive moral code Listening to young people in casual conversation I often heard the expression, 'pepelo 'oe' You're a story teller! This was a frequent response to someone embellishing an account of an everyday incident. Risque stories are the spice of life for many Samoans. Did the young Margaret Mead give enough weight to ambiguity in the responses of Samoan informants wanting to impress an American scholar inordinately Separated by temporary blinds when I slept in the Church House, it did not escape my attention that several teenage girls were under the supervision of the Pastor and his wife during the hours of darkness. To be chaperoned in this way was normal practice. Formalised behaviour patterns, upheld by sanctions, were necessary in these closely knit communities. I found that my regular visits along a plank to the toilet located over the lagoon were clearly visible, and neighbours were aware of each other's movements day and night. I was sensitive at first about a bodily function usually associated with privacy, but the exercise quickly became a formality like everything else. Could it be that sexual activity was regarded in the same way. Further comments on the issues raised by Margaret Mead's book are found in Chapter 12 under the heading 'Programmed sexuality?'

Trouble brewing

Returning to Pago Pago on the island of Tutuila after 3 weeks spent in Manu'a the desperately slow Motor Vessel Samoa, smelling of rancid copra, made my stomach turn with every lurch sideways, before plunging into the depths once more. The Examination Group prepared for the next stage of the month - long journey (malaga) on the larger island. Tutuila was politically divided into two regions by Pago Pago Bay one was known as the Sua ma Vaifanua towards the east, and the other district, Fofo ma Itulagi in the west.

Manu'a behind us, we were to begin in the village of Masausi at the eastern end of Tutuila Island. According to the legends of 'Old Samoa', the chiefs of Tutuila were regarded as inferior by those in Manu'a 60 miles to the east. Chicfs of Tutuila were also regarded as subservient to those of A'ana, a district on the island of Upolu in Western Samoa, less than forty miles to the west. During the 1950's, the highest chiefs of Tutuila Tuitele, Maunga and Le'iato did not have the same prestige as the chiefs of A'ana to the west, or Manu'a in the east.

Writing down two main impressions gained through evening conversations with Manu'a chiefs,our malaga group agreed that the tension at the heart of the Samoan Church's unity which included American and Western Samoa, had increased considerably. We had been reminded that six out of the seven Districts in the All Samoa Church, (E. and W.) were located in Western Samoa. American Samoa was the seventh Church District, relatively small and insignificant. Several Manu'a Chiefs / Deacons maintained that the Central Office, Printing Press, High School and Theological College intended for the benefit of seven districts, were all concentrated in Western Samoa. The chiefs claimed that the building of these essential institutions relied on dollars raised in American Samoa, and their families living in the USA. Unfairness in the apportionment of total Church resources was leading to growing resentment among Manu'a chiefs, most of whom lived in Tutuila, close to the seat of the Government of American Samoa.

The second impression I gained from the Examination Malaga was that of a desire of Manu'a chiefs for a greater measure of self government in both Church and State. Moves towards political independence in Western Samoa, (achieved 4 years later),had raised questions about the political and economic future of Tutuila and Manu'a. An Independence movement begun in Western Samoa in 1928 had been known as the Mau, but leaders had been working toward greater self-government for many years earlier. Thwarted in that intention, much of the drive towards having a greater share in determining their own future was funnelled into creating indigenous structures within the L M. S. Church, or the Lotu Tahiti, as it was popularly known.

A largely autonomous Church in both E. and W. Samoa had been the result of the Independence Movement. Long accustomed to village churches being brought together into Pulega (sub districts), along the lines of ancient political sub districts, groups of local church representatives met regularly to bring up matters for the consideration of each of the five Pulega, when they came together to form the American Samoa District Council (Fono Matagaluega).

Pulega Meeting brought the concerns of roughly 12 local churches to the District (60+ churches), whose members could reject or recommend that they be passed on to the Fono Tele or General Assembly meeting in W. Samoa. Consideration of the subjects submitted occupied the attention of representatives from the seven Church Districts drawn from all the Samoan Islands, who met annually in Western Samoa during May each year. Church policy agreed at the May Assembly flowed back through the system in the opposite direction, through a District Assembly to the Sub District (Pulega) Meeting,and through its representatives to finally reach and affect local congregations,where the process had begun. It appeared to be a good example of a democratic process,except that the participants had to be lesser or greater chiefs.

Home truths

When anybody went on a journey in Samoa, short or long, those staying at home would cry out, "Ia manuia le malaga', (Have a good journey) and the traveller would call out the ritualistic response, 'Ia manuia le fa'amuli' (Good on you who stay behind). In what has been written earlier in this chapter, reliance has been placed on a personal diary, and various reports made soon after the Examination Tour, and these give an impression of always being on the move. The entries made by Eileen my wife in the same diary, show what life was like for her living at home in Fagalele, whilst I was travelling throughout Manu'a and Tutuila.. The Samoan word for wife is 'faletua', or 'the back of the house', where it was said the really important decisions affecting everyday life were made. I knew that a welcome mat always awaited me when I returned home to Fagalele.

Eileen had received her teacher training at All Saints College in Tottenham, in the same area of North London where John Williams, the Apostle to the South

Seas had been an apprentice engineer working in an iron foundry. A qualified teacher, Eileen's contribution to Fagalele Boys School was appreciated by those in a position to recognise her professionalism. It made it easier for me, released from schoolteacher duties, to understand better the changes taking place in village and urban life. In return for her unpaid service, domestic help was given by two or three boys appointed on a rotary basis. They had the opportunity of improving their use of the English language. Samoans do not have servants in their homes because it is understood that every member is responsible for performing clearly- defined family duties, known as (tautua i le aiga). In return the family,as a group, undertakes to take care of them.

Often on her own in a large rambling home isolated from other dwellings, where fishermen, or older teenage students, took advantage of my absence to fish at night from the rocks in front of the house. They occasionally played heartless pranks, such as leaning a fishing rod against her bedroom door, to disturb her peace of mind when she woke in the morning. Toby, a stray became her watchdog,and a constant friendly companion. The houseboys whose ages ranged from 15 - 19 years of age could be helpful, friendly, sulky or uncooperative as any teenager.

On Wednesday the 4th of July 1956, after I had left for Manu 'a, Eileen wrote in the diary that 'A teacher named Siota hasn't turned up. I don't like the idea of being responsible for three boys /young men. Liu was lazy about garden- ing, and wouldn't help other schoolboys to clear the small plantation next to the house, where papaya, taro and bananas are grown. I don't think we have done him any good, because he is quick to take advantage of a helpful attitude on my part. I heard him banging on the piano before I had a chance to show him how to play it.' (The boys quickly became rude and offhand if Eileen or myself attempted to appeal to a sense of responsibility. Only orders such as 'Do this', or 'Do that' got a ready response !)

An entry the following day read, ' Liu and Matagi took the only pressure lamp, and used it without permission for fishing last night. Greeted with the news that it had fallen over on the reef I asked 'Did it break?' 'No' was their reply. 'Will it work tonight?' 'No, it is too old!'. I asked them to repair it, but they said that the generator was blocked,and they could do nothing further about it'. Their indifferent attitude towards Eileen living on her own with only candle light in a large dark house for several nights, was inexcusable. On a more positive note, Eileen also recorded that another boy named Mailei had with great patience helped her pick the seeds out of pods from the Kapok tree. The pods contained a creamy white silk, which separated by hand from closely packed small seeds, was used as filling for cushions and pillows.

Another boy named Aifiti was usually willing to get on with any job without constant supervision. He had an open friendly face,which we thought expressed clearly what he was thinking and feeling, yet he could readily swing to a gloomy remoteness. 'He's musu', meant that he would not speak or co-operate with anyone. It was difficult to fathom what was going on. Asking others what was wrong they would reply 'Ta ilo', meaning 'Don't know,' which marked the end of the conversation. This lack of curiosity about inner feelings, or the possible cause of an emotional 'shut down',continued into adulthood for many of the Samoans I came to know.

Several entries in the diary at that time referred to Numia, another teenager, whose remote, undemonstrative character baffled our understanding. Ioasa, a reliable likeable lad, immensely strong physically, said that he was 'fiasili', meaning that Numia thought of himself as being different from everybody else. He appeared to be 'stuck up', which together with the charge of meanness is the worst thing that one Samoan can say about another. Teenagers are difficult to cope with at the best of times, in any culture, so we probably expected too much of them.

Living in a Samoan community meant that you helped yourself if you needed a particular tool or item of household equipment. Cutlery, hammers, pots and pans etc were often missing when needed. R. L. Stevenson, when living in Samoa wrote: "Asking for help from someone who can't refuse is but a step away from taking what you want, or stealing". On the other hand the recovery by Ioasa and Matagi of stolen hens from a neighbours patch, provided a welcome bonding experience with our adopted 'children'. Our Diary also refers to a young man named Fainu'u showing me how to shred halves of coconuts over a sharp pointed stick. The result provided good food for the hens and our dogs.

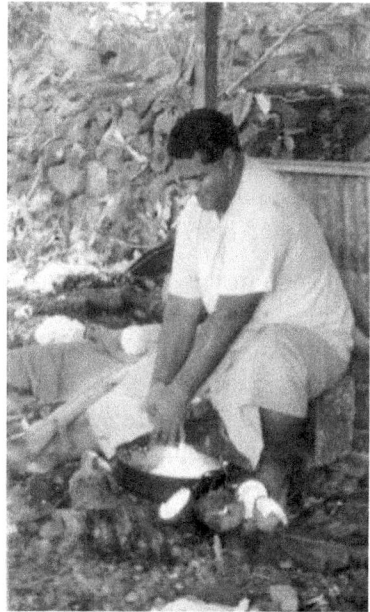

Shredding coconut

115

Our houseboys boys regularly earned our admiration as they shinned up the coconut trees with a piece of tough cloth tied between their ankles. This allowed them to make 'kangaroo' jumps upward with long bush knives between their teeth to hack at the fronds whilst perched dangerously high above the ground. From there they threw down the nuts in quick succession before descending to grate the nuts.

An entry in the diary also mentions Matagi's arrival from his home, 12 miles over the mountain in the village of Fagasa, seated on a horse carrying 30 coconuts to feed his, or were they our chickens? Ioasa. Numia, Matagi, these names, and many more besides, are a warm reminder of a dozen or more young men who came in and out of our lives over a period of three years. All of them went on to Honolulu and California. Strange to think that they are now past retirement age, many of them having served in the US Armed Services.

Both of us had moments of exasperation as we lived alongside young people about to come of age in Samoa. The contrast between the way in which Samoans reared children and young people, and that of our own youth intrigued us. Reared in communal surroundings with shared tasks, several adults watched over the offspring of family members. They provided strict discipline, dried their tears, over-indulged them, or withdrew favours. One-to-one relationships were made within peer groups, The Samoan household was really an extended family unit in which all adult relatives exerted a measure of parental control over their young charges. For the duration of their stay in Fagalele School, it was assumed that we had become part of a network of adopted parents. Coming from widely-scattered villages,the boys and young men, aged between 12 and 20 years, had not known each other previously.

Apart from the rapport found in a manual task such as grass cutting, I was rarely able to get alongside the boys on a personal level. Cutting through the bush and weeds in the school plantation, their long knives swishing through the air in unison,they were in their element. Such group activities gave them great satisfaction. Invariably the rhythm was energetically provided by sticks beating on an empty canister, or another improvised drum. The cohesiveness of their social system was far beyond the reach of someone like myself coming from a more individualistic way of life. The positive benefit of the Samoan solidarity was the powerful sense of belonging that it gave them, which was powerfully demonstrated through team games such as rugby football. No prisoners were taken, as many World Cup International sides readily testify. Manu Tuilagi playing for England in the 1911 World Cup, is the latest example of these formidable rugby players.

We experienced the downside of corporate strength, which was often shown in an undeveloped sense of individual responsibility. On the one hand as 'family' we could choose to go along with the cultural norm, where guardians said 'Do this or otherwise you will be an outcast'. Alternatively an appeal could be made to an individual's growing sense of right and wrong. In those early days we struggled to get the balance right, but fragile 'one to one' relationships fell apart at the seams. A desire for informality in relationships was attempted, but I now realize that we expected too much. Would I attempt it again today, despite the likelihood of disappointment? I hope so.

Nuisances

Pests around the house received short shrift. The mention of kapok seeds earlier is a reminder of the attraction that these seeds had for the large long tailed rats around our home, who quickly got wind of them. It seemed to drive them crazy with desire. Cockroaches found everywhere were the bane of our life for many years until pesticides came on the scene. Venomous ants (loata) had a painful sting. We had no idea in the mid 1950's, when the chemical was liberally sprayed in our home, that it would be banned later for its toxicity. Centipedes (alualoa),found in corners throughout the house received the same treatment. They had 15 to over 100 legs, and although they did some good in eating slugs, their poisonous jaws gave a very painful bite. In later years when our children ran about the house barefoot, they were told that 'if a centipede settled on the arm or leg, they were to brush it off in the direction in which it was going, to prevent hooks being left.

During 1956 I became accustomed to chasing large marauding pigs, especially on moonlight nights as their keen sense of smell told them where old yam roots and tubers were to found under the grass lawn around the house. Rooting around under the mango tree on our side of a boundary fence was a special delight. They ploughed up the grass nearby allowing troublesome weeds such as Nut Grass (Mumutu), and the prickly Sensitive Plant (Vaofefe), to flourish. Afterwards they ruined the little garden in which an attempt was made to grow tomatoes, carrots and pineapples. A succession of bad nights, with the dog barking at a large boar,sent me to a neighbour's home to remonstrate with the family about the animal's unrestricted wandering habits. I held them responsible for spreading hookworm, a health risk which carried a fine of $200 payable to the Village Council.

More than fifty years later I do not know how it was possible to find a shotgun with shells at short notice in a Mission House, of all places! (Shades of Henry Nott p.30). However it happened that at 2am on a dark night, I saw a large pig eyeing me at 25 yards, took aim, and shot him dead. In the resulting confusion I was threatened with violent reprisals. Stones were hurled onto the roof throughout the night, but after a week the stormy protest had blown itself out. A hurricane a few months later uprooted the huge mango tree between the house and the hedge, its branches narrowly missing the house where we were sleeping. The pigs no longer had a place to hide, and the firearm had long disappeared, never to return.

A few day's later I disturbed a hornet's nest with my naifi (bush knife),when clearing undergrowth near the hedge boundary at the point where the school plantation overlooked the reef, 15 feet below. The stings felt like a succession of painful hammer blows on my arms and legs. When hornets sting, the tail end opens, and a sharp pointed sting punctures the skin allowing a poison to hit home. It hurts, but you usually live to tell the tale! On another occasion at the same spot I slipped on the cliff edge, the volcanic rock made smooth and slippery by a combination of heavy rain and algae.

Welcome guests

A Frangipani tree grew next to one of the corners of the six-foot wide verandah of our Fagalele home as it faced the sea It had a short trunk with branches spread out like the fingers of an open hand, at the end of which were groups of thick hairy leaves and tiny fragrant yellow and white flowers. A cherished memory is that of watching a couple of kingfishers (Ti'otala) in the early dawn as they took turns to swoop in flight between the Frangipani and a Morinda (Nonu-togi), a small tree with a smooth and greyish white trunk situated 30 yards away,near the cliff edge. A Ve'a (Banded rail), a shy bird that seldom flies would be seen scuttling away into thick undergrowth at the slightest sound. This would be followed immediately by a brief glimpse of the deep red-black plumage of the tiny bird, the Cardinal Honey Eater. Memorable sights such as these rewarded an early rising.

There was also the week-long experience of nursing back to health an injured Frigate Bird (Tata'a) found on the grass surrounding Fagalele House. A large bird with long pointed wings and tail, it had a long thin bill with a sharp hook at the end,which it used to rob other sea birds of their catch as they struggled to gain height after plunging into the depths of the sea. The aptly named man o' war, or frigate bird, would then soar away from the scene of the crime, making use of the upward air currents. I can still see in my mind's eye our 'patient' taking off slowly and majestically from the front lawn, flapping its healed wing in unison with the other,circling high and wide over our home before disappearing gradually into the distance.

A minor nuisance, before a hurricane struck, had been the noise of quarrelling flying foxes (pe'a), roosting together on the branches of the massive mango tree near the house. When the fruit ripened, dozens of them bombarded our home with partially chewed fruit. Together with bats, the flying foxes are the only mammals that can drop the mango from the folds of its wings whilst in flight, Released, the fruit thumped on the corrugated iron roof at irregular intervals throughout the night. We were soon to discover that there were other things that went bump in the night. .

A Fagalele guest in November 1955 was George Milner, a linguistic scholar and a Fellow of London University's School of Oriental Studies. George, a dapper looking gentleman, with a high forehead, a flourishing beard and horn-rimmed glasses, was engaged in the mammoth task of revising Pratt's Samoan Dictionary, a book that had been completed 100 years earlier. To do this work he sought the help of Talking Chiefs (Tulafale), the custodians of proverbs, ancient legends and genealogies.

In a orally transmitted culture,the forming of opinion leading up to a decision, had become an enthralling mind game for those involved. Enlivened by an artistry in expressing thought, an orator was applauded for the substance of what he said, but also for the nuances of meaning he squeezed out of words to both enlighten and confuse. George was to spend hours noting the competitive spirit between orators using the disguised ploy, the subtle innuendo, devious double talk and the subtle bending of a familiar words to slide off a wily politicians tongue.

The purpose of Milner's visit to our home was to ask us to provide lodgings for Dr. Jasper Buce, his colleague in the Dictionary project, who arrived in December 1956, and stayed in our home until June 1957. Although we shared meals, and often played cards together, Jasper was deeply immersed in the detailed recording of words and phrases and rarely 'switched off' after working hours. Simply a working arrangement, his company was different from the deep friendship made with Bud Cole, a retired Chief Petty Officer, U.S. Navy, who lived with us for more than a year.

I remember that Jasper would not stay in Fagalele overnight because of an eerie, even frightening experience that he had when Eileen and I had gone to

Western Samoa for the General Assembly. He woke up in the middle of the night with the hairs on his neck standing on end, likewise those of our dog Toby. I don't know if the boys had been telling him about the 'aitu' or ghost said to haunt the property and surrounding land, but he travelled over to Apia, post haste, on the next boat, and vowed that he would not repeat staying overnight on his own.

We were reminded of strange happenings, such as barrel bolts slipping down to lock doors from the inside of a room, making entry impossible without causing damage. Searching high and low for the missing half of a sponge cake, just out of the oven, was another strange incident, which seemed to be of little consequence yet begged for an explanation that was not forthcoming. Dismissed unconvincingly at the time as a mischievous prank by someone unknown, such incidents continued to rankle as we looked for a rational explanation. Trivial losses upset our equilibrium. A key seen to drop on a particular spot, then to disappear without trace was disconcerting but normally shrugged off. Missing keys were put down to 'going troppo' (experiencing tropical fatigue).

Unexpected draughts on otherwise airless evenings, would make us stop what we were doing, and ask each other 'What was that?' The occasional smell of pipe smoke on the verandah during the evening caused a similar comment. Again we dismissed such unusual happenings with a laughing aside about a 19th century former resident missionary named Thomas Powell 'at it again' and assumed that there was a rational explanations. The distinctive smell of pipe smoke was a reminder of colleagues from the past. We likened it to the day when our well-used piano arrived from London. As the lid was lifted, and the keys struck, an unmistakable smell of sooty London smog emerged from inside. Old scenes and familiar faces came to mind.

A new friend, not an apparition, who frequently made his presence known by arriving in his priestly garb, was Father Louis Beauchemin, a Roman Catholic priest,whose Samoan name was Tovi'o. Born in New England, possessing that state's pleasant accent and manners, he said that he looked forward to sharing afternoon tea with us on our verandah overlooking Leone Bay. (The study groups from the American Community Church ,also visited Fagalele for meetings, and always enthused about our quaint Olde Worlde custom.)

Tovi'o began to visit us soon after we had moved into Fagalele. This was four years before the Second Vatican Council heralded a new openness between Catholics and Protestants. I remember him telling me that the R. C. intention of appointing a new Bishop from among the indigenous leadership had stalled, but had recently come back on track. Five years later Tovi'o was a member of an ecumenical team appointed to make a Common Bible in the Samoan language for use in Protestant and Roman Catholic churches. Although Protestant churches had used the complete Bible since 1884, the Catholic Church used only small parts in its own translation. During our conversations I 'confessed' to Louis my dissatisfaction with the job I was doing.

Appearance is everything

The truth was that I spent long and often boring hours inside places of worship, and experienced at close quarters the personal rivalry between pastors. The gossip, intrigue, and card playing bonhomie surrounding the 'Big Tent' occasions, as we waited for the toll of the bell announcing the readiness of visiting choirs to perform, seemed to be an irrelevance to a young man on a mission! Dedicating church buildings,commemorating numerous anniversaries, honouring the installation of important chiefs, appeared to be excuses for feasting and displaying wealth. It struck home that I was a complete misfit in a sacerdotal society ; a nonconformist within a religious establishment.

There was nothing new here. An entry from the diary of Churchward, the British Consul written on October 22 1882, described one of these large gatherings.'They come to hear the yearly report of the amount of the sub-scriptions received, to listen to various addresses and to take part in hymn singing and prayers. Known as the May Meeting, it is a grand opportunity for showing off. Great are the exertions made to raise the necessary dollars to appear fearfully and wonderfully adorned at this yearly festival. Each company of ladies, regardless of expense, comes out in some distinct uni-form of brown and sober hue, to be transformed later by a gorgeous raiment dazzling with every colour of the rainbow.' Eighty years after Churchward had described the whole rigmarole, it hadn't changed.

The May Collection (Faiga Me) was still the most colourful and important of the local pageants during which money raising was dressed up in religious garments. Throughout the 1950's I felt that I was being asked to preside at the equivalent of a small company's Annual Board Meeting. It was as if minor shareholders were encouraged to think that they had a say in the company's business. Letting the imagination fly even further I thought of the congregation as stakeholders as they listened carefully for a percentage rise or fall in contributions given by other villages, or made comparisons with last year's contributions. In the case of the 'Me' (pronounced May) gathering, an attempt was made to give the occasion an aura of sanctity. Village choirs singing sacred music intended to be uplifting became competitive, and unintentionally entertaining, sometimes hilarious to a secular sceptic.

A particular Church Opening Dedication (Fa'aulufalega),in the village of Taputimu sticks in my memory. Several choirs from different villages had tried to outshine each other, both in the volume of sound, and the complexity of their syncopated music making. It was their way of congratulating the villagers of Taputimu, who in various ways had contributed to the construction of their pride and joy. A young man played the xylophone with great dexterity as he accompanied the choristers. When he began playing, dozens of children's faces appeared at the open windows gazing at him with open-mouthed amazement, only to bob down out of sight as the hymn finished.

Struggling to get up to announce the next reading, I was held fast to the back of the seat by recently applied varnish. Levering myself free, I was aware that I looked like a recently escaped convict from prison, due to the stripes down the back of my white suit. This was a minor problem compared with that of the Taputimu villagers hoping and praying that the financial contributions of guests would cover debt repayments at the Bank. Rather than maintain the fabric in a sound condition, the complete rebuilding of the largest and most costly building in the village, often took place after only 10-20 years of use. The profligacy, which ignored repairs, and the waste of hard labour in raising the money, drew critical comments from the American bank officials present. Despite these reservations, 50 years later I'm still full of admiration for the skill of the builders, and the strength of structures, which were able to withstand the shock of severe earthquakes.

The stability of Samoan Church buildings was underlined for me one Sunday morning in Leone Church as the minister, Liaiga, an old man who was the School Chaplain at Atauloma School, was leading prayer. We were suddenly aware that the pew was shaking violently. We then experienced similar movements to those felt by passengers standing on a railway platform as an express train hurtles by. The vibrations seemed to suck us forwards before blowing us backwards. Self-preservation prompted us to fly out of the nearby doors, whilst others were diving through the open windows. As we slowly returned to our former positions, we saw Liaiga, apparently unconcerned, still leading us in prayer from his lofty perch in the pulpit. The elongated prayer ended with the congregation joining together to say the words of the Lord's

Prayer, 'A ia laveai mai i matou ai le leaga,) Deliver us from evil).The service then continued as if nothing had happened.

Wake up call

The launching of the unmanned Russian satellite called Sputnik 1 on the 4th October 1957 was a personal wake up call. Looking beyond the reef and upwards into the clear night sky, some of us saw what appeared to be a shooting star, travelling from one horizon to the other. In another forty five minutes, Sputnik would be over Europe, where we had begun our 7 week long voyage more than 2 years earlier. Blast off had been in Kazakhstan, moving across other Soviet Republics, to be followed by the Pacific Ocean to the Magellan Straits, then north crossing both Africa and Europe. Travelling at 17,400 miles an hour, and 188 miles above the earth, it orbited the earth for 3 months. The Space Age had arrived. It provided a vision for thoughtful people below its flight path,whether they lived in congested cities, or isolated islands, that everyone lived in One World of inter-dependence, – or mutual destruction.

Previous to this event the light given by a full moon had been the main source of wonder. I would read an English newspaper sitting on the rocks overlooking the reef in front of our island home. In bright moonlight I read news,which was only 6 weeks old ! Although detailed comment about the Suez War, and the Soviet destruction of the 1956 uprising in Hungary came from out of date, papers and magazines, the B. B. C. World Service kept us up to date with world events. The arrival in Pago Harbour of a U. S. Navy ship crammed to the gunnels with the latest tracking technology re-enforced the latest headlines about the Cold War. The U.S. Navy visit was linked to U2 aircraft spying on the Baikonur space launch facility in Kazakhstan.

DAILY EXPRESS

No. 17,844   SATURDAY OCTOBER 5 1957   1 a.m. forecast: Some drizzle; bright spells later   Price 2d.

The first 'Flying Saucer' travels at 17,000 m.p.h.

SPACE AGE IS HERE

Soviet satellite circling world in 95 minutes

| Mrs. Mike Parker names woman | THAT 7% WILSON: I've evidence leak was political MACMILLAN: I'll act | Warsaw rioters stone police |

The moving dot of light across the night sky did not convey 'a sign of things to come' to most Islanders but it proved to be a 'wake up call to political and church leaders, who were sleepwalking through a rapidly changing world. An Assembly Meeting had decided that improved training for ministers was listed as a top priority. I had cause for satisfaction as a District representative that work was to begin on developing 'In Service' training for ministers, plus an emphasis on partnership in learning between pastor and people. Work among children and young people was to be stepped up.. As I prepared for the return voyage to Tutuila I was heartened by Assembly's approval for a car, money for a film projector and tape recorder to help with a Youth Club Work, and a willingness to support moves to start a Bookshop in the Bay Area.

Passed 'on the nod' by representatives from the seven Districts, the grants may have been a ' sweetener' to partially satisfy a demand in American Samoa, that money be spent in their territory. Encouraged by the use of the Samoan proverb 'Ia tupu e pei o le taro i le fusi'. (Grow as taro in a swamp). I was not so sure about the weather forecast. Rough seas were pounding the Apia waterfront as I waited to board the Sulimoni (The true Heir Apparent) bound for home. Many passengers had the 70 foot yacht named Joyita on their minds.

On October 3 1955 the Joyita, a similar sized boat to the Sulimoni, had left Apia for the Tokelau Islands, about 270 miles away. She had been carrying 16 crew members and 9 passengers, including a government official, a doctor, a copra dealer and 2 children. Expected 48 hours later, the yacht did not arrive. Five weeks later the Joyita was sighted 600 miles from her planned route, partially submerged and listing heavily. There was no trace of any of the passengers or crew.

A subsequent enquiry found that the vessel was poorly maintained, and probably the engine broke down. It also came to the conclusion that the fate of the crew and passengers was 'inexplicable on the evidence submitted'. Three of the life boats the Joyita carried were missing, but it would not make sense for the people on board to abandon it voluntarily. Fitted out for carrying refrigerated goods, her holds were lined with cork making her almost unsinkable. Further buoyancy was provided by a cargo of empty fuel drums. Responsibility for the tragedy was placed on the captain for setting out on a voyage in a ship that wasn't seaworthy..

Travelling on the Sulimoni a year afterwards, some of us were aware that the Joyita Inquiry was still taking place. Meanwhile our small craft began to 'ride the white horses' as she left the reef behind, for the ship were battling against the tail end of a hurricane. We heard later that the storm had struck Manu'a. Soon the squeals of frightened pigs, and the increasing stench of rancid copra became a reminder of similar rough crossings, and heaving stomachs. Many of the fourteen journeys I made on the 80 mile long route between Apia and Pago on the M. V. Samoa, the Isabelle Rose, or the Manu'a Tele, had been uncomfortable. This one was different in scale.

Passengers were truly scared when the cargo broke loose, and we heard it rolling about alarmingly. Waves rushed through the space where we were lying down, first throwing us one way, and then the other, as the tiny vessel lurched and dipped. Then a great grey sea broke over us pressing the ship down until it seemed that it would never come up again. She did, and shaking herself she went down into the depths again, and again. I can't believe it now, but at the time when all seemed lost, I thought 'get it over now'. Eventually the storm subsided, and 12 hours later the Pago Harbour beacon could be seen as the Sulimoni crossed over Leone Bay. Soon after our dousing in the deep waters, I began negotiations with the Government about a lease of land in the Bay Area for a Bookshop.

During the conversations about a Bookshop location Governor Lowe asked me to be the Convener of the Alcohol Control Board. Heavy drinking was a huge social problem and I had previous experience of disciplinary cases involving High Chiefs who were also deacons in the church. It was a poisoned chalice in many ways, but I did my best. The Alcohol Control Board taught me a number of things,but most drinkers knew them already, and it did not stop alcohol abuse. I did not further the cause of moderation in all things, including alcohol consumption, when at a Board meeting I was foolish enough to suggest that, in future, all government functions should be liquor free. I deserved the report in the local newspaper, where in the Samoan translation, I was reported as saying that there should be free alcohol at all government functions!

Perseverance rewarded

Alongside the hugely popular Pago Bar, and its raucous clientele in down-town Fagatogo, food stores, a police station, bank, and government adminis-tration building looked out on a large oval shaped grass space regarded as sacred (malae). On the opposite side was a Fale Tifaga (cinema) built in 1942 for the benefit of U.S. Marines, and a scruffy- looking cobblers shop. Intended to repair the boots of long departed naval ratings, the business was short of

customers. The leaseholder let it be known that the flip-flops worn by local people as suitable for a wet and hot climate, made his work largely redundant. He was therefore preparing to leave shortly for Honolulu. In the heart of town, it was an ideal site for a Bookshop. After preliminary conversations with Governor Lowe, his Deputy, Macquarry, and Baird, the Attorney General on the 21st of June 1956, I was asked to draw up plans ,but on the 26th, objections received by Baird led to further delay. After I'd lobbied against several delaying schemes of the Attorney General, the Governor finally gave the 'go ahead' on January 23rd 1957.

Samoan Bibles, Hymn Books,Sunday School materials and equipment, as well as an agency for obtaining church organs would be part of the service. From January 1957 onwards books were being ordered from many different publishers in the States, Australia and Britain. The initial stock was purchased with money granted from the L. M. S. the United Society for Christian Literature and the Samoan Church. Extra cash flow was created before the official opening in August as the result of securing large Government High School orders for textbooks. Local Roman Catholic priests, Joe Heslyn and Louis Beauchamin favoured us with several bulk orders for Catholic schools. This support ensured that money was available to order books covering a wide range of authors and publishers before the shop was opened to the general public. 'Did Bookshop orders with British and American publishers past midnight' was a regular entry in the diary at that time.

Initially we were ordering three copies of titles such as 'The Quiet American' and 'Dr. Zhivago' to ensure that we had an eye-catching variety on the shelves. We had to run the risk of little depth in numbers if some titles proved more popular than others. I was thoroughly enjoying the experience of being a bookseller. It meant trying to gauge what would sell to Americans living far from home and picking up a book on impulse, and at the same time attract Samoans who had entered a wider world through reading. A few individuals had specialized needs such as car maintenance, puzzles or cooking, which we tried to meet, and the tourists from the luxury liners were always looking for a relaxing read.

Mainly paperbacks were sold, with some hard covers about travel in the Southern Hemisphere, 'Kon Tiki' for example, and a few specialist books on Old Samoa. These included several rare books, one by Dr. Kramer listing the genealogical trees of Samoan families, was accompanied by photographs of the highest quality. This volume was for reference only. By Opening Day over six thousand books, excluding the bulk orders, had been unpacked, indexed, priced, and displayed. I remember that the Longmans series of books in easy English proved popular, as was the case with Classics Illustrated, and three books translated by Fana'afi Maia'i into Samoan, 'King Solo-mons Mines, Treasure Island, and the Black Tulip.

'One Bookshop for twenty thousand', was the headline in the Pacific Island-Magazine (PIM) reporting the official opening of The Bookshop on August 1st 1957. Representatives of the Church and Government gathered outside the building painted pastel blue, located in the centre of town next to the open expanse known as the Malae. It was an ideal situation.

Governor Peter Tali Coleman, the first Samoan to hold that office, recognised the benefit it would bring to the Samoan people through a wide range of literature available at reasonable prices. He was particularly glad that the island's bookshop was in the hands of those who cared for the true wellbeing of all Samoan people. I recognised the gentle prompting of our mutual friend Father Louis Beauchamin.

Doubts and misgivings

In early 1958 I was always working to meet a deadline. At five thirty each morning I would be in the study on the corner of the verandah where the swooping kingfishers suggested the need for some fun and space in life. I had agreed to support the writing of a series of commentaries on a new Statement of Faith. I ground out a commentary on Regeneration, and tackled Faith and

Repentance with little enthusiasm. The themes selected were ridiculously inappropriate for a jaded spirit. Rough Samoan copy needed constant revision, often inaccurate the writing lacked vitality..

In late 1957 into 1958 I noticed 'near enough' practices creeping into the running of the Bookshop. The stock control system required every title to have a matching card giving the selling price, number of copies in stock, and the date of sale. Made aware of varying stock flow, and the date when books were to be re-ordered, it was possible to operate the business satisfactorily. Spot checks, the clearing of shelves and relocation of book sections, (fiction, non fiction,travel etc.) took place regularly,and kept staff on their toes. Despite these safeguards it was obvious that when the first full stock check took place, many books were missing ; either that, or they had not been entered on the stock cards as paid.

The success of the enterprise was in jeopardy as a result of a casual attitude (fa'ama'ia'i), dishonesty and ineptitude. 'Near enough' was not good enough if a business was to remain solvent. After all these years I still find it hurtful to recall missing cash from sales, and casual malpractice by trusted colleagues. This happened as the background work of accountancy and ordering stock, required considerable time and effort after business hours from Eileen and myself.

We wanted to hand over the Bookshop to the Samoan Manager in good order when we took a break in Australia. With 3 months left, alarm bells began to ring. Scribbled notes left in the till read 'borrowed $5 to be paid back tomorrow'. Lunch time food bought with Bookshop money was becoming a habit. Two Fagalele students acting as assistants confessed that they had been bribed with food to keep quiet. Pressure exerted by family members on the staff was the usual cause of discrepancies in the takings. An attempt to explain that the Bookshop was for the benefit of a wider community fell on deaf ears. Family came first.

It was important to maintain stock levels, and ensure that there was enough money coming in to keep the business going for the three months while we were on leave in Australia. This meant that considerable forward planning had to be done in cooperation with the Assistant Manager. The situation was complicated by our desire to transfer the daily operation of the business to Samoans as smoothly and rapidly as possible, whilst not running away from our responsibility to provide a promised service to a mixed community.

Over the next few months financial losses continued, goods was not replenished, but the ailing fledgling survived. The Manager, Aifiti and Matagi (2 ex-Fagalele schoolboys), worked well together. Scraps of paper indicating '$ 5 borrowed' appeared. The hours of opening and closing the business became 'hit or miss' for many irate customers. Eventually the Manager resigned saying that the Bookshop was not a suitable job for a pastor (the reason given for departure),and the family returned to Western Samoa. The final comment of his wife, on what had been an uncomfortable time for all concerned was that her husband was regarded as 'Misi's slave'. She meant that he had not been given enough responsibility.

This episode was stressful because I had obviously contributed to a poor working relationship. A partnership between a 'White Man' associated with a colonial era, and Samoans aspiring to leadership in government, commerce or church, was always going to be a tough assignment. Trying to make a positive contribution in a transitional period, foreigners like myself were likely to misunderstand signals. Building relationships based on 'give and take' required sensitivity. Thankfully most Samoan colleagues made it clear that they did not want a 'Boss man'. Neither did they want someone who said 'Yes' to everything that had 'Samoan Way' stamped on it. Working relationships based on trust required a willingness to accept inadequacy and competence, whatever custom was cherished, or language spoken.

Refreshment needed

The gradual renovation of Fagalele begun in 1955 went on in fits and starts due to the cost of carpentry, plumbing, paint, and roofing iron being greater than what had been estimated. Many Saturdays scraping loose plaster and whitewash from the inside walls of the high rooms ready for painting meant that the rambling farm house by the sea was gradually becoming a home.

Petty irritations had begun to get on top of me. I resented missionary colleagues asking Leslie Brame, the Secretary, to put in writing their reservations about the amount of time I was devoting to the Bookshop enterprise. It was suggested that I should add to my District travels, a visit to the distant Tokelau Islands ; moreover I should consider looking after the Apia Protestant Church for several months, The task in American Samoa seemed to be relatively unimportant. Adding insult to injury it was said that I should exercise greater care in submitting estimates for what had become extensive works on our Fagalele home.

With the wisdom of hindsight it had been a mistake to agree to a haphazard method of house renovation,overly dependent on voluntary help and an intermittent cash flow. Decision time in July 1955 meant that there was no practical alternative. The situation cried out for a business manager. It was also unfortunate that I had grown up with a view of missionary service, which not only accepted hardship, but looked for it. I had given myself too much to do. During one rain sodden weekend I knew that Tutuila' s high rainfall and humidity should have provided a sufficient challenge for anyone..

An average rainfall of 24 inches each month from January to March,with 15 inches the average monthly amount until mid June. July and August had 10 inches of rain. Highs of 20 inches monthly returned for the rest of the year, with the occasional hurricane and tropical squall thrown in. According to U.S. Navy meteorologists, prevailing easterly trade winds encountered a distinctive counter- trade current at 16,000 feet in the immediate area sur-rounding Tutuila. Our island home had 267 inches of rain in 1956 compared to 120 inches only 80 miles away in Western Samoa. Such conditions affect physical and mental performance was the conclusion of a U.S. Navy report. We needed a break.

The outline of this chapter was suggested by floor mats of different shapes and sizes being brought together in a bundle before storage. A sequence of events describing personal experiences from 1955-58 have been brought together in a similar fashion. Just as mats unrolled carelessly fall into a messy heap on the floor, the chapter ends in some confusion. 'Ua solo le falute' The roll of mats had broken apart. I needed to be put together again.

Section headings

Round trip - Importance of ceremony - Honour satisfied - Challenge of Youth - Trouble brewing - Home truths - Nuisances - Welcome guest Appearance is everything - Wake up call - Perseverance rewarded - Doubts and misgivings - Refreshment needed.

Chapter Ten

1958 - 1961 - Well done the rowers

Samoan proverb. *Ia lafoia i le alogalu.* 'May you be thrown (lafoia) by the crest of the wave (alogalu)', is the literal translation. Get through the passage in the reef with the boat and crew still upright, is the hope expressed in the proverb. Applied to everyday life it means 'May you overcome all difficulties'. Normally a word of encouragement, a slight change allows it to become one of congratulation. Ua lafoia i le alogalu. 'All obstacles have been overcome'.

Faith and reason

'Gusty south-southeast winds travelling 20-25 mph at times 30, Seas rough. Swells of 10 feet. Subsiding by tomorrow. A trough of low pressure to the north of Samoa is moving on.' The evening weather forecast on Radio Station W.V.U.V. for Sunday, 27th July 1958, promised unsettled conditions as the Motor Vessel 'Samoa' left the shelter of Pago Harbour a few minutes before midnight. The hour of departure allowed sufficient time for the vessel to arrive in Manu'a at daybreak. Permission granted by the Harbour Master for the trip to go ahead had been received on the recently installed radio equipment. Lessons had been learned from the sinking of 'The Joyita' (p124) The faint hilly outline of Aunu'u could be seen as our coastal vessel, unsuitable for ocean travel,chugged slowly past the small volcanic islet one mile south of the main island of Tutuila.

Two years earlier, on a similar Examination trail, I had journeyed by rowboat from Auasi on the mainland to Aunu'u, where a tragic incident had taken place on a previous 'Faiga Suega. Pastor Keriti's son had drowned as the boat overturned passing through the reef channel. The lights seen on the Aunu'u' shoreline from the M.V. Samoa,was a grim reminder of what could go wrong on the seriously overloaded boat carrying us forward. Too many passengers, pigs for welcome ceremonies, barrels of salt beef and cases of pilchards or tuna intended for the small stores in the Manu'a group, all contributed to the ships slow progress. Despite the overcrowded conditions and the stench of the copra, its movement lulled me into fitful sleep.

Soon after four am I became aware of a speck of light, as the day was about to break. Towards the east I saw a solid mass of volcanic rock emerging out of the darkness to form a shape gradually defined by bright gold and fiery red shafts of light. They cut out an outline of the mountain fortress of Olosenga. It was as if a curtain was being drawn back to reveal the opening scene of a brand new production, which was the picturesque Samoan way of describing sunrise, 'Se'ia tafa mai ata'. I was overawed by the unfolding drama of a new day emerging from the depths of a dull grey sea. Slowly and surely the sombre waters gave way to the colour of azure blue.

Nothing could have prepared me for the awareness of a tremendous mystery unfolding around our tiny vessel. Several years later I read an account by Robert Louis Stevenson (Tusitala) of a similar experience on the 28th of July 1888, which in his words had 'touched a virginity of sense' He wrote 'Although the dawn was preparing by four, the sun was not up till six, the day two hours a-coming'. Stevenson's sympathy towards natural theology began with such wonders of nature and scientific discovery. Such experiences led him to believe that God exists. For him natural science seemed to support the truth of the Bible and Christian revelation. Seventy years, to the day, after Stevenson's epiphany, I felt that I had been given an equally awesome experience of the wonder of creation.

During this journey among the islands of Manu'a I was constantly reminded of the pioneer missionaries scientific interest in unusual plants, as well as the different creatures found in the South Pacific Islands. The Missionary enterprise had begun with the scientific research of Sir Joseph Banks with regard to exotic tropical plants, including breadfruit. Specimens can still be seen at Kew Gardens. A succession of L. M. S missionaries, such as W. Ellis in Tahiti, acclimatized species of fruit and vegetables, adding to those already available. Another named Buzacott propagated the sweet potato to feed starving Hervey Islanders, and so combined an expertise in horticulture with the requirement of the biblical message to love your neighbour. Although many of the pioneer European missionaries in 1792 had lacked a formal education,their successors such as William Ellis, an expert in horticulture, carried out a scientific investigation into Polynesian fauna and flora(1820's).

Thomas Powell (1809-1887), a Welsh Calvinistic Methodist, who lived in what became our home at Fagalele,was an ardent botanist and zoologist. From 1852 onwards until the early 1880's, he travelled to Manu' a to encourage pastors and deacons in their work, checking progress in understanding and applying the Christian teaching, conducting examinations in Scripture, Samoan language, and some elementary Maths and Science. I was relieved to learn that knowledge of Samoan plants and 'creepy crawlies' had slipped out of the Pastor's Schools curriculum before I came on the scene.

Powell was fascinated by the natural sciences, and carried out field studies during the District Examination period. He compiled,translated and published a 330 page zoology manual entitled 'O le tala i tino o tagata ma Mea Ola Ese'ese'. The book began life as a resource for graduates of Malua Theological College, who needed a sound knowledge of plants and creatures mentioned in the Bible. A vast treatise, it dealt with the relationship between the various species, included detailed sections on human anatomy, and bodily functions. Published in 1886, a year before Powell's death in Penzance, S.W. England, it was a systematic scientific work written in the Samoan language.

A section in Powell's book showing the movement of the hydra provides an example of his love of detail. Biologists are especially interested in hydra because they appear not to age, or die of old age. When hydras move they bend over and attach themselves to a firm surface with the mouth and the tentacles, (Ua ia tu'u ifo lona gutu i le mea ua ia tu ai pe tautau ai.), and then release the foot, which provides the usual attachment. The body then bends over and makes a new place of attachment with the foot, (ona tu'u mai ai i o lona i'u e felata' i ma lona gutu). By 'inch worming' or 'somersaulting' a hydra was able move several inches.

Ata 10—O LE HAITERA UA FEALUMA'I.

Writing in the journals of the Linnean Society London, in 1866 about unusual Samoan plants and their vernacular names, Powell also contributed articles on the structure and habits of creatures such as the Coral-reef Annelid, or Palolo viridis. (Palolo is caviar to Samoan taste buds). As a Fellow of the world's premier society for the study and dissemination of natural history, he classified discoveries in the biological sciences, and was necessarily conversant with the theory of evolution and biodiversity. Born in the same year as Charles Darwin in 1809, Powell lived five years longer, and retained a life long interest in botany and zoology which informed his theology. (Darwin was influenced, when studying for Holy Orders at Cambridge, by John Henslow, a clergyman who linked his parish duties with a University Professorship of Botany. Darwin lost interest in theology, and came to deny its value).

During those years theology had to come to terms with the theory of evolution challenging the reliability of the Bible account of creation. The revolutionary concept also required Christians to recognise weaknesses in the argument from design, known as Deism. Many engaged in scientific research were still impressed by the apparent traces of purpose and harmony in the universe, but a growing number found dissonance, irregularity, and chaos. Although different conclusions were drawn from the data obtained, the intertwining of missionary work and scientific activity remained constant.

Powell, and missionary colleagues in Samoa such as Pratt, Whitmee, and Turner, who shared similar scientific interests, were persuaded that both reason and revelation had important roles in discerning truth. A commitment to Christian core beliefs, and a search for meaning in both the transcendent and the immediate, sustained them throughout thirty years work in Samoa. A valid criticism of the Church as an institution, would be that it concentrated on human sin and salvation and ignored a exploration of a theology concerned with ecology, and a sustainable environment begun by the early missionaries scientific interest.

Powell was also a prolific hymn writer throughout those long years, drawing on the imagery of the Bible, which resonated with his experience of wonder in the natural world. Despite losing my well used hymn book Pese 83 'Vivi'i atu ia', (Let us praise) and 370 'Lo'u Ali'i ua fa'afetai', (My Lord I give thanks), the words still reverberate in my head. A down to earth character, Thomas showed his strong humanitarian instincts by campaigning against the infamous activities of a recruiter of slave labour for the Queensland sugar plantations, 'Bully' Hayes.

Sea captain Hayes, was imprisoned when he visited Pago Pago in 1870, but was allowed to escape from custody, much to Powell's dismay. He wrote to M. P.'s in London and the Directors of the L. M. S. 'It will be a lamentable inconsistency of the British and French governments, if this iniquitous traffic be allowed after their intervention to put a stop to Peruvian activities of the same kind' As I sang along with the children of Manu'a the hymns attributed to T. P., and looked at the movement of the hydra that he drew in his text book owned by the village pastor, I recalled his many gifts. There were times at our Fagalele home when I thought that I detected a whiff of his pipe smoke along the verandah in the late evening - an elusive senior partner perhaps! A rational explanation was to be found in the bindweed growing nearby.

On a high

Reversing the order followed on the previous year's malaga, the 1958 Visitation began at the far end of the Manu'a chain at Ta'u Island, which lies about seven miles east south-east of Olosenga. The majority of the eight villages on Ta'u are on the west side of the island, but our first landfall was to be at Fitiuta at the northeast corner. On four visits to Fitiuta in Manu'a, a deep visual impact was made on me by the central open space of the village (malae), surrounded by several thatched houses, balancing each other in size and shape, the spaces between them being proportionate.

The Minister's dwelling, proudly provided by the village, was regarded as best equipped for receiving foreign visitors, and I remember with gratitude the generous hospitality I received. A slightly wrinkled white suit was washed and ironed before I could say 'it doesn't matter.' Whenever I sat down to a meal, a daughter of the 'Feagainga' (Pastor), usually a past student of Atauloma Church School, would hover nearby with a fan to keep the flies away, and to ensure that a smooth efficient service was provided.

Faleasau five miles to the east along the coast from Fitiuta was the next village on our itinerary. Our journey began at dawn, 'i le vave ao', or in the hour of 'quickening cloud'. I could hear the young men of the village preparing the longboat in the dark watches of the night, 'leoleoga o le po', seemingly unaware of the disturbance they were causing. As I emerged from the pastor's house the fautasi (longboat) was carried to the edge of the lagoon, prior to being paddled at low tide towards the reef passage and the open sea. Sitting amidships the morning air was cool and bracing as the longboat glided slowly over the crystal clear waters, through which I could see in the early morning light the sea anemone (lumane), jelly fish with a painful sting (ala'ala), and the small cylindrical parent coral known as 'amu', with the coral budding on its side ready to form a new colony.

Bright blue and red coloured fish, such as the Fuga and Tifitifi, (the Butterfly and Parrot fish to give them their English names) darted about before hiding beneath the rocks, and provided a necessary distraction as the open sea awaited us beyond the reef. Along the coast towards Si'ulangi Point, heaving seas with waves that did not quite reach breaking point developed an uneasy 'roller coaster' momentum, even on the smoothest crossing. These swells rolling towards the rocky promontory became inflated like a gigantic balloon. On their way back after thumping the headland the movement made the boat rise and fall alarmingly.

Beyond the surf, at the beginning of a two-hour journey, the sixteen oarsmen rowed steadily to the sound of a large empty biscuit tin being hit repeatedly and rhythmically with a teak rod as we moved slowly, a hundred yards from the edge of the reef, towards the rising sun. Bounced back and forth as if we were made of cork the waves passed beneath us on their way to crash against the coral barrier, immediately followed by a thunderous crash. A wall of spray flying upwards, made a loud hissing sound as if to say 'I'll get you the next time'. The crew showed that they were equal to the challenge of the journey as they took part in a well-practiced exercise designed to encourage and inspire each other, and those who heard it. The captain at the helm would chant the words, 'Well done the rowers', (Malo fa'auli),and they would reply as one man, 'Thank you for you encouragement.' (Faafetai tapua'i).

A little further on the rowers would call out in unison to the helmsman, 'Well done the captain', Malo le tautai, and he would reply, 'Thanks for your encouragement.' Fa'afetai tapua' i. The man hitting the biscuit tin, who provided the rhythm was not forgotten in the mutual encouragement., 'Malo le ta mea'. The final word was for me when they called out 'Malo Nimese. Malo tapua'i.' (Well-done Neems. Well done the one praying.) This Samoan liturgy of the deep was repeated frequently as we surged forward towards our destination. It also provided me with food for thought..

'Tapuaiga' the Samoan word suggested inspiration from beyond the physical world, freely available to enliven human endeavour. Deeply embedded in the Polynesian psyche was the belief in transcendence, of getting in touch with a spiritual dimension,as the key to satisfaction in any human enterprise. This attitude was summed up in the Samoan proverb, 'E le sili the ta'i i lo le tapua'i.' (Physical effort is itself less important than the spirit upon which it relies.) I was reminded of the older men thoughtfully rolling sinnit on their knees as they sat in the Meeting House, while the young men were engaged in a strenuous fishing expedition beyond the reef. 'Malo tapua'i.' (Well done those who pray for our success).

Approaching Faleasau I felt the boat drawn towards the land by an undertow created by a freshwater stream, which over thousands of years had meandered through the barrier reef at that point to create a narrow, rock - strewn passage leading to the safety of the lagoon. As the boat entered the slipstream flowing from land, erratic movement was corrected before the helmsman ordered the crew to row in a wide circle before pointing the boat towards the passage. He shouted 'Sauni!',(Prepare for landing). Looking over his shoulder the leader at the helm scanned the horizon for the 'Big Wave', and having made his decision he told them to get moving, 'Alu!' (Go!), he shouted, then counting the strokes for the oarsmen, 'Tasi, lua, tolu, fa, tasi, 'he repeated the numbers 1-4 several times with increasing urgency.

Sitting close to the centre of the action I watched the 'Big One', a massive wall of water piling up behind the helmsman. Relying on 'tapua'i', and his skill in choosing the right wave, we anticipated 'lift off' which would happen if the boat and the crest arrived at the passage entrance at the same time.

At such moments I remembered previous land falls, such as when a dislodged coral rock had been deposited across a direct run in, where only the largest waves enabled a heavily laden boat to surmount the obstacle. Another passage quickly flashed through my mind. It was the one approaching the village of Sili where a following wave had forced the boat 'broadside on' to be crushed by the jagged reef. I was thrown into the water, to be immediately held aloft by strong arms, and goodwill. The landing here at Faleasau meant going in at a great pace, the wave taking us up and over, and throwing us thankfully into smooth water. 'Riding the wave',or enjoying the moment, epitomized my experience of life during those two or three years in Samoa.

The thrill and appreciation of a boat journey on the high seas did not end in Faleasau, for after visiting on foot the villages of Si'ufanga, Fagamalo and Amouli on the west side of Ta'u, I boarded the fautasi again for the voyage of seven miles across the open sea between the islands of Ta'u and Olosenga. A deep-sea voyage, and the prospect of a hot sun beating down later, were good reasons for making an early start before the sun rose. As the longboat moved in a westerly direction with the rowers facing east,the sun began to rise. While the boat glided through the water the helmsman and I faced west to become gradually became aware of the glimmer of a new day reflected on the rowers palm oiled bodies, now sweating profusely from their exertions, Slowly the colours of day breaking moved up their straining torsos, until the mirror image of the dawn's rays in the longboat's wake, was reflected on the rower's faces and arms. This experience of the new dawn in Jesus Christ, daily mentioned in welcome ceremonies, encouraged me to look for further evidence of 'Reflected Glory' in the lives of Samoan people. In later years when disillusionment and despair threatened, I recalled with gratitude the vision granted on those journeys between the islands of Manu'a.

Opening minds

In late 1958, the advantage of a town centre position for the Bookshop was being exploited to the full. Pastors and teachers searching for ideas and materials to enliven Christian Education found visual aids such as flannel-graph, posters and pictures readily available. Representatives of congregations from local and remote villages requiring hymn books, Bible Lesson notes,commentaries and prayer books, and literature from the Church Printing Press in W. Samoa, had their needs met. The news stand become a meeting place for Samoan political leaders and stateside employees of the Government, who liked to talk over issues raised by international books and magazines. Time and Newsweek, plus air mail editions of The Guardian Weekly, provided food for thought. People of all shades of knowledge and opinion appreciated the Bookshop's easy accessibility and usefulness. 'Opening minds' was not welcome in all quarters.

At that time restrictions were in force under both government and church authorities concerning what was written and printed in the Samoan language. The United States Navy administration was responsible for the production and distribution of their official newspaper, 'O le Fa'atonu'. Significantly this meant, 'The Director'. An educated elite thought that they knew what was best for the wider public. In the 1930's the Samoan Legislature asked the U.S. Navy Governor to allow them discretionary powers to regulate written material about their culture that was to be used in schools (Section 582 Code of American Samoa).Censorship was necessary, according to the chiefs, because unauthorised observers might misunderstand the customs,culture and traditions intended to provide social harmony.

The roll of censor was also exercised by an educated Church elite who controlled the distribution and sale of the Bible and derivative literature such as So'o (Disciples) and 'O le Maumausolo' (Pilgrim's Progress). Some educated leaders were uneasy about the wide variety of books and magazines available through The Bookshop. They had assumed that mostly religious literature would be sold. Literature other than religious books in the Samoan language, R. L. Stevenson's 'Bottle Imp' for example, were stored in family treasure chests and rarely read. A translation of 'Lamb's Tales from Shakespeare', occasionally saw the light of day. Dusted down, the stories formed the basis of Samoan plays produced for money raising 'malaga' (tours) of neighbouring villages.

Trusted colleagues

Ioane (John) Liulemaga was appointed Bookshop Manager in February 1959. Direct in speech, solid in physique and character, Ioane was a tower of strength as the Bookshop began to develop a sound economic base helped by the sale of postcards and boxed note-lets using photos taken of places seen on Examination Tours. Games and activities for Youth Clubs,Children's Play Group,orders for church organs also enabled the business to expand without losing sight of its main role of providing good reading material in the battle for minds and hearts. John was a trustworthy partner, who was good to have around later, when the going got tough.

Savali Sunia was another example of an admirable co-worker. The daughter of Samoan missionary parents in Moru, Papua New Guinea, she was given the name of the inter island vessel of the London Missionary Society, 'Savali o le Filemu' or 'The Messenger of Peace'. Savali helped to mould the character and values of three generations in the 41 years she worked along-side her husband Fiti Sunia in the town centre church of Fagatogo. Teaching arithmetic, hygiene, and oral and written forms of the Samoan language, she also shared her love of Bible study and prayer,whilst using her gift of storytelling to captivate young people. Through her work with the Girls Life Brigade she drew out of young women a talent for homemaking, and encour-aged professionalism in teaching and nursing. As a 'messenger' in name and disposition, Savali was an inspiration to others engaged in similar work.

Savali provided leadership in a Sunday School Teacher training programme held in the Fagatogo Church each Friday morning in the early 1960's. Teachers from many villages in the District came to these gatherings. With more than fifty teachers present, Savali was an enthusiastic advocate for the use of flannel-graph, posters, cut -out stories and other visual aids obtained from the Bookshop. 'Word Alive' was an accurate way of describing the imaginative methods demonstrated by our team as they worked together. With other teachers, mainly women, Savali worked tirelessly to enrich the lives of young and old alike.

Open Forums for lay people and chiefs, took place in Fagatogo, at the heart of island's life, across the road from the Bookshop. Fiti Sunia, Ne'emia, and

Panama Mutu were responsible for organising the weekly Friday morning events. Paul's first letter to the Corinthians enabled those present to hear what was claimed to be God's word to men and women who lived in a sleazy port where cultures clash.

Paul the Apostle set out clearly the challenges and opportunities of living in New Corinth, an island port in the Mediterranean. A thriving commercial centre with many prostitutes to service sailors, it was home to a mix of dislocated people trying to put down roots. Paul saw the debauchery, but disassociated himself from the censorious attitude of his Jewish compatriots. Corinthians and ourselves were challenged by Paul's painful letters to understand the difference between freedom and licence, also to move on from an understanding of faith as conformity, limitation and habit. Those of us who could hear the loud noise next door in the Pago Bar, when a cruise liner berthed in Fagatogo, appreciated the Apostle's word 'you cannot withdraw from the world.'

Between

Two

Worlds

Discipline an issue

Listening to the responses of Chiefs, their wives and family members in these 'Open Forums', it was obvious that there was growing alarm at the exodus from villages of the 'aumaga', or young men, who had been its strength. In the urban centre and many villages, the traditional Samoan way of life had been weakened. Among young adults there was a desire to get away from the family system with its demands on the individual to share possessions. Young married couples wanted to have their own things, rather than share everything with other members of the community. The education young people received about American values and aspirations widened the to villages, 6- 10 miles outside the increasingly urbanized Pago area. Beginning in Fagaitua, and nearby villages in the Eastern District, ably supported by Luavasa the Senior Minister, new style youth programmes were introduced. They were to be thoughtful and entertaining in presenting alternative attitudes and behaviour to alienated young people, who no longer took notice of their elders and traditional values.

To start a new organisation in a village, approval was sought from the Council of chiefs. I suggested that present-day village youth might respond to a church- related activity, which was different from one that had served an earlier generation. After the usual courtesies of the Kava ceremony, a question and answer session followed. Proceedings began with the assertion that new wine needed new wine skins to contain it. The biblical allusion, and the awareness that the new wine of youth was running to waste, led to a lively discussion. One benefit of a stratified social organisation in Samoa for someone like myself was that I was given the courteous and fair hearing. This was granted to a foreigners associated with health and education. Having access to an enclosed world, I gave thanks for missionary forbears.

Dark evenings from 6.30 onwards meant that use was made of Fact and Faith films, which explored the wonders of outer space, and the microscopic world of nature. Films about medical discoveries and the Olympic Games, film-strips about postage stamp designs using Pacific mythology, and another entitled 'Taking a drink?', added to a wide range of topics. These proved to be lively starters for exchanges in a mixture of English, Samoan and American languages.

Arriving in a village after school hours it was possible to arrange games of mixed volleyball, baseball or cricket for children of the village. Older youth stayed for an evening of discussion and games of musical chairs and statues, of 'Simon says' and attempts made to dance the Virginia Reel or a similar fun dance done to Samoan music. The evening ended with prayers and a hymn. Novel methods (hopefully avoiding mild cultural imperialism), were the attraction, but the underlying importance of these visits was to give a clear signal to village and church leaders that work among young people was in need of urgent attention. Pastors Schools were not enough.

One evening following a thunderstorm I was returning home late after an evening among young people at Lauli' i on the eastern side of the island. Approaching Leone, and attempting to avoid pot holes caused by heavy rain and floods, I saw that several logs had been placed across the dirt road. Remaining in the car I took the turn off right, going down the track to the village of Taputimu to return to Leone village another way. An ambush intended for a rival group bent on violence reinforced a conviction that away from the mission compound such traps were a fact of life. Behind a facade of smooth talk and a smiling faces, tribalism often reared its ugly head. Retribution awaited outsiders who offended the honour of a family grouping by unwanted sexual activity. Suspected cheating in sports among participants in local competitions often led to brawling. A continuing challenge faced those who valued self discipline, and the benefits of cooperation.

In 1959 a leaving student from Malua Theological College named Misipele became a helpful colleague as he prepared scripts in Samoan, then tape recorded them to accompany films and filmstrips made in Britain, and the USA. Questions to prompt discussion as part of a balanced Youth Club evening programme were also prepared to suit the age range and location, in the urbanised area and isolated village. Our hope was that 'coconut wireless' (word of mouth),would encourage representatives of other villages to attend training sessions in youth leadership. The Youth Club Organisation in American Samoa began to grow in size and influence.

Maverick Chairman

One afternoon in early January 1959, The Bookshop doors had to be closed due to high winds, and a drenching downpour. With a weather forecast predicting a hurricane brewing north east of Manu'a I prepared to travel to Apia on the small motor vessel, 'Sulimoni' for Church Executive Meetings. I was about to experience what had become a familiar experience, that of being thrown in at the deep end.

During those early years the annual appointment of Chairman of the Church alternated between a missionary and a Samoan. As I was the only missionary available I had been elected Vice Chairman for one year, before taking the Chair of the General Assembly the following year. In the year of office of the previous missionary occupant of the Chair, John Bradshaw, several radical policies had received Assembly assent. However resistance to the decisions taken grew steadily in the following months. Vaguely aware of a storm brewing I wasn't particularly concerned because I thought that anything could happen in the year before I moved over to the 'hot seat'. Sufficient unto the day is the evil thereof' was my spurious comfort. I was prepared to s sink or swim in the depths of Samoan Church Assembly politics.

A deeply divisive incident happened at the January Meetings. One of the Senior Ministers named Tupe, Chairman of the General Assembly from May 1958, disobeyed a decision of that august body, which required ministers to retire at 75 years of age. Senior Pastor Tupe, having broken a rule made at the previous Assembly was therefore not allowed to preside over Church business. In effect I became Chairman of the Assembly for eighteen months, (Jan. 1959 -May 1960). I knew Elder Pastor Tupe quite well because we had travelled together on the inter-island boat, the M. V. Tofua, on her way to Samoa in 1955. On that occasion he had made me feel like one of the many green bananas in the ship's hold. Struggling to understand and speak Samoan fluently, I was now Chairman of the Assembly.

Behind the dispute about retirement age was a protest by councils of village chiefs who objected to a centralised body, in this case the Established Church in Samoa, telling local chiefs what to do. The Feagaiga, (binding mutual agreement), between a village and an individual minister,whatever his age,was village business. A Church Assembly decision stated that 'The Samoan Way' of conducting local church and village business no longer applied to ministerial training. Was the crack in the edifice binding together the Samoan Church with Samoan culture and traditions about to split apart? Would the centre hold ? Others thought that an opportunity for creating a more flexible organisation, was present within the anticipated turmoil.

My immediate concern as Chairman of the Assembly was to remain afloat in a sea of trouble. What a hope! In assemblies Samoans often 'speak to the gallery' without giving a clear indication of the way they would vote. Flying kites on hill tops and jousting had been the sport of Samoan kings. An opinion could be wrapped up in vague allusions designed, it seemed, to confuse, rather than enlighten. Often when I turned to an interpreter for help, he would declare that he was equally mystified about what was being said.

Leaving room to back-track when majority opinion seemed to be going in an opposite direction to that being proposed,was an all important consideration for any spokesman. Being left high and dry damaged the speaker's dignity, and this was to be avoided at all costs. Long after it would have been of use to me as Chairman' I heard a common saying, 'ne'i te'a ma le fainga,'. It meant 'don't be far from the large basket when a fishing party deliberately disturb the water's surface'. Go with the big fish! To continue the fishing analogy, great efforts were made in a public discussion among Samoans to 'get everybody on board', - and this took time, not always available.

Throughout the Assembly I was out of my depth. The frustration aroused by those members opposing the rule applying to 75 year old Pastors rankled representatives on both sides of the dispute, throughout the week. Many of the powerful family alliances were drawn into contention, and the voice of dissent was heard beneath the consideration of 'domestic' issues affecting the organisation of church life. Threats of withdrawing or reducing finances (Taulaga) collected in the Districts were heard. These were side-tracked into loud complaint about a growing desire for control from those serving in central church administration. Fortunately the point of no return had not been reached, and the Church officials in a position to know believed that further room for manoeuvre had been created. Verbal assurances given by representatives returning to their villages in the next few weeks would be crucial.

Squabbling with a neighbour

After a rough sea journey back to American Samoa I was soon caught up in a dispute of my own doing. Our home at Fagalele was built fifty yards from the edge of a volcanic outcrop, with a drop of 20 feet to the sea below. A fisherman's path along the cliff top meant that our sleep was occasionally disturbed. It was only a minor nuisance, for it was believed by locals that Tuiatua, a powerful Spirit (Aitu) who demanded that quiet should reign, rested on rocks close to blowholes beside the path. On most nights of the year our welcome guardian did his work. However on one night in the year all caution was thrown to the winds.

As regular as clockwork, at dawn on the day before, or the day after, the last quarter of the moon in the months of October and November, noisy activity took place. On one of those four days, when all the conditions for the event had been met, the Palolo worm, which lived among the coral all the year, released its hind end, and then swam in vast swarms to the surface where they spawned. When this happened the local people went wild, rushing to scoop them up in baskets to eat as a delicacy, the texture and taste said to be akin to caviar. Most of the time, depending on the phases of the moon, mutual consideration, and making allowance for minor disturbances, Fagalele was a peaceful place.

When Susan, our firstborn, was two and a half months old, boisterous fishermen did not help her colic restlessness in the middle of the night. When I asked them to move on from the Fagalele property, I discovered that one of them was our close neighbour, Talking Chief Fega. An argument followed during which he repeated what he had said in previous debacles with teachers of the school. He intended to revoke the easement of a fifty-yard long double track over his family land granted by his ancestors. Because the means of access had been used by members of the school community for over a century, it was an empty threat in law. Unfortunately my dog growled menacingly, whereupon Fega attempted to slash Spotty with a bush knife.

We exchanged strong words. It was a serious mistake because Fega had been ostracised by the Council of fellow chiefs responsible for the village social order (faiganu'u), after he had served a sentence for manslaughter.

The next morning I saw him carrying a shotgun on the other side of the compound, near the house of Iakopo, the Headmaster. Fega then moved in our direction, and nearing the house called out that he was going to shoot Spotty. He also threatened to do the same to me if I stood in his way. Iakopo, who had raced from his home, was able through the constant repetition of words such as 'Susu le Fega o Atua'(honorific title), to pacify and eventually persuade him to leave the school compound. The power of other key words used in explosive situations, gave me a lesson on how to diffuse tension leading to conflict.

Living in small island communities there was no chance of escaping person-ality clashes, emotional outbursts of bad humour and behaviour. Responsible Samoan leaders had learned that in heated moments you did not say the first thought that came into your head. Instead words such as 'fa'amolemole, lau susuga. Ia malie lou finagalo' (Make smooth your honour. Be calm your will), were of primary importance in dispersing hostility. Spoken by someone who was respected, and a person prepared to ingratiate themselves, hot tempers were cooled and anger made manageable. I was much indebted to Iakopo.

Communication among the 'elite' in Samoa relied on the lubricant inherent in ancient formal phrases intended to relieve tension and aggravation. As the years passed I came to appreciate the skill of Samoan orators during subtle verbal exchanges. The dexterity with which innuendo was concealed, or irony expressed with a subtle nudge, was appreciated by their audience. Awkward in comparison, the exchange with Fega and Iakopo meant that he went away mollified for the moment.

Apparent reconciliation did not stop him blocking the access track for vehicles on to the School property (including our home), on subsequent occasions. Following Iakopo's suggestion, I went to Fega's house and pre-sented him with cotton material for a new lavalava, or wrap-around. This episode with my near neighbour showed that I had much to learn about living in close proximity to others on a small island. William Golding's 'Lord of the flies',a novel which we sold in the Bookshop, should have taught me that raw aggression could lead to violent death when space was confined.

Dog Watch

Iakopo's help did not end with the gun incident. Accustomed to being wakened early when called upon to do the 'dog watch' hours in Navy days, I spent time preparing a handbook for the Watchers Prayer Union. This was a society of men and women who met daily around dawn in every village throughout Samoa, to pray for 'all sorts and conditions' world wide. The London Missionary Society had planted the seed of the Gospel in five continents,and a network of churches had come into being, many of which were members of the World Council of Churches, based in Geneva. Plans were being made for the First Conference of the Pacific Council to be held in Samoa.

In the early morning, I would prepare Samoan text with a distinctive English 'voice',which began to have an authentic Samoan sound when Iakopo ,who spoke 'broken ' English, had finished with it. Between us we were able to create comprehensible copy to be sent to an impatient printer in Apia, waiting to meet a deadline. After one late night session, Iakopo walked out of my study onto the verandah, misjudged the position of the steps,and fell six feet to the ground below. Fortunately he emerged unhurt from under the frangipani tree, only for the students to tease him the next morning about drinking something stronger than cocoa.

A example from of our partnership in prayer is found on page one of the 1960 handbook.'Before we begin our prayers each day let us remember what we are doing, and the reason why we are doing it. Let us recall that our lives, and the lives of those for whom we pray, are included in the loving purposes of God.' In a prayer for the Samoan Church meeting in General Assembly, found on page 6 of the same book, readers were bidden to pray 'We pray in your presence that all hatred, and evil and the causes of disturbance may be removed from your Church.' It was encouraging to know that groups met at daylight in Pastor's homes in Samoa to unite in prayer using these words. I dare to think that without their prayers,matters might have been much worse as Chairman of the General Assembly of the Samoan Church.

Bad to worse

The controversy surrounding Elder Pastor Tupe was unresolved at the time of the 1960 General Assembly. Long past retirement age; he was still unwilling to accept a majority decision, which meant breaking an agreement binding him to a particular village. Another controversy was brewing related to Samoan custom and the control it exerted over wider Church discipline.

John Bradshaw, the Malua College Principal, asked the Church Assembly to provide overseas scholarships for two students, who had been marked out as showing particular promise. The request was refused because a designated sponsorship would have gone against an established Samoan custom.

When a Samoan was convinced that God had called him to be a minister,his sense of vocation was tested by recognised assessors,both individuals and groups. If accepted for training, a student became an offering made by his extended family,who would support him financially throughout four years of study. On completing the college course the student might receive an invitation to enter into an agreement (Feagaiga), with another village whereupon the approval of a student's wider family would be sought. Because such arrangements often created new family ties, or conferred reciprocal benefits, according to Samoan custom, the scene was set for a head on collision in the Assembly when the Theological College brought a resolution for approval.

In a new age of wider educational opportunity, Malua College recognised the need for a few candidates to do further study overseas. They would be selected and sponsored on the basis of academic promise. The intention was that those who were selected would keep abreast of scholarship students in government service who already received grants for further education. In due course the scholarship students would serve the Church,whose leaders recognised the need for comparable high standards. The Church through its General Assembly would be responsible for providing the necessary financial help.

The resolution was lost and John resigned as Principal. It was painful all round. For the next five years J. B. was the leading figure among those responsible for a new Church Constitution, preparing a Statement of Faith, and also producing a well used Book of Public Worship. Besides being an influential member of a new Bible translation committee, he continued to be a powerful voice in the life of the Church and Nation, in particular with regard to preparations leading up to Independence Day in Western Samoa.

Flavour of the decade

A journey to the United Kingdom in 1960 after an absence of 5 years was a welcome break for our young family. Our return to American Samoa coincided with the arrival of a powerful hurricane. It began on the night of

Saturday the 24th of January 1961,and continued throughout the following day. Our daughter Susan celebrated her second birthday as the storm threatened to break, the first of three 'blows' of similar intensity experienced by us during the next seven years.

The 1961 tempest was described by Pitone Leauga, a Samoan schoolboy as beginning at two in the morning. He captured the sense of overwhelming awe that came over him as the wind grew in force. 'Everything was still, there was no sound, and nothing moved. The air was hot, and the appearance of the trees and the sea looked strangely angry. Following an eerie silence, seeming to last an eternity, a mounting crescendo of noise announced the arrival of powerful gusts in quick succession from all points of the compass. Concentrating on becoming a single howling monster, and accompanied by drenching rain, the hurricane destroyed houses and uprooted plantations'.

1961 was to be a year of upheaval and new growth too. Some observers of Pacific Island life in the 1960's,consider that the movement towards Church Unity provided an important element in the flavour of the decade. During the Sixth Tidal Wave described in Part One of this book(p47), the steady growth of the Tahitian Mission spread into Melanesia. After broken comity agreements in New Zealand,Australia and Tonga had spoiled relationships, the Anglican and Methodists gradually learned to work reasonably well together, without a sense of competition. Eighty years later the time was right for a Regional Conference of Protestant Churches, mainly Anglican, Methodist and Congregational, to take place between the 22nd April- 4 May 1961 at Malua College in Western Samoa. Roman Catholic observers were welcomed. A team of outstanding Island leaders came to the fore at that time including the Samoans, Mila Sapolu and Vavae Toma. The Pacific Council of Churches was born, and the United Theological College located in Fiji became more than a dream.

About this time a major change took place in the relationship between the Church in Samoa, and the London Missionary Society, which had been instrumental in the church's foundation. The Congregational Christian Church of Samoa was recognised as a member of a family of churches, not only in the Pacific, but throughout the world. Whereas Samoan colleagues in 1955 had used the deferential expression, 'The Elders in London' (Au Matat-ua), the new constitution recognised Samoans and Europeans as Partners in Mission.

Big brother

American Samoa was about to receive special treatment from an unexpected quarter. In March 1961, John F. Kennedy was elected President of the USA. Three months later he announced an economic plan to raise living standards in Central and South America, which was intended to unsettle President Castro's government in Cuba. Unsuccessful in that regard, it nevertheless prepared the way for an injection of considerable financial aid in the U.S. dependent territories in the Pacific, such as Guam and American Samoa. Nations critical of U.S. in the United Nations Assembly accused the super power of negligence in furthering self government within its territories.

In May 1961 Rex Lee was appointed Governor, and four months later a large grant from Congress set in motion a series of projects aimed at improving health, education and public works. Tourism was to be at the heart of the economy, and a thorough clean up programme was set in motion. During Governor Lee's first year in office, a bitumen paved road was laid, which stretched along the length of one side of Tutuila Island, connecting eastern and western districts. New terminal buildings for the International Airport at Tafuna were constructed to give the impression of a Samoan village. Beams of pre-cast concrete supported shingle roofs to resemble thatched homes to provide a welcome contrast to 'identi-kit 'airport terminals.

Improved berthing facilities were created in Pago Pago Harbour to enable more cruise vessels to call. Regular visits of the Matson liners Monterey and Mariposa continued. Two large dredgers were used to scoop coral rocks from the foreshore to create a strip of landfill joined to a small islet called Goat Island, formerly the site of the U.S. Navy Clubhouse, and Commissary. A sandy beach bordered by waving palm trees completed the impression of a South Seas Paradise.

The foundation for a luxury Intercontinental Hotel with 97 bedrooms completed, the dredger moved on to make several sandy beaches and other landfill sites for The Turtle Auditorium and the Television Centre. Most of the buildings constructed by the Government during this rapid expansion programme were of Polynesian design imitating a traditional Samoan thatched roof dwelling.

The hotel was the main showpiece. Built at the cost of $2 million on land leased from the Government the enterprise was largely financed by the Economic Development Corporation of Washington D.C. and the Wells Fargo Bank. Air-conditioned throughout, with a large attractive swimming pool, the hotel was managed by a subsidiary of Pan American Airways, before that company went out of business. A layout for a new Hospital, and High School Campus in the Bay Area, became the next objective in upgrading the territory's public services.

A Big Brother's sense of responsibility was behind the U.S. Government's attempt to strengthen representative government in American Samoa. Governor Lee,an American Democratic Party nominee,had to come to terms with a resilient Samoan hierarchical system possessing elitist traditions and attitudes. Locals came to know that Lee meant business as he pressed for a more egalitarian system that was more acceptable to his compatriots back in Washington. Strong resistance was encountered over land possession. Land tenure in Samoa continued to be vested in heads of families, and caused bitter disputes among its members, that kept the Office of Samoan Affairs working at full stretch. As more money circulated,the number of legal wrangles increased due to the number of American style residencies being built on disputed land. Numerous legal battles awaited settlement in court, with the result that many houses stood incomplete to become an eyesore.

Aware of the reluctance of the Western Samoa Parliament to extend the franchise to anyone outside the ranks of traditional chiefs, Governor Lee wanted to encourage American Samoans who had achieved some movement on the question of voting rights. A limited franchise was now open to women and untitled men to enter The Upper House or Senate. Progress towards the coexistence of traditional and democratic procedures was seen in decisions made by secret ballot in the Legislative Council,or through a show of hands. Possible closer relations between the two Samoan administrations was regarded as loose talk because Western Samoa legislators would never agree to any move towards an open franchise. Big Brother attitudes by Western Samoan leaders towards their kith and kin across the water in American Samoa had a long history. (see below)

Encouragement was given by the U.S. Department of the Interior for the people of American Samoa to have a House of Representatives acting alongside the Senate jointly conducting government business. An attempt was to be made to run the modern alongside the well tried. The Senate elected members from the traditional leadership of village chiefs,whereas all adults voted for Representatives. Land rights vested in the name of titled men were to be non negotiable. Nonetheless chiefs recognised that stateside education had begun to change attitudes towards long established forms of social control relying on elitism. As economic progress enriched more local people, communal unrest seemed inevitable. An Upper House Senator was heard to say 'that in a time of rapid change when one is uncertain, it is always best to hold on to what one has'. (Apron strings !)

Following meetings in the Assembly Hall next door, Members of the Legislative Council often called in the Bookshop for their newspapers and magazines. I heard expressions of unease about the fast pace of economic, educational and social change brought about by 'Big Brother' in Washington. American Samoan leaders looked over their shoulders at the cautious approach of the Western Samoan Legislature to restore a broken unity.. However further reflection reminded them that such a move would confirm their lower status in an All - Samoa Parliament in which Western Samoa would replace Uncle Sam as Big Brother.

The subservient attitude of American Samoan chiefs towards their Western brothers was well known. Samoa orators,who are the guardians of tradition,excel in distorting ancient folklore to the political advantage of their own districts, yet all of them accept that the main island of Upolu, in Western Samoa, had long been divided into three separate districts. (1) A'ana in the west was nearest to Tutuila, American Samoa. (2) Tuamasanga the central district enjoyed the benefit of Apia harbour, and (3) Atua in the east. Each had a separate paramount chief. Incessant rivalry and warfare occurred between these powerful groups. (Map p64)

The domination of Tutuila by Tuamasanga was forcibly removed through the defeat of Tuamasanga by the combined forces of the other two districts. Humiliated, Tuamasanga was threatened with annihilation,or pay a ransom (togiola), which was to be the island of Tutuila. The result was that many of the village names and chiefly titles of Tutuila, American Samoa bear witness to their origin in Upolu,Western Samoa. 'Ua tosi fa'alauti le eleele o Tutuila' (Tutuila has been torn to shreds as the strands of a skirt). On 17th April 1900 the overlords of A'ana District in W. Samoa lost control of the islands of Tutuila and Manu'a and were replaced by the US Navy. In a reversal of fortune, the domination of A'ana was over. However eighty years passed before Tutuila family links with California proved stronger than the deep family loyalties that had existed between Tutuila (American Samoa) and nearby A'ana. (Western Samoa).

Samoans living in Tutuila and Manu's still experienced a strong pull of the umbilical cord towards their Western Samoan cousins as they sat through the New Constitution Church Assembly of 1961. However when these same Samoans from the American group had recovered from a rough sea trip home from Apia to Pago, they woke up to the fact that their affections were mainly drawn to their American sons, daughters and cousins, now citizens of the USA living in Hawai'i and California. Regular visits between relatives using the Pan American Airline were taken for granted. Digging beneath the surface of an outward show of support for an All Samoa Government, which favoured kinship groups based in Western Samoa, the chiefs of American Samoa knew that their 'bread and butter' concerns were elsewhere. They received sustenance from the special treatment given to them by the USA, a World Power, with apparently limitless resources. A united Samoa was for another time. (se isi aso).

American Samoan leaders attending the 1961 General Assembly, where I had been Chairman, saw that a give and take attitude and generosity towards their own district,was sadly lacking. They felt sore because reciprocity in relationships was dear to Samoan hearts. American Samoans were aggrieved because they were paying more than their fair share for the impressive new office in the centre of Apia. It gave further offence that the massive building programme to upgrade Malua College and Leulumoega High School was all one way traffic. Old resentments emerged as questions were asked about fairness in the distribution of joint resources at the church's periphery.

Late in the day many members of the American Samoa Legislature realised that they had agreed to the Church's New Constitution, which had been made and delivered in Western Samoa. It had failed to address the distinctive nature of American Samoa's social and political upheaval. A tidal wave of dollar millions, T. V. technology and an appeal to individual gain, threatened to sweep away a culture based on sharing wealth that was common property. The Eastern group of Samoan islands needed a different response from that of Western Samoa for the challenges facing the newly Independent State were real enough, but not potentially overwhelming. Samoan leaders, whether in Church or Nation, could not have anticipated the extent of the changes brought about by President Kennedy's election victory. A greater flexibility in the way that finance was allocated by Big Brother based in the Church H.Q. in Western Samoa, would have helped considerably.

California. Land of promise

Numia, a Fagalele schoolboy adopted as one of our family in 1956-7 left Samoa for California in 1959. Our nearest neighbour, a woman schoolteacher named Fausaga left for the USA soon afterwards. She was the daughter of Chief To'omata (Susu oulua Ilaoa ma To'omata), whose family a century earlier had given their land to allow Fagalele to become a place of learning. Anoa'i, a close neighbour belonging to the Leoso family,known as master builders, had been ordained as a Samoan Minister. He joined what appeared to be a mass exodus to San Francisco. After their departure I heard from family members that the three of them had immediately linked up with relatives already settled in the city's suburbs. A good description of the Samoan family is that of 'a community who use the same cookhouse', and this applied in California as it did in Leone,our local Samoan village.

In the village situation the cookhouse served perhaps twenty people living in two or three homes situated nearby. The group would have at its heart a grandmother, or a great uncle, to whom all were related in one way or another, a niece or nephew, cousins close or distant, plus a few adopted children. This extended family system of mutual benefits and responsibilities also operated on Californian soil. Because churchgoing was a strong element in sustaining a corporate sense of identity, Samoan families met together initially under the auspices of the Southern Californian Conference of Congregational

Churches. The Congregational pattern of worship was familiar to them, and a well-understood organization of ministers and deacons took care of financial and pastoral concerns.

San Diego was the most popular port of entry. During the 1960's, it was the home port of 175 Navy ships, covering the full range from L. S. T. (Landing ship tank) to enormous battleships. In addition 235 ships of the 'Mothball Fleet', made redundant after the Second World War, were moored in long rows at the Naval Station in San Diego Bay. 142,000 sailors, marines, and civilians living in San Diego County, were on the Navy payroll. Many of them were Samoans.

When the Naval Administration left Pago in 1951, nearly 1,000 Samoan men, wives and their families left their own land for Honolulu, and many moved on to San Diego in the following months and year. This led to an exponential growth in the numbers of Samoans living in U. S. cities and towns. Settling in areas where they could meet to socialize, and continue to take part in worship following a familiar pattern, they were supported and encouraged by members of the Conference mentioned earlier.

Links having been made on the American mainland with the Southern Conference, Tutuila and Manu'a District leaders back in Samoa sought to encourage former members of their congregations to consolidate this relationship. Since 1945 attempts had been made by American Samoans to obtain the services of a minister/teacher from the USA rather than one from Britain. Western Samoans with a majority vote had discouraged such a move. This did not prevent the American Board, as the overseas arm of the Congregational Church body with Headquarters in New York, maintaining close contact with the General Secretary of the London Missionary Society to further that aim. For nearly 10 years both organisations anticipated that an American missionary would be appointed to Samoa.

The American Board was aware of the pastoral needs of Americans in the administrative and business community working in Pago Pago, and awaited an invitation from Samoa. London was sympathetic, but maintained that such an appointment must have the approval of the Samoan Church in the Islands. When Western Samoa achieved Independence in 1961, it revived concern among American Samoans in the Islands and the USA that a possible closer partnership with a mainstream church in the USA was slipping away.

The District leaders including the Senior Ministers (Toeaina), the District Treasurer, Fiti Sunia, and the District Secretary, Panama Mutu, were under mounting pressure in 1961 to make up their minds, now or never. Would it be possible to look both ways, towards W. Samoa, and the USA? The proposed New Constitution, awaiting ratification at the 1962 Assembly, had resurrected earlier resentments, and stirred up threats of non co-operation in collecting a Church Tax. Powerful voices in the Legislature maintained that with greater autonomy, American Samoa would be able to build on fraternal bonds already made with the Church in the USA.

I was asked by the Au Toeaina (Senior Ministers), and other District Officers to prepare a District Constitution. In broad outline the proposal would affirm the unity of the Church, whilst enabling the District to have its own committee structure to spend a block grant of money on projects relevant to a rapidly changing social situation. These would include improving on the successful 'Word Alive' Christian Education programme for all ages, and expanding Youth and Sunday School activity. Inter-dependence rather than Independence was at the heart of the document.

There was alarm in London. Questions were asked about the direction taken by the Church in American Samoa. I wrote reports and letters providing background information about the proposed District Constitution to missionary colleagues, and to Stuart Craig an Overseas Secretary of L. M. S. with headquarters in Westminster. Stuart replied in a letter dated 17th November 1961, 'I should like to know more of the pressures which have caused things to move on at what seems to me a somewhat alarming rate.' After commenting favourably on the possibility of having an American missionary to work in Tutuila, he wrote that 'what is now taking shape as set out in the report, is not a constitution for a district within a church, but is leading to a separate church, which might for purposes of convenience and fellowship, do certain things such as ministerial training and oversight together with the Church in Western Samoa'.

John Bradshaw also wrote recognising the grounds for a genuine grievance, but believed that the unity of the Church would be best preserved by the district adopting a 5-year plan, that is a special dispensation given by the whole church, to focus the District's energies, including financial resources, on a programme of renewal.

I deserved the sting in the tail of Stuart's letter, which at first seemed to be a 'throw away' line. 'On a tiny matter of detail', he wrote 'in any form of constitution, whether District or otherwise, where the membership of the body is set out, the missionary should not come at the head. This is very much out of date.' It was a mistake on my part, because as Stuart pointed out, it would suggest that I had given 'this particular proposal a good deal of personal support and pressure.'

He was right, for the Constitution 's draft form suggested that I intended to be the Captain of the boat, whereas the heading at the beginning of this chapter, 'Well done the rowers' drew inspiration from a longboat journey in Manu'a. Shared responsibilities among those on board the fautasi had enabled the crew with one passenger to cross the open sea, and surmount the barrier reef. Because the document had been conceived in collaboration with Samoan leaders, Stuart's apparently innocent aside struck home. I should have concentrated on defining the underlying issues at stake in a controversial debate, rather than be open to the charge of instigating a political row. Although Stuart did not state as much, 'The messenger, not the sender, is often shot dead when powerful people receive unwelcome news'.

Partnership elusive

From September 1961 onwards I got on with the job of visiting villages to work out a youth programme with local leaders. Walking the mountain trail to Fagamalo, again in an incessant downpour, I was given a courteous reception at a kava ceremony. Having previously made a note of the order of precedence when referring to the chiefly titles of the village 'Afio mai (Your Presence) Fa'asisina,' ma (and) 'Maliu mai (Your lesser Presence) Moi and Faletogo'. Respect being another word for love had begun to be understood.

When the orator responded using the now redundant title 'Ta'ita'i a le Matagaluega' (Leader of the District), I sensed that it was done 'for old times sake' to show respect to missionaries who in past generations had sat in front of the post assigned to honoured visitors. They made it clear that genuine partnership required trust in the missionaries who had gone before me. I heard again an exhortation used on many occasions when cooperative effort was needed on a fishing 'drive' or during a building programme. 'Se' i tatou galulue felagolagoma'i i ai.' (Let us work together, trusting each other).

Partnership was easily misunderstood. When in September 1961 Iakopo, the Headmaster of Fagalele' received an invitation from the village of Amouli to be their minister, the group of senior ministers and myself appointed as supervisors for the 'Aufaigaluega' (Ministers in pastoral charge), felt that the transfer should not take place until a substitute was appointed. Sese, Iakopo's wife, taunted the Au Toeaina with the charge that 'There are four of you, and you can't stand up to one missionary.

Many shared Sese's opinion, that partnership was a vacuous term hiding a struggle for dominance. There were some who thought that leaders should walk in the shoes of some authoritarian 'fathers' of a bygone age. Their view was that 'In times of upheaval, Samoans wanted to receive firm directions from their overseers'. Often such sentiments were a rebuke aimed at the perceived ineffectiveness of the present day leaders who preferred to consult, rather than direct. During lengthy committee meetings I found it particularly unnerving to observe one Samoan leader, who regarded a missionary of an earlier dispensation as a model leader.

Tapeni Ioelu, who was frequently Chairman of the Church during the 1960's, had been brought up in the nearby village of Leone, before becoming a student at Fagalele School. Fifty years afterwards Ioelu reflected the doctrinaire habit of mind of his long dead former Headmaster and Mentor, Misi Uafa. (Hough). Some of Hough's opinions are revealed in the minutes of the Western Samoa's Board of Education in 1924, and his overbearing demeanour portrayed in a newspaper photograph of that year. The appearance and views of the 1960's Samoan leader were remarkably similar to the those of the 1915 English Headmaster. For better or for worse some old missionaries lived on.

Long established downward command structures of leadership continued to exist alongside an equally ancient collective style of decision making practiced in Church, Village and Government Assemblies. I was grateful for Samoan colleagues who were prepared to build relationships based on mutual trust. The courage of those prepared to try out new ideas, or learn from mistakes,stood out among many conformist brethren. Valued colleagues wanted to read widely,to learn from each other's insights, and to make time to attend further education courses.

This chapter began with the account of a sea journey in Manu'a with the words 'Well done the rowers' (Malo le Fa'auli) ringing in the ears. That deep-sea experience in July 1958 spelt out a need to create partnerships where appreciation was expressed for each other's efforts. Leadership skills were not confined to one individual or group. In particular I was drawn to the man hitting the biscuit tin who called out 'Malo tapua'i',or 'Well done Encourager' at a time when I was physically inactive in a boat with so much strenuous effort going on all round me. Everyone had a part to play.

Encouraging Prayer, (tapua'i) meant a sympathetic identification with fellow crew members, but more important, 'tapua'i' was the alignment of the group with a Higher Power, 'Le Atua Silisili Ese' The words of a proverb rang in my ears 'E le sili le ta' i i lo le tapu'a' I' (Effort is not more important than the source of inspiration,God Himself). It was a reminder, that inspiration comes before perspiration, and our lives are in His hands.

Two and a half years later in December 1961, despite failures and misunder-standings, I had been involved in several cooperative ventures, which hope-fully had made a useful contribution to the Island's life. A partnership in prayer had been developed with co-translator Iakopo. Because of the books we prepared together a special link had been forged with people waking up bleary eyed to the daily discipline of group prayer. The Watchers Prayer Union book was used in many villages throughout Samoa. Youth Work with Misipele had made a good start, and relationships made through the Book-shop, and the work of Ioane, particularly with Island's leaders, was promising. Word Alive gatherings on Market Days in the Bay Area were welcomed, and the sharing of helpful insights on teaching material used in village schools reached a wider audience. Partnership with Samoan colleagues began to be more relaxed and some mutual benefit was enjoyed.

Chapter Headings

Faith and reason - On a roll - Opening minds - Trusted colleagues - Discipline an issue - Maverick Chairman - Squabbling with a neighbour - Dog watch - Bad to worse - Flavour of the decade - Big Brother - California .Land of promise -Partnership elusive.

Junior Partner

Chapter Eleven

1962 - 1964 Proceed with caution

Samoan Proverb. Ia seu le manu, 'ae silasila i le galu. Catch the bird, but watch the waves. Sea birds rest on the rocks near the shore, and become prey for trappers with nets. 'Catch the bird' applauds the spirit of adventure, but warns the hunter to watch out for unsuspected danger. The seaweed and algae make for slippery conditions, and powerful waves can catch them off guard.

Independence Day

January 1st 1962 was celebrated as Independence Day by the people of Western Samoa. A few days earlier I had arrived in the capital to assume pastoral charge of the Apia Protestant Church for three months whilst the resident minister was on furlough. A five-day programme of parades, fire-work displays, sports and competitions of all kinds culminated in a boat race (fautasi),with crews of 18 rowers. The contest was followed by an evening garden party at Vailima, the former home of Robert Louis Stevenson.

Prime Minister, Fiame Mata'afa spoke of the new Government's responsibility to 'fa'afoe lelei le Pulega o le Malo o le atumotu mo ona Tagata uma', that

159

is, 'to steer well the rule of the Government of the country for all its people. Western Samoa was the first Pacific territory to emerge from a period of colonial rule, and was also first in possessing full control of its external relations in addition to its internal affairs.

A mischievous reporter of the Pacific Islands Monthly asked the Prime Minister, 'Had any of the Communist countries indicated that they would be coming to the Independence celebrations?' He replied that as far as he knew, they had not. The interviewer said that he thought that it was strange because Russians in particular had pressed hard in the United Nations Assembly for early independence for Samoa. (Soviet Bloc countries, derided as an Evil Empire, were keen to embarrass Western Powers with former possessions in the Pacific). Mata'afa responded to the effect that invitations had been confined to Samoa's Pacific neighbours. 'But Germany is coming'. Poker faced Mata'afa replied that Germany was a special case. Not to be outdone the reporter asserted that Russia had also shown a lively interest in the occasion. 'It was strange' agreed Mata'afa, still speaking with a straight face.

What Mata'afa said to the reporter, and the manner in which he said it, agreed with what he had said in 1960 to the United Nations Fourth Committee on Trusteeship. 'Helped by our gradual assumption of political responsibility over the past 14 years, and by our friendly cooperation with New Zealand, we should experience little difficulty when the moment for independence comes. For that reason, I would suggest that you should not look for any spectacular or revolutionary change in our way of doing things when we become independent. Such revolutionary changes have been made unnecessary both by the strength of our traditions, and the good fortune of our circumstances. Rooted in tradition and responding to the invigorating influences of the modern world, the Independent State of Western Samoa will grow and flourish.'

The dominant note struck by the Prime Minister on Independence Day was of optimism and openness to the future, but the note of caution was present too in what he said to his own people 'Ia outou migao ma fa'aaloalo i le pule mamalu a matai i o outou aiga.' (You must respect and honour the dignified rule of the chiefs in your families.) In other words ,Western Samoa remained apprehensive about egalitarianism. J. W. Davidson, who had great sympathy with Samoan aspirations, and was a contributor to the negotiations leading to independence wrote 'The dominant tone of Samoan politics is not reactionary, but it remains conservative'.

160

In another passage from his book 'Samoa mo Samoa' he wrote,'The Samoans, like all conservatives, run the risk of retaining the form of traditional institutions when their spirit and purpose have disappeared and, in doing so, failing to satisfy contemporary demands. Because of its political traditions, Samoa is well protected against the tyranny and disorder that have marked the early years of many other new states. For the same reason, it is in danger of failing to keep pace with events'.

The English speaking congregation of the Apia Protestant Church included Ted Annandale, the executive head of O. F. Nelson, Ltd., one of the overseas trading firms similar to Burns Philp Ltd. and Morris Hedstrom Ltd. who had a good business reason for expressing confidence in the newly constituted Government. Olaf Nelson had married the daughter of a leading chief of Safune in Savai'i in 1871, and established himself as a trader. His knowledge of English , Samoan language and culture, enabled him to act as a mediator in local disputes. In the 1920's a bitter relationship developed between businessmen of mixed race, and a New Zealand Administrator who was insensitive to Samoan aspirations. This group thrust Nelson forward as a key member of the joint Samoan-European Independence movement, known as the Mau ,with a slogan 'Samoa for the Samoans'. In practice, the Mau seemed bent on bringing about 'Samoa without New Zealanders.'

When Nelson's successor,Ted Annandale, was asked during the first week of Independence 'What is the new state going to do for money?' he replied 'The same as they have always used, because they are not going to lose anything in the changeover'. He was referring to the huge accumulation of Samoan properties- mostly plantations, which New Zealand had received as reparations from the Germans after the 1914-19 War, and administered for 30 years as the N. Z. Reparations Estates. The organization's profits were returned to Samoa, and in 1957 the whole valuable set-up worth one million pounds was presented by New Zealand to the Samoan Government, and worked profitably as the Western Samoan Trust Estates Corporation.

Ted was also aware that the Bank of Western Samoa would guide the government. He commented that 'The Bank of N. Z. had a 55% interest, and would not allow wild financing'. Like America Samoa, more conspicuously in the grip of the Almighty Dollar, Independent Western Samoa had discovered that there were financial strings attached to their newfound freedom. However the business community was largely supportive of the newly independent state, and wanted it to be stable and successful.

Fast pace questioned

The rapid speed of change affecting both Western and Eastern groups of Samoan islands was evident in a new means of travel introduced during our stay in Apia. For the previous five years sea journeys had been endured, but now we were returning in comfort with Polynesian Air Lines, (P. A. L.) to Tafuna in Tutuila, where ongoing passengers connected with New Zealand's International Airline,Teal. Introduced in 1937, Pan American Clipper Flying boats had provided an aerial trade route from San Francisco to Sydney, calling at Pago Pago harbour, that is until the Second World War .

Recommencing the service in the 1950's, a regular Solent flying boat service known as Teal's Coral Route operated between N. Z. Fiji, W. Samoa and Tahiti, but it was discontinued after experiencing financial difficulties. In the 1960's several small airlines attempted to cash in on what seemed to be a lucrative opportunity, with varying degrees of success. On the flights to and from Tafuna Airport, I felt the rush of air into an open cockpit. I had a similar experience flying in a bone rattler airplane over the sugar plantations near Nandi, Fiji in 1958. Sitting next to the pilot in the nine seater Percival Proctor 5 aircraft, I was able to open a side window to take photos from the air. These appeared later as postcards and boxed note-lets sold in the Bookshop.

Very shortly afterwards all Proctor aircraft, (basically the same as the pre-1939 model), were withdrawn from service. Several aircraft had been lost because of the failure of glue joints in the tropical heat. Polynesian Airlines used Proctor 5's at first, then changed, as did their rival, Samoan Airlines, to wartime Douglas Dakota's (D. C. 3's). On one flight the pilot was able to land safely despite the fact that the passenger door had not been closed properly by attendants. This had broken loose hitting the tail-plane. The carelessness of ground staff was corrected, but the swirling currents of air created by the surrounding mountains, coupled with the prevailing winds from the sea, continued to make take-off and landing a shaky experience. U. S. pilots in World War 2 had encountered similar sudden updrafts resulting in many crash landings.

Bumping down on familiar territory in late March, I soon received news of unfinished business. A decision had been taken in February by the District Council, to press ahead with the subject of a possible separate constitution for the churches in American Samoa. Several months earlier I had prepared a three-page background paper giving reasons for bringing this issue before the whole Church. In the preamble a plea was made for representatives on both sides of the political divide to recognise the rapidly changed circum- stances of American Samoa. The District Constitution did not reach the floor of the General Assembly for debate. The reason given was that there was already too much business to deal with, especially the all-embracing Church Constitution for the seven Districts including the one in American Samoa. A resolution was passed to 'ta'atia le mataupu i le laulau.' (Leave on the table). 'Not so fast' was the message.

It was not only in Church circles that families felt that they had enough on their plate. Political leaders in American Samoa were also saying that the population at large could not cope with the turmoil going on around them. Many of the chiefs recognised that a genuine attempt was being made to put things right after years of neglect regarding the Island's social and economic infrastructure. Samoan land rights were being safeguarded, the Economy strengthened, Health Care improved, and the Public Highway put in better shape. Education was next in line, but they wanted a breathing space.

The pace of change was ringing alarm bells in the clubs and bars of Pago despite a recent affirmation of trust in Government Administration made by the local Legislative Council. Samoan chiefs had given their favourable response to a request from the United Nations Assembly meeting in New York. 'People of American Samoa value their American nationality, and do not wish to take any action that would weaken the relationship of the territory to the USA.' Nevertheless, after one year of intense building activity, critics were lining up against Governor Rex Lee, and he was obliged to take notice of those who said 'Watch your back!' His positive response was to make a radio broadcast before setting off for Washington in June 1962 for Budget hearings on the U.S. Fiscal Year beginning July 1st. 1962. He reaffirmed his intention to stay as Governor until he'd completed the task given to him.

163

Lee said on the local radio station W. V. U. V. broadcasting on June 18th 1962, that he was confident that approval would be given for additional road paving, a sea wall for the airport, a new power plant providing electrical power to every village, more modern elementary /secondary schools linked to an Educational T. V. system, and in addition he had been told that the Federal Aviation Agency, and the U.S. Weather Bureau, would be spending large sums in the territory. His confidence that finance for these large projects would be forthcoming proved to be justified, despite the blocking efforts of some members of the Samoan Legislature . Senators had travelled to the East Coast of the USA. to give an alternative message to Republican Party members of the Department of the Interior's Budget Committee.

Before flying to the USA, Lee did not endear himself to many who listened to a radio broadcast during which he spoke about the Islanders irresponsible use of Government money. Drunken, antisocial behaviour by some chiefs, and the spoiling of an attractive environment by villagers was deplored. The whole speech was made available in a written bulletin and distributed throughout the island. It referred to 'Garbage and sewage, unpainted, half finished stores and shanty type housing had been built disregarding planning and sanitary regulations. Course behaviour by a few chiefs would mean that tourists felt unwelcome,at a time when attracting tourists was essential to the creation of a sustainable economy'.

Governor Lee stirred up a hornet's nest as he concluded his message. 'All building permits have been suspended to within 400 feet of the paved road, and most of the Bay Area. To deserve the respect of future Samoans, we must plan carefully, and build well'. A direct criticism of 'anything will do' (so'ona fai) housing for the majority, was not well received. In fact several houses in a grand style had been erected in prime locations as a focus of tribal pride. Powerful status symbols, they had been constructed by members of the wider family (tribe). Lower in the hierarchy, the builders felt bound to accept a system in which heads of an extended family received praise on their behalf. Group pride in an impressive edifice, while most of them lived in ramshackle housing,was acceptable . But the times were a changing !

The road that raised clouds of dust with every passing bus was about to enter the 20th Century. Sadly a new tar-macadam road would take an increased toll of human life. One evening I received a disturbing message from John (Ioane), the Bookshop Manager, to say that his son Tomasi, (Thomas) had been knocked down by a bus on the road near his home at Iliili, and was in a serious condition. When I arrived it was obvious that the 5 year old lad was dead, for he had been placed outside their home, stretched out on pillows. On a hot humid night it would not be long before his body, anointed with turmeric and rubbed with oil, would begin to decompose as he lay there looking so calm and serene. Earlier in the week he had been chasing around in the Bookshop.

People of all ages numbed by the abrupt nature of the tragedy sat outside family homes around the village green known as a malae. They were trying to absorb the effect of the young lads's death. A constant refrain could be heard as adults spoke quietly with the grieving parents. 'Pule lava le Atua', (Everything is in Gods hands). Job's words after all his children had been stricken dead were also used. 'The Lord has given, and the Lord has taken away, Blessed be the name of the Lord'. (Job 1:21.) John and Mafuli's grief over Tomasi's death was palpable,yet they both seemed impassive. I recalled seeing them playing with the lively lad. Now their calm exterior told me that a protective community shield had been put around them. The murmured words of condolence merging into an acceptance of, 'that's the way it is' stayed with me.

I did not get beyond a formal expression of sympathy, 'Talofai.' (I'm so sorry.) which sounded so empty and meaningless. Giving them a ceremonial fine mat, and asking a blessing served to underline the inadequacy I experienced as an outsider in their midst. What I received from them was a strong sense of the dead Tomasi being present ; that the bereaved were visited by those who had passed on. Raymond Firth in his book on Polynesian ritual and belief recorded a conversation between a dying child and his mother, 'I shall go among the spirits and look down at you sleeping on my mat.' The passage from the book had given me as a glimpse into another world, but now I had come face to face with it.

One consequence was that the Communion of Saints element in Christian worship became more accessible. Thinking things through later that evening I retreated to a quiet spot on the lava rocks near our Fagalele home. The waves pounded against caverns created by volcanic lava flow meeting the ocean in prehistoric times. Plumes of water rose high into the air. A narrow overgrown path hugged the coastline before plunging down to a rugged promontory overlooking the spectacle.

Peering down through the corals of many colours, shoals of bright metallic blue fish sparkled like diamonds in rock pools. Contemplating the sea's changing mood was my way of sorting things out after receiving news, good or bad. Often I had mulled over decisions taken at meetings, which left me feeling depressed, perplexed and sometimes satisfied.

After Tomasi's death I sat and stared towards the reef in the middle distance trying to come to terms with fatalism, or predestination of 'whatever will be, will be'. 'Accept those things, which cannot be changed' seemed to be empty words. Surprisingly I found the words of Margaret Mead's book entitled 'Coming of age in Samoa' helpful. She wrote of her experience in Samoa in 1925 'that the facts of life and death are shorn of all mystery at an early age'. The lack of privacy within Samoan homes meant that death was a matter of fact experience of daily life. It is quite different for anyone brought up today in America or Britain where many people rarely see a dead person on public display. Assassination before our eyes shocks us.

The fast pace and danger of living in a global village was reinforced by the lighting speed in which the news of President Kennedy's assassination arrived in Samoa. News of the attempt was signalled during the afternoon of November 22nd 1963, early Friday evening local time, when most people had gone home for the weekend. As I prepared to meet Governor Rex Lee in his office on Monday morning November 25th 1963, the members of his staff had returned to work after two days coming to terms with the shattering event in Dallas. They were visibly distressed and talking together in small groups.

Rex Lee, was still in a state of deep shock, whilst those around him attempted to reconstruct the sequence of events surrounding the President's death. This was done by means of radio reports and information coming direct from the Department of the Interior Office in Washington. In a highly charged emotional atmosphere,many reacted to the President's sudden death with uncontrollable grief, utter disbelief and a desperate search for an explanation. 'Do something !' The air of resignation surrounding Tomasi's death had been so different. Instead a desperate attempt to save J. F .K .'s life went into overdrive, in which the very best hospital facilities and medical skill were pressed into service immediately.

Health concerns

As an active supporter of the U. S. Democratic Party, Rex Lee believed that adequate Health Care available for everyone at the point of need was a goal worth striving for. He made clear his admiration for the National Health Service in Britain, with its comprehensive organisation of financial and human resources on behalf of all its citizens. Plans for upgrading the hospital in Utulei, a village in the Bay Area, were translated into action in the first year of Lee's administration. It soon became apparent that the building of a new hospital, or Tropical Medical Centre, in nearby Faga'alu Valley, near the mouth of Pago Harbour, was a long-term aim.

In the 1950's our family had an insider's knowledge of the hospital, and the need for an efficient Community Health programme. In 1959,when Eileen was in hospital expecting the arrival of our firstborn, Susan, she saw rats at play among the dirty bed linen. We had also been shocked to discover an enormous worm in the toilet, after it had lived inside a family member's body for many months. Community Health relied heavily on a long established voluntary group known as the Women' s Committee, with branches in every village. They provided considerable financial and practical help to maintain good hygienic practice in the home, and at the workplace. An impressive 'special' building in the Bay Area belonging to the Women's Committee was called The House of Watchfulness. (O le Maota o Mata'aga).

Hookworm infestation was common, although there had been an improvement in safety measures since 1909 when Dr. Rossiter discovered that at least half the population of Tutuila harboured the worm, which breaks through the skin of the shoeless. Individuals walking barefoot were at risk, and the use of latrines was made obligatory by law. Five years before our arrival in Samoa, the campaign had been judged a failure. In 1950, 22 per cent of patients admitted into the Hospital were carriers of hookworm. Frequent attendance at feasts, meant that my body often succumbed to microbes in the 'pink peril' drink. It was made from packets of 'Kool-aid", coloured crystals mixed with water that had not been boiled.

On the Fagalele School compound the boys toilets were wooden cabins located over ' blow holes'. Waves pounding on the crumbly volcanic rock at the seashore had created underground caverns going inland. Water pressure had then blasted vertical shafts upwards through the porous rock. Unusually strong tides forced columns of water through the caverns, finally to shoot up into the air. Normally the rhythmic lapping of waves provided a satisfactory system of sanitary cleansing, but stormy conditions rocked the cabins,and drenched the backsides of those sitting inside.'Waterproof your bums' was the jocular instruction given by teachers when students complained.

Leone village was the first place outside the Bay Area to have a water treatment plant, making it possible to pump clean water through pipes to the Fagalele School compound. Gusty winds and heavy downpours often clogged up the system with polluting debris. At such times people living on the school compound depended on two large coral concrete tanks adjoining our house, serving as catchments for rain water. Most of that water had been in the tanks for a long time. To safeguard good health,every drop of water drunk in our home at Fagalele, piped or stored, was boiled first on a paraffin stove. Typing these words a question crossed my mind about the old water tanks, and whether they provided a breeding place for the filarial bearing mosquitoes. Did I adequately cover the gap where the rainwater ran down the corrugated iron roof to enter the tank? Too late now.

Mosquitoes were always a nuisance,and in addition threatened us with ill health. Sleeping away from home I knew that although they flew mainly in the hours of darkness, the shadows of noonday created opportunities for them to bite in broad daylight. The female mosquito transfers the filarial parasite of a sick person to another person, or animal, as it sucks their blood through punctured skin. From the 1906 records of the dispensary, I found out that 45 amputations to remove the scrotum had been carried out that year. This was the result of the parasite working through the body of its victims. Although the number of such operations had decreased, the elephant like appearance of the legs of many Samoan's legs in the early 1960's were a visual reminder of the task of eradication waiting to be done. We poured kerosene on pools and boggy places to prevent the mosquito larva and pupa from breathing air, but our best defence was keeping the area round the house clear of large leaves. The work of completely eradicating the mosquito from the island had to wait until the year 2000.

Yaws had been the most common forms of sickness,but in the late 1950's arsenic based drugs produced in American laboratories had effectively dealt with the crusted body sores on those affected, which left untreated, led to deformity in bones and joints. Conjunctivitis, often leading to blindness, was still a problem for Dr. Brennerman, previously a missionary in India, who became our good friend in June 1959. Mentioning health concerns to another Doctor named Bert Williams, we learned that Samoan medicine was far from dead. He told us that on one occasion he had to invoke the law to stop a bush doctor practicing exorcism on a patient, who was later cured of meningitis with a sulphur drug.

An improved Government Health Service with modern hospital facilities, depended on nurses making sure that the treatment prescribed by doctors was carried out. Before 1960, strong loyalty and concern for family members meant that the Fa'a Samoa way of caring for the sick existed alongside Stateside practice towards patients in hospital. Two or three relatives would accompany each patient, to take up temporary residence on a ward, where others were also receiving treatment. The relatives cooked and brought food to the sick room, and gave the proper pills at the right times as ordered by the doctor. The use of Samoan herbal prescriptions and treatments was discouraged in a hospital environment,but were in fact often included in a mixed diet of pills and potions.

Concern for the welfare of the whole person, appreciated by American and Samoan medical practitioners alike earlier in the century, had become too casual through the passage of time. Nursing Sisters such as Pepe Haleck, Fe'iloiga and Initia, who had received their early education at the Church Girls School at Atauloma struggled to draw on the best in Samoan hospitality, whilst maintaining professional standards. In 1961 a new code of nursing practice was introduced, and the wives of chiefs and talking chiefs (Faletua ma tausi),were critical of the proposed changes. These prevented the use of the Samoan Way (Fa'a Samoa) of nursing the sick during their stay in hospital. Governor Lee's administration in an attempt to model health provision on the same lines as the State of California came up against formidable opposition. Both sides in a disruptive dispute soon recognised that the goodwill of village Women's Committees, with their delegated powers ensured sensible health practice where people lived and worked, had to be accommodated. Compromise won the day.

Village Women's Committees were mainly concerned with hospitality,child

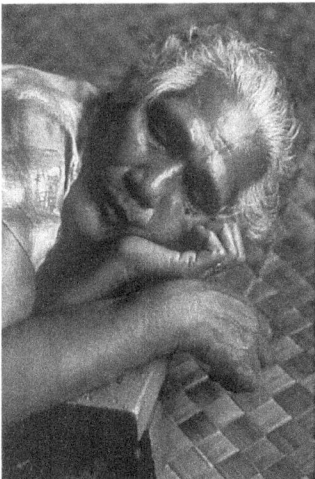

care, village cleanliness and hygiene. No male would interfere in what were regarded as women's exclusive spheres. These included making tapa, weaving mats, cleaning the house and doing the washing. 'Faletua', the word used for a chiefs wife, literally meant the back of the house. 'Tausi'(care) described the hospitable, dutiful concerns of orator's wives. These married women,Faletua ma Tausi, provided the top echelon in Women's Assemblies. The' aualuma', or unmarried / unattached women were included in the organisation as a kind of junior section providing additional clout in any power struggle. Wearing a matronly uniform, the colours of which differentiated them from representatives of their organisation in other villages, Committee members had an unmistakable air of authority, awake or asleep.

In addition to health concerns which were their exclusive domain, women had an opportunity, along with the untitled young men, to express views on rules and regulations considered by an all male Village Council. Women made their opinions known through the wife of the High Chief. As the senior woman she was expected to find a way, through her husband, of bringing women's concerns to the fore. In a blend of feminine wisdom, and insights gained from a Christian education at Atauloma School, many Samoan women proved to be anything but docile onlookers when village and district business was being discussed.

The withdrawal of women's approval in naming a new chief could be decisive. Vaoita, was the wife of Alesana, a renowned orator recently returned from missionary service in Papua in 1923, who later became an outstanding leader in Malua Theological College, and Church Assemblies. Vaoita persuaded her husband Alesana to relinquish a recently acquired senior title of Fai'ivae in Leone. Women's influence increased during the intervening years, so much so, that in the 1960's I heard chiefs complaining about women who were getting above themselves,and would soon cause an imbalance in Samoan society.

Achieving equilibrium applied to other areas of Samoan life. The overall authority of the High Chief in settling community policy was counterbalanced by the Chief Orator's attention to detail. A particular person's weighty voice in discussion could be corrected by an alliance of chiefs lower in the hierarchy. They would speak with a combined voice sitting next to their assigned posts facing superior titled chiefs in the oval Meeting House.

Upper crust members of Samoan society also recognised the need to balance rival claims to regal power made by children of male and female lines of descent. Two interconnecting royal family lines known as Samalietoa and Satupua, co-existed with the orator groups,Tumua and Pule. They provided a strong framework for opposing factions to jostle for increased influence, without the struggle getting out of hand. Strain or imbalance between these groups was contained by this aristocratic Upper House of Watchfulness' The authors description.(Maota Maualuga o Mata'ala).

South Pacific Forum

In 1955 I was told that it was sensible to get the faletua (wife) 'on side',when advocating an innovative course of action. The strongest influence was not always the person 'up front'. When the South Pacific Commission brought together representatives from territories across the region in July 1962, one of the subjects chosen for debate was 'The changing role of women'. Meeting every three years, beginning in Fiji in 1953, the Commission had been set up by former colonial powers France,the U. K., and the USA, with its Head-quarters in Noumea, capital of New Caledonia. Intended to be a mutual support system for countries facing similar problems and opportunities, it was to be more than a 'Talking Shop'.

Attending a Commission Assembly in 1962 I remember hearing Mr F. Bagotu from the Solomon Islands quoting a Maori proverb, which commended a woman's unobtrusiveness. 'If a hen crows ring its neck'. When the Masiofo (Leading Lady) Fetaui Mata'afa, wife of Western Samoa's Prime Minister, was elected Chairman of the Social (Tausi) Committee, many thought that the appointment recognised the Samoan nation's enlightened position on women's rights. Actually it was a token gesture. The real reason had to do with her husband's being the Prime Minister, that Fetaui was a bearer of an important title in her own right, and that male Chiefs didn't concern themselves with 'Social Concerns'. Fetaui Mata'afa had received a college education in New Zealand

Participants at the Conference revealed that most of them had received their education in Christian schools and colleges founded by British missionaries. Delegates welcomed the ideal of men and women being one another's helpmate, and this included fathers accepting responsibility for the rearing of children. (As a young father in 1962 looking after two daughters on regular trips to work at the Bookshop, I was never questioned, or ridiculed). A list of what representatives considered were feminine qualities, confirmed that listening, providing support, and caring came out on top. In other words women attending the Conference chose to side step an issue that challenged the cultural norm.

Given the opportunity to suggest an alternative model, an educated feminine elite could not find it within themselves to question the view that large areas of Island life were reserved for 'Men Only'. Significantly the politically powerful portfolios of Trade, Finance, Education, Fisheries/Agriculture within the Commission, were all occupied by men. Social issues were important,and women were expected get on and do the work.. The appointment of a Woman Chairman, of the Social Committee actually reflected their acceptance of the status quo.

Islanders Voice Ignored

Under the watchful eye of ex colonial powers,who were supreme exponents of the mantra 'Proceed with caution', the South Pacific Commission went about its important, but non-controversial business. The political 'hot potato' of a Fisheries policy to curtail tuna fishing with drag lines, did not see the light of day in discussion papers. There was no chance that vested interests in the fish canning industry would be disturbed by questioning.

Similarly the 'guiding' ex colonial powers ensured that the sensibilities of Britain, France and the USA were not bothered by political controversy surrounding 'controlled' Nuclear Bomb tests in the Pacific. French tests in Tahiti, the British test on Christmas Island, and the 23 atmospheric USA tests from 1946- 1954,on Bikini and Eniwetok in the Marshall Islands went ahead as planned. Such major concerns did not feature on the Commission's agenda. The Bravo test in February 1954, which vaporised 3 islands,and spread radioactive debris over 50,000 square miles was ignored. Threatening to escalate out of control, the scientists present could only watch in horror as a massive chain reaction took place.

A light brighter than a thousand suns, two seconds long, was seen on November 8th 1957 by people living in Samoa. British and American scientists had detonated a nuclear device above the remote Pacific atoll known as Christmas Island. Living many hundreds of miles from 'Operation Grapple', onlookers in American Samoa were startled by the intensity of light blazing beyond Amanave, a small village across Fagalele Bay in front of our home. Those who were much nearer to the explosion spoke of the tremendous heat of the fireball, of actually seeing the shock waves, and watching the mushroom cloud forming at 80,000 feet.

The fall-out affected not only the armed services personnel, but also Gilbert Islanders and their livestock. Fishermen, going about their business in the vicinity, were also enveloped in an eerie green-grey cloud. Seven hundred miles away in Hawai'i electrical equipment stopped working, street lighting and house power cut out. Scientists concluded that if a similar nuclear bomb exploded over the centre of the USA, it would knock out electrical power for the whole country, and Canada. Aircraft would be unable to take off, or remain airborne over U.S. airspace.

Prevailing trade winds blowing across the Pacific Ocean from the N. E, and. an annual rainfall of 263 inches could be expected to cause risks to health from nuclear fall out. Local government officials questioned about health checks were unhelpful. The former colonial powers, Britain, France and the USA had poisoned fish stocks that had entered the food chain to cause cancerous growths, disfigurement and deformity among the island people. Sadly it was difficult to stir up interest among Samoan politicians, for what seemed at the time to be a remote concern. Ten years passed before the Government of Western Samoa, at the South Pacific Forum meeting in Apia in 1973, was authorized to make an appeal to France. Samoans asked the French to heed the call of the United Nations to refrain from nuclear testing in the atmosphere of the South Pacific. They were ignored .

The Missile Crisis of 1962 brought the subject of M. A. D. (Mutually Assured Destruction) even closer to home. Unlike American Samoa, Cuba did not want to be included in President Kennedy's plan, announced in 1961,to raise living standards among people living close to the USA. After the exiled Cuban's failed attempt to invade Cuba during the Bay of Pigs fiasco, the Soviet Union was worried that the United States would make another attempt to oust the Communist leader,President Castro, from power. To prevent this the Kremlin ordered the building of missile sites on Cuba, from which rockets capable of carrying nuclear warheads would threaten the U.S. Mainland, only 90 miles away. So began a worldwide walk with extinction, which began on October 19 1962. President Khrushchev on the 24th October ordered the ships carrying missile transporters, back to Russia.

To keep abreast of world wide events a radio aerial stretched from our living room to the top of a nearby coconut tree to bring us good news as well as bad. In late 1960 we listened to broadcasts direct from B. B. C. in London, followed by British newspaper comment. Although reception was patchy in the evening, Radio New Zealand was loud and clear in the mornings in broadcasting Children's Programmes. At 10.30am we would break off from what we were doing,and take part in action songs with daughter Susan, led by 'Mary and Elsa', the names of the co-presenters. 'Down by the station early in morning, See the little engines all in a row'. Watch the engine driver pull the little lever toot toot, puff puff, off we go.' Two years later Susan began a Correspondence Course with the N. Z. School of the Air.

The correspondence columns of the First Edition of the Samoa News, with Fofo Sunia as its Editor provided an opportunity to raise a controversial issue. I wanted the first independent newspaper published in American Samoa to flourish, and during its first few weeks of life, the Bookshop acted as its agency. Doing my bit by writing an article 'People not Profits' I asked a question about the material benefits accruing to the business community as a result of the U. S. Governments vast economic programme. 'Is an interest in profits for the business community, balanced by a genuine concern for the well-being of the island's people?'(Provision of Sports facilities etc.)The local Chamber of Commerce denied that excessive profits were being made. Their Secretary sent a Letter to the Editor on May 6 1963, which at the same time cut me down to size. A sharp criticism suggested that the Bookshop was making exorbitant profits. I learned quickly that free speech would promise a rough ride.

Attempting to open up discussion on public affairs, newspaper editors like Fofo faced problems of inadequate finance, lack of trained editorial and technical staff, inadequate distribution facilities, and limited interests among the wider public. There was little incentive for business to spend money on feeding the mind rather than the body. The first aim of any newspaper was survival, and in developing countries coming to terms with a wider world, this led inevitably to journalism on the cheap. It was relatively easy to follow the example of the tabloid press in the U. K., with its diet of half-truths, sensationalism and gossip. Samoan editors had an additional hazard to face.

The boundaries of discourse using the democratic process were tested in articles appearing in the Samoan News of April and May 1963. Serious charges of drunkenness and lewd behaviour were made against other Chiefs in the Senate by fellow members of that august body. Eventually Fofo, and the Editor of the Western Samoan newspaper 'Samoana', R. Rankin, established ground rules for free expression. Leaders were to be accountable for derogatory remarks made in print about rival chiefs, and there was a beginning of an understanding of everyone having the right of reply. Access to the facts about proposed legislation,and ensuring that members of the public were able to express an opinion about them was more difficult.

The Editor of the newspaper, Samoana, went on record as saying that Samoa still had a long way to go on the matter of accountability. He cited the Prime Minister, Fiame Mata'afa who claimed that the press in its criticism of authority was alien to Samoan custom, and should perhaps be closed down. That nothing like this happened revealed that the Government did not want to go down the same road as some emerging African states in the way that they clamped down on press freedom. However when an educated Member of Parliament, Afoafouvale Misimoa, was asked what he thought was the view of fellow politicians, and their supporters, about the possibility of threatened restrictions on reporters, he replied, 'Most of them couldn't care less one way or the other'.

There were other threats to press freedom. According to Rankin, the editor a representative of a big local firm,was guilty of exerting improper pressure on the press. The businessman who had close family connections with the new hierarchy of government, complained that,'The paper should help the progress of independence by not criticizing.' 'Should the truth be hidden?' he was asked. 'It's not a matter of hiding the truth. Just tell it at the right time', was the reply. Taking a risk the editor printed the substance of a critical report on collusion between Government and Commercial interests. Overnight the 'Samoana' lost $1,500 of badly needed advertising revenue. A newspaper editor was obliged to follow the new Government's watchword, 'Proceed with caution'.

Who do you believe?

The question raised by newspaper censorship had a wider application. Explanations given for customs,traditions, and shared beliefs are often contradictory and prompted the question 'Who do you believe?' In conversation with George Milner in late 1956, he said that care was needed in making generalisations about Samoan culture. Responsible to two Governments, and the Oxford University Press for compiling a new Samoan Dictionary Milner found that at first the social organisation appeared to follow a regular pattern. Later it turned out to be a more fluid reality. Ancient rituals had a common basis, but there were many local variations. 'Ua tofu le nu'u ma le agan'u.'

George expected to find several differences of pronunciation. However, the meaning of proverbs,which at first appeared straightforward, turned out to be capable of several interpretations. It was disconcerting to discover that regular patterns in the structure of the Samoan language, masked a complex range of permutations. George found that this variety was usually due to family groups insisting that they had possession of the secret key to unlock unusual conjugations,which had been revealed, and entrusted to them alone. Finding ways to identify the best available authority to get an understanding of the construction of a Samoan orator's speech proved to be extremely time consuming. Going round in circles they seemed to create ambiguity. Individuals or family groups in a position to share what they knew, would not do so because they feared that their interpretation would be disputed by others. Influential leaders were not prepared to face the possibility of ridicule.

A dictionary compiled nearly a century earlier by George Pratt, an L. M. S. Missionary, captured the nuances of meaning, present at that time, in the words used by natural orators, who used words to mean more than what was being said.. In attempting to pinpoint a word's present meaning, some cases showed that over the passage of time a more precise meaning had emerged, that had lost a former elasticity. Tiresome it may be to mention the word Feagaiga again, but in Old Samoa the word had to do with shifting relation-ships enabling the elite class to enter new marriages without threatening public social order. In the 20th Century, the older interpretation has given way to one, which means a legal contract with no loopholes. The emphasis on relationships has been superceded, yet both meanings are still available for use. Compilers of dictionaries can be compared to fishermen at work on shifting sands.

Holding together different linguistic interpretations of 'agreement' for exam-ple, or accepting various explanations for particular Samoan customs and traditions, may suggest a way of answering the question 'Who do we believe about everyday concerns such as an individual's well-being, and the health of a community. Should traditional methods of healing be combined with modern medicine, or should they be kept separate ?

Traditional medicine

'Soifua maloloina', in the Samoan language describes an individual's 'well being',whereas maopoopo refers to community's healthy state. Separate conditions, they merged and affected each other, with both words indicating a stable situation where disturbance was minimal. 'Storms and calm are neighbours', (tuaoi afa ma maninoa), is a proverb that gives another clue for appreciating that good health is about getting the balance right. A residual condition of unease is waiting for the chance to upset an individual's equilibrium and contentment, or to spoil the health of a community.

Limitations on individual freedom enforced by the Village Council attempted to contain a sickness brought about by disagreements. Always a major concern in close knit Samoan communities, the managing of disruptive stress between individuals and groups looked for compliance to an imposed discipline. Disturbance in the village 'Ua f'aavevesi le nu'u' was one form of 'ma'i' or 'gasegase' Samoa (Samoan Sickness), that couldn't be cured by a pill prescribed at the Dispensary.

Responsibility for dealing with the effects of a dispute in a community usually fell on the chiefs and the Faifeau (Pastor). A family head would try to restrain hotheads,and identify malcontents within his group. As a last resort a chief, or chiefs in Council prescribed a penalty. The main emphasis of the pastor's role was that of prevention, which he exercised through regular teaching and preaching on peace, forgiveness and reconciliation. When relationships finally broke down, pastors acted as mediators. It might happen that one family group involved in an argument about land rights had gained an unfair advantage over another. Hopefully the Faifeau could lead all concerned towards an act of reconciliation, (fa'aleleiga) to mark the end of what was considered to be a social illness.

Another cause of sickness was demon possession. Most Samoans believed in a Christian God as the supreme being, but this did not prevent many from believing in supernatural agencies (aitu), who were unpredictable in their activities. Whereas an Englishman would touch wood and whistle as a safeguard, many Samoans were not so lighthearted when holding on to such beliefs. More recent folk memories of a world of capricious spirits prompted many to believe that a possible explanation for a disease was an aitu who had taken offence at something said or done to villagers under his, or her control. If infection spread to others in the victims family it was because the power of the aitu had increased.

An out of the ordinary kind of event such as a suicide or fatality sometimes triggered 'sightings', (or what others called coincidences), which indicated that a troubled spirit was roaming. 'Sightings' led to unusual behaviour, or fever in those affected. When treatment based on modern methods failed to provide a cure, a healer (taulaaitu),could be called in. The Samoan word meant 'an anchor secured to the disturbed spirit' which prevented the person-moving on. Broken conventions were often at the bottom of sickness because a person at odds with himself and fellow villagers couldn't function as a healthy person. Modern medicine's insights into mental illness overlap the work done by these indigenous healers.

Earlier in this chapter it was said that Women's Committees (Komiti Tumama) remained effective channels for the extension of modern medical practice, and public health initiatives. Many of the women who played an important role in this work, were well known traditional healers. Their enthusiasm and commitment to Government health programmes did not stop them from using traditional methods, whenever they seemed appropriate. Known as a fofo, or 'taulasea', their 'hands on' healing methods contrasted with those who dealt with aitu. Instead they recognised and treated aches and pains with herbal remedies, or common drugs from the Government pharmacy. After attending short intensive Government sponsored courses, some had limited access to equipment and medicine. The two systems,traditional and modern co-existed.

Massage for muscular discomfort was a powerful weapon in the armoury of traditional healers. Kneading in a way similar to a baker working dough, delivering short sharp blows with the edge of palms,or teasing out soreness with gentle finger tips, the massager was worth her weight in gold to the arthritic. Poultices for ulcers, and vapours for the relief of respiratory problems, were made from a variety of creeper plants. Some indigenous plants released anti inflammatory compounds, and the anti-HIV substance Prostratin was also isolated. A herbal medicine presently used to treat hepatitis has been used in the treatment of Aids. The compound is an extract from the bark of a mamala tree.

Accepting that there is much to be commended and admired in traditional medicine, there is a calculated risk to be made in accepting the coexistence of modern and traditional ways of healing. Who do you believe? Part of the answer could be that without careful supervision the mixture is toxic. Evidence is available to show that superstition and fear wrecks communities where traditional methods are used exclusively. On the other hand the easy availability of various pills in bottles , and an emphasis on administrative tidiness can also create dysfunctional health care. A cautious, mixed approach towards health and healing was the one, which many Samoan health workers adopted. An interactive process, which accepted the attraction of opposite methods informed their everyday response to illness. Appearing to be a smooth accommodation, hidden rocks could nevertheless trip up the unwary.

Hidden rocks

Our neighbour named Fega,-the fisherman who threatened me with a shotgun,- had sporadically shown his displeasure towards the Fagalele School authorities living next to his property. Since our arrival 7 years earlier we had rubbed along well enough with occasional spats. His horses ate the grass, cantered occasionally between the coconut trees to shake off the flies, thereby encouraging dogs on the school compound to bark and howl. I thought that things had settled down. Fega must have got wind of news that 'my boss' Stuart Craig, L. M. S. Secretary, S. Pacific was on the way to stay at Fagalele, because he had carefully prepared a rough passage for the car carrying our guest along the track leading to the Church land. He had hidden rocks covered by coconut fronds along the final stretch before reaching the blow holes, making sure that our visitor had a bumpy ride.

Our neighbour probably intended to give him a simple message that I was unpopular, but he was also making a point about the land on which our home was built. The forbears of other local chiefs had given the land for a Church School, but because the Mission House was now the home of someone other than a Headmaster of Fagalele School, our neighbour believed that the original land agreement was no longer binding. Fega, through the means of access to the Mission House, was raising questions about land ownership, an issue thought to have been settled in 1924. In 1963 the Government had taken out a 2 year lease on the Fagalele School buildings, while Atauloma had been improved at government expense to be used as residential quarters for several stateside teachers. I know them as friends.

Six years earlier I had received a request from the National Council of Churches in the USA and had agreed to serve as part-time minister for 75 or more American families in Pago Pago. One result was that we got to know families such as the Niederholzts, Rothchilds and the Stoltz's., all of whom made us very welcome in their homes. (The young lad Eric Stoltz became a Hollywood film idol.) Accepting an invitation to be their minister, it was hoped that increased numbers, and improved finances, would lead to the appointment of a full-time American pastor working together with the Samoan Church. 'If invited' was an important proviso in Stuart Craig's thinking. He had taught in a Chinese University during the years before the Revolution,when colonialism was a dirty word.

Colonial trap

Stuart Craig was concerned about a colonial attitude among some American Church leaders, and wanted to ensure that the autonomy and maturity of the Congregational Christian Church in Samoa was respected. Genuine partnership

would be welcome, but any suggestion of a 'take-over' by any American religious denomination or group of churches would be resisted. Craig wrote to the United Board of World Ministries at Riverside Drive, New York 27, dated 21 02 1962 declaring that 'The Church in Samoa had long been in charge of its own affairs, and had indicated its autonomy by taking a distinctive name.'

Dr. Carroll L. Shuster, the Moderator of the United Presbyterian Churches in California had 'colonial' aspirations . He had taken a personal interest in the Americans in Samoa, and had been pressing the United Presbyterian Commission, and the National Council of Churches at their respective Headquarters in New York, to support him in a major effort to build a new church for the American congregation in Pago Pago, and to supply the congregation with a full-time minister from the mainland. This was one of several initiatives made by various denominational leaders in the State of California to move into American Samoa. As a Brit living in an American territory, the jibe of being a colonialist was often made. I rebutted this accusation by saying that colonialism meant the transfer of a dominant population to a new territory, where the new arrivals maintained political allegiance to their country of origin. I believed that 'I was a sojourner in a strange land', and had to respect its ways.

Both of the nation-wide United Church organisations in the USA stood firm in their insistence that church expansion from California should not be attempted without giving serious consideration to the relationship between the English-speaking congregation, and the churches of Samoa. Paul Gregory in New York writing to Stuart in London wrote, 'I am certainly grateful to you for insisting to Hugh Neems that the filling of this particular post may require more time than any of us would regard as ideal'. Developing a sensitive partnership between different churches working in widely dispersed locales, Samoa, U.S. and the U. K. took time and effort. Nearly 10 years after my arrival a common view emerged in 1964, that the time had come at last for an American to be appointed to American Samoa.

Consistent with what had been said to the Churches in the U. S A., that they should respect and work with the Church in the host territory of Samoa, Samoan congregations in the USA, were encouraged to do the same in the host country. After several years of stop-go attempts to forge links between

Samoan congregations and the long established Congregational Church in California, Craig conceded in correspondence that 'we have failed to carry this point'. He added that 'the most recent word from the Church in Samoa on this matter, was to reiterate its intention to combine the congregations in the USA into District Eight of the Samoan Church, located in the South Pacific. Some of the attractions of this are not difficult to imagine.' This was Stuart's diplomatic way of saying that the Church Treasurer in Apia would be rubbing his hands anticipating a financial windfall of American dollars.. The Samoan Church had decided to adopt the way of colonialism.

A strong criticism of the move to create District Eight of the Samoan Church (Mother Church) in the USA came from other groups of American Samoans also residing in California An alternative suggestion was made to the Californian Conference through the Senior Minister (Toeaina) Luavasa, of Fagaitua, a village 9 miles from Pago in Tutuila. The 69 year old Luavasa had been a helpful colleague, when he stood beside me quietly guiding when I was struggling in the late 1950's to conduct Holy Communion in the Samoan language at District Assemblies,with 300 people present. (p92)

Elder Luavasa now explored the possibility of the congregations in Tutuila and Manu'a, (one of seven Districts of the Congregational Church back in their Samoan homeland), becoming an integral part of the United Congregational Church Conference in Northern California. Samoan churches in California would be included in this proposal. Nothing came of the suggestion because the alternative view had won the day. District 8 (California) was to be an integral part of the Church based in the Pacific Islands..

In May 1963 a group of American Samoan colonists, living in California, but owing allegiance to Mother Church in Samoa, were representatives at the Assembly meeting in Western Samoa, having turned their backs on the Congregational Conference in California. At the same time historic American churches in California were involved in long drawn out discussions leading to the appointment of a minister to the same Mother Church in Samoa. The American missionary replacement was to serve that organisation plus the American colonists settled in Samoa. The skies over the Pacific were crowded with all of the coming and going! Was it necessary for Samoans, now living in California, to hold on so tightly to mother back in Samoa, and return to her annually for sustenance?

A similar question was asked of the American churchgoers living in American Samoa, who were hanging on to their mother's apron strings back in the USA.

181

Replying to such a questions Dr. Donald Rothchild, the Director of Education in Pago Pago gave the National Council of Churches in Riverside, New York, a description of 'Our little congregation away from home', when replying to a question about the need for an English speaking padre or minister.

'First of all, we are a mixed denominational group rather evenly divided as far as church preference is concerned. Second, most of us are on temporary assignments from the States, and the average tenure runs just a little over two years. Third, we are a well-educated group where a person without a college degree is the exception. Fourth, we are a somewhat adventurous lot. That's why we are here, and therefore it should be pointed out that some of our mores must be overlooked. We work hard when we work, and play in our free time.' The Colonial Trap had already done its work among Samoans living in the USA. Now it claimed more victims among the Americans working in Samoa. At the time I was walking into a well laid elephant trap.

As the Samoan Church Assembly of 1964 drew nearer the representatives knew that the explosive issue of District Constitution had been 'left on the table' for another year. Stuart Craig had written advising me not to disturb matters as negotiations were going ahead regarding the appointment of an American minister. The usual hassle of getting the Bookshop's accounts prepared for the Church Auditor stationed in Western Samoa, meant that stocktaking had to be done. Although strictly speaking Ioane was the Manager, as a long standing member of the Assembly's Finance Committee, I was held responsible for presenting the Bookshop Report.

Eileen did the hard graft of checking the accounts with Ioane, who was his usual conscientious self. This meant that when the Finance Committee received 'with gratitude' the Statement of Accounts, and the accompanying progress report they were received, Tapeni Ioelu (p157) was preparing to step into the shoes of the outgoing Chairman of the Assembly. At the same time Vavae Toma the General Secretary was leaving to take up a new appointment as Secretary of the Pacific Council of Churches in Suva, Fiji. He was to be replaced by Etene Sa'aga who vehemently opposed Interdependence between American and Independent Western Samoa. All change at the top table spelt trouble for me.

Leadership

It was said of a long lived turtle that regularly appeared on the village shoreline near our home (Vaitogi), that it made progress by sticking its neck out. In order to eat, the turtle had to leave the safety of the shell, but in doing so it was vulnerable to passing predators. The Samoans who were willing to leave the comfort zone of a familiar culture in order to explore a European education, became their country's leaders. After being actively involved between 1843 and 1855 in the translation of the Bible, a small number of Samoan pastor's families came to appreciate the value of a wider education. Over successive generations these households produced many leading politicians, establishment figures, schoolteachers, civil servants as well as pastors.

Many provided the ballast for steadying the Samoan ship of State as it sailed through troubled waters. They were outstanding in the work of government and church as they attempted to preserve their language, customs and traditions. Other contributed to the work of government and church through their adaptability and willingness to explore ideas and schemes associated with the Colonial Powers, Germany,Britain and America. The homes of Pastors became renowned for competence in financial matters and negotiating skills. Consequently they produced some of Samoa's most effective and best-informed political and church leaders as both of these institutions moved steadily towards Independence.

Often the men appointed to be Village Pastors were bastions of conservatism. They occupied a position of dignity and influence similar to that enjoyed by the country parson in 1870's England, described in 'Kilvert's Diary'. English parsons were dependent on the local gentry, as indeed Samoan pastors were on their village chiefs. Secure in their social position, and prone to complacency, the influence of pastors was generally to buttress the existing order. Openness to new ideas was also found in such an environment, and there were conspicuous examples of men and women from these backgrounds who became prime movers for change. Both progressive and conservative attitudes were present among the educated elite, (sometimes through individuals in the same family). Intermarriage with families bearing the highest hereditary titles in Samoan Society extended the caste system.

In the Samoan social and political arena the balance of tribal influence was always tipping one way, and then the other as new alliances were created through marriage, death, changing political fortunes, new titles and consequent realignments. These brought about a range of choice when electing someone to an influential position. Sensitivity had to be exercised on account of tribal rivalries. Representatives of rival administrative and political groups held Senior Offices of Church and State in rotation which proved to be a useful way of preserving long term harmony. The rotation of the office of

Chairman of the Church was a carefully designed vehicle for recognising the influence of various factions within Church and Society. Satisfaction, or dissatisfaction with moderate or conservative policies came to be identified with particular individuals.

Elder Pastors Tupe and Alesana were still formidable figures in the Councils of the Church when I arrived in Samoa in 1955, and although both of them looked and sounded to be in their sunset years, people listened to them with care and attention. 'Ua tu'u la le va'a tele' (The large boat has furled its sails) applied to them as they took soundings, then pronounced, bringing discussion to an end. There was no point in others speaking afterwards. Sitting next to Pastor Tupe when he defied the Assembly over the 75-year rule on retirement, he was clearly 'a big boat'. Sadly he had allowed himself to become isolated as he defended what had become a sectional interest. Leaving the matter unresolved until a consensus was reached would have been a better option but he was not to know that. He was pressurized to withdraw from the Chair with a consequent loss of face, but traditional support for him did not disappear altogether.

Elder Pastor Poasa was another Chairman who appealed to the status quo, believing that introducing complexity into decision making would create instability. Poasa thereby alienated those who wanted to see moderate changes in line with the movement towards independence in both Church and State. By contrast Alesana, another large boat, seemed to strike a balance between competing interests, often disarming his critics by unusual imaginative ploys. I was amused and instructed at the end of a meeting when Alesana, who had been in the Chair, turned to Amerperosa, an Elder Minister who had been querulous throughout the discussion, and asked him to close the meeting in prayer. Consensus was restored, as if by magic.

Tapeni Ioelu, Chairman at regular intervals throughout the 1960's, was for several years the minister of the Samoan congregation in Apia. He imbibed the tense atmosphere of pre-1947 years when there was justifiable doubt and suspicion about the intentions of some New Zealand Government Officials regarding Political Independence. Ioelu later gave up this prestigious 'town' appointment, and that of Elder Minister, and moved to Malua as the Manager of the L. M. S Printing Press. He strengthened its reputation for keeping alive traditional values through the distribution of the Samoan Bible, plus the publication of the bible based commentaries and set books used for a many generations in Pastors Schools. The Press was a centre of power in church and society.

Printing the Sulu magazine (Torch) with a large circulation reporting news of people and events dear to the hearts of traditionalists and progressives alike, Ioelu appeared to be willing to move with the times. Financially competent, like other outstanding leaders, his detached manner and bearing commended him to the conventional, whilst his occasional bluntness gave rise to a hope for change in those of a questioning disposition. His clear thinking and awareness of the serious challenge facing the Church suggested a reformer, but crucially he had the solid support of traditional Samoa previously invested in men like Tupe. Ioelu's polite and gentle exterior was compared to a velvet glove covering an iron fist.

Fiti Sunia was a 29 year old student at Malua Theological College when he married Savali the 19 year old daughter of Alesana and Vaoita, teachers at the college. ' E le o se tagata e tele na'ua ni fa'a matalaga, ae sa agamalu ma le tausa'afia. He was not talkative, but he had a quiet and unassuming manner' she recalled in her memoirs. Fiti was the Treasurer of the District, for approximately 15 years. I used to call on him before 7am after catching the early morning bus from Leone to find him poring over the accounts. With Savali his wife he would have been awake before daybreak for the Watcher's Prayer Meeting. Both were devoted to a daily discipline of prayer, which they maintained set them free for a full and worthwhile life.

At the centre of the heated controversy surrounding the proposed separate Constitution for the churches in American Samoa, his disposition led him to proceed with caution, and wait on the gradual unfolding of events. 'E tapena malie ma mae'a mea uma e ala i fonotaga ma malieliega fa'atasi'. Essentially conservative in attitude towards Samoan culture, and its relationship to Christian belief and practice, he was nevertheless open to new ideas. He was a liberating partner for his wife Savali, who travelled world-wide, developing and sharing her gifts and concerns for work among young people..

A 'younger' generation of leaders in the emerging Western Samoan Government after 1947, men such as Luamanuvae and Fiame Mataafa, had their counterparts in the Church leadership in Mila Sapolu, Vavae Toma and Etene Sa'aga, a capable and conscientious government officer, who became the Church Secretary. 'Younger' was not a reference to physical age, but to people who were most in touch with the modern world, who at the same time retained a deep knowledge of Samoan tradition and custom. Mila Sapolu, who was a Chairman in the 1960's, attempted to reconcile the conflicting claims of an ancient culture with an independent nation moving into the modern world. Vavae Toma understood the Samoan Way of negotiation, and how to get things done, whilst remaining objective about the social system.

Vavae had no need to pack up everything when he moved to Suva, Fiji to be the General Secretary of Pacific Churches, whereas L. M. S. rules and regulations required missionaries to store away all their belongings in their Samoan home on the assumption that they might not be coming back. More than ten years may have seemed quite a long time to us, but to our Samoan colleagues we were 'birds of passage'. They knew that our contribution was ephemeral. Eileen became an expert packer after doing it on three separate occasions. When the bulk of our personal effects had been put away in boxes and cartons in 1961, '64 and '68, we left for the airport, our home left bare awaiting further occupancy, by us or possible successors. We were aware of being dispensable despite gracious departure speeches and the processional farewell, during which we were draped with floral necklaces ('ula).

Togafiti (Trickery)

While I was in London I received a letter from Ioane, informing me that Chairman Tapeui Ioelu had been in Pago soon after I had left. He had sought Ioane's agreement as Manager to remove me from the Bookshop. I took the precaution of showing the letter to Stuart Craig in London. Ioane reported that Ioelu thought of Neems as a disturbing influence in the life of the Church. (Ua fa'avevesi le Ekalesia).

Dr Alford Carleton, General Secretary of the Congregational Church in the USA (United Board) was in London, and I was invited to meet with him and Stuart Craig to discuss the issues raised by the American congregation in Pago. There was mounting concern among leaders of the mainstream churches working for Church Unity, (National Council Office in Riverside, New York), about the activity of some congregations in California wanting to establish 'American Christians Abroad' on a firmer footing, including the provision of a church building, without first consulting with the indigenous Samoan Church.

Dr. Kenneth Jones, who had worked with an Evangelical Medical Mission in India before being employed in the American Samoan Hospital, was now associated with a Presbyterian congregation in California, and was keen on such a development. Dr. Carleton wanted clarification on the relationship between the American congregation and the Samoan churches. Was it feasible for an American pastor to serve local churches in Christian Education and youth work, and to give attention to Americans living abroad? It was agreed that he would recommend to the Board that a candidate be sought.

In view of the contents of Ioane's letter I expected trouble on our return to Samoa, and this was quickly confirmed by the news that my friend and colleague, Fiti Sunia, had been removed from the office of District Treasurer after the visit of the Church Auditor from Apia. However, in less than a year Fiti had been elected and installed in a prestigious position as a Toeaina, (Senior Minister), by the Bay Area ministers and deacons. (Fagaloa ma Itu'au.) The compensatory mechanism, that is to say the need to balance competing interest groups, was still alive and well in Samoan society. It did not apply to overseas nationals.

During early April I was asked to meet with the Attorney General in Pago (p.vii) to discuss a written request made by the new treasurer, Tulafono, who had replaced Fiti as District Treasurer. Tulafono had requested permission from the Government for the Church to build a large permanent Office next to the Pago Hospital, because its present location was small and restrictive, being included within a temporary Bookshop lease negotiated 5 years earlier.

While I was in Britain in 1961 the District Meeting in Pago had agreed to a recommendation made by the newly appointed Treasurer to move the Church Office from the Bookshop to another location. It was hoped to 'match' the splendid edifice in Apia, Western Samoa. This development would go some way to meet the criticism of those who thought that little money had been spent on projects in American Samoa. Such a move would also strengthen the control of an organisation based in Independent Samoa over their American Samoan counterparts. At the meeting with the Attorney General, I was told that after reviewing the law concerning the alienation of land for a Church Office to be built on a new site, it would not be possible to grant the request. In addition the previous permission to have space for an Office within the Bookshop had been withdrawn.

The arrangement made by the previous Attorney General, to include a Church Office in the lawfully permitted Bookshop, had been unlawful with regard to the Office. Preferential treatment had been given to one church denomination, and the concession had therefore been withdrawn. Unfortunately I conveyed the news to the Treasurer with the words that he was 'to clear out'. I would deeply regret that a personal disagreement had ended in discourtesy on my part..

Disgraced

On his second visit in 7 years, the Church Auditor H. Betham, based in Western Samoa, scrutinised the annual accounts submitted by the Manager, Ioane and myself. Required by the Attorney General's Office to produce Annual Financial Statements,we had already submitted these, and they had been approved. Detailed answers to questions on book keeping regarding business transactions were given in meetings on the Bookshop's premises. An explanation given for the difference between the Bookshop's items for sale, and the strictly religious nature of the Methodist Bookroom in W. Samoa was also provided.

Two weeks later I was disturbed to receive a letter from Mr. Betham asking me to bring detailed accounts to a meeting in Western Samoa,which was to take place immediately before the Assembly. Realising that there was more at stake than Bookshop business, I obtained letters from the Bank Manager in Pago Pago, and the Attorney General of American Samoa, giving assurances that the Bookshop's finances were in good order. Their concern was that dollars would not be transferred to the Office in Western Samoa.

At a specially convened meeting in Western Samoa, Chairman Tapeni Ioelu accused me of incompetence, and I was charged with operating the Bookshop in contravention of the rules and procedures of the Church. It felt like a 'show trial'. The committee could not agree on a course of action regarding the Bookshop, and discussion moved on to the subject of a new Office in American Samoa. It was asserted by the Chairman that 'the cause of the removal from the old Office was Nimese, (my Samoan name). A proposition that a new Office be built in Pago was approved,which included the statement 'Therefore the care of the Bookshop should be given to someone else, and Nimese should give his single minded attention to spiritual work, according to his appointment as a missionary'.

The meeting then considered a District motion brought by representatives from American Samoa. It sought approval from the Assembly for a specialist in Youth and Children's work, presently a minister belonging to the United Congregational Church in the USA to work in co-operation with the Samoan Church. A telegram had been received by, Secretary, London on the 13th of May 1965, 'Confirm Carleton conversation London. Have since pursued matter and have U.S. letter dated 4 May reporting growing support for appointment. Candidate being sought. Please convey our warmest greetings and assurance of prayers to the Assembly. Craig.'

Little interest was shown in this topic, and Ioelu said amid laughter, 'If Nimese cannot do the work himself he should resign, he is obviously not equal to the work.' He also roundly condemned me for working 'round the back way' in bringing the 'American' subject to the Assembly. At 10pm as the meeting was turning into a marathon, with the curfew bell about to be rung on the Malua College compound. It had already tolled for me.

Returning to the subject of my removal from the Bookshop, the Chairman further expounded on a theme used earlier. I was described as a disturber, 'ua fa'avevesi le Ekalesia'. He then appealed to the words of Caiaphas the High Priest as a justification for the action of the Church. Ioelu said 'ua aoga pe a fano se toatasi e sui a'i le nuu.' (It was expedient that one man should die for the people. John. 18:14.). Of course it was inappropriate to compare my discomfort with Christ's death on the cross, but it did reveal a person deeply disturbed by the prospect of the Church falling apart.

'Proceed with caution', the theme of this chapter, was writ large into the character of Ioelu. A different observation was made by Savali Sunia, 'Ai lava, e le o ona aso ia.' (Probably it was not the right time.) Fifteen years later in 1980 a complete break took place, and talk of unity based on inter-dependence between the Eastern and Western Samoan members of the Church was silenced. The big fish had spiked each other.

Chapter Headings

Independence Day - Fast pace questioned - Health concerns - South Pacific Forum - Islanders voice ignored - Who do you believe? -Traditional Medicine Hidden rocks - Colonial trap - Rivalry among leaders - Trickery - Disgraced.

Chapter Twelve

1965 - 2012 A Durable Network

A Samoan proverb, *'O le upega ua tautau, 'ae fagota'* means that a torn fishing net can be repaired so that it can be used again. Do not allow yourself to be downcast by failure.

The chapter begins with the practical task of mending a fishing net for an unfinished task. Beginning with the language of Lake Galilee, and Samoan fishing traps, ' A Durable Network' takes us into the Internet world. 'Out of the loop', explores the common experience of rejection, which leads to the next section about 'connections' made with the outside world through tourism.. The Island's educational television's failure to deliver, and its return to a 'default' position is examined. Attitudes to sexual behaviour, and suicide rates among Samoan adolescents raises a question about Islanders being 'programmed'. A review of positive and negative features of world wide 'systems' is followed by the final section giving a brief survey of one world wide network which provides mutual support to its members.

Hung out to dry

What sounded like a ripple of applause disturbed our sleep. The sound was made by groups of fishermen cupping their hands downwards before smacking them against the surface of the sea as the tide ebbed to reveal the coral reef of Leone Bay. It was a necessary prelude to a method of fishing known as 'lauloa'. Making a clatter in unison, a group of twenty adults drove a shoal of fish towards a stretch of shallow water in the lagoon. There a barrier made from coconut fronds was waiting to guide the thrashing flow, mainly mullet (anae), towards a large net.

In 'lauloa' fishing a group of men, each one holding part of the rim of a large net, known as a 'tapo', waited for their breakfast to arrive. As some fish took fright, and jumped out of the mainstream carrying them towards the 'tapo', other fishermen caught them in small hand nets (alagamea.). The large net loaded with fish was dragged toward land risking the possibility of becoming entangled, then ripped apart by jagged coral slabs. Stretched to breaking point the net often snagged on submerged volcanic rocks. The task of mending the 'tapo' would be tackled later. Following repair work, the treasured net was hung up to recover tensile strength in readiness for the next fishing expedition.

I had been well and truly hung out to dry by a decision of the General Assembly of the Church, of which I was a member. Repair work was needed. Instructed by the Chairman to cease all activity in areas of the Church's life deemed to be secular, I had to concentrate on spiritual work,that is preaching, conducting Holy Communion, and providing pastoral care. It was a time to mend nets and reflect on an opportunity missed. How much I was to blame? Had I sought personal satisfaction when as an alien I should have been more in the background to encourage American Samoans stand up for what had been their decision. Fed up with an institution, which allowed its appointed officials to misuse their power to crush and humiliate a fellow worker, another Samoan proverb summed up my bitterness. 'E sola le fai, ae tu'u le foto'. A sting ray escapes, but leaves its sting behind'.

A story from Samoan mythology with strong echoes of one of the Gospel stories also came to mind. It was of the god Pili, who was supposed to have taught the Samoans to fish with nets. He spread out a large net and so many fish were caught in it, that the boats could not contain them. Many fish had to be thrown back into the sea. Called an 'upu fa'anoanoa' (tragic word),it was recalled when an anticipated benefit was snatched away at the last moment. The parable also applied to a group of people who had an objective within their grasp, and then had lost it through failing to act together. I felt both remorse for the mistakes I had made, and a sense of being betrayed by colleagues and friends.

The compensation of a more relaxed family life was realized during the following weeks. Brother Canute's beach at Le'ala was part of the coastline of Tutuila, two miles east from our home, deserted and irregular. The 'beach' was a stretch of jet-black rock worn smooth by the Pacific rollers, slippery wet and ideal for sliding. Rock pools of various sizes, that had become home to crabs (pa'a) sea shrimps (ulafiti) lobsters (ula) and spiny-skinned starfish (aveau), provided opportunities for our children to splash each other. Sea crabs scrambled across the lava rocks as the waves receded, and then held on for dear life as the rollers crashed back again. Their activity spoke to my condition. The shouted warning 'watch your backs' was heard repeatedly.

Chasing the toads as they jumped about in the miniature lakes on the front lawn,created by sudden downpours, was great fun for our daughters. Leone, became attached to scaly, croaking toads, stroking them as pets, and getting reactions of disgust from others. Sue had a preference for the grasshoppers, green in colour and veined like a leaf enabling them to hide among the convolvulus. Listening to the whirring sound made by the male rubbing its hind legs quickly against its wings was a soothing experience for jaded spirits.

The house lizards (mo'o) and the outdoor ones (pili) proved fascinating to our infant Rachel as she looked up at the 'creepy crawlies' playing around her pram. Lizards climbed up smooth walls with claws and suction pads on their feet. A narrow body with a long tapering tail helped them to hide in shaded corners to dart out rapidly to catch flies, mosquitoes and stick insects. Coloured shades of yellow and brown, with purple eyes surrounded by deep orange folds, the mo'o had a habit of shedding its tail when provoked. Their constant activity, blending with the girls riding their tricycles, or pushing toys along the wide smooth verandah, kept me going. Near one of the corners was the study/office, with overhanging frangipani and hibiscus flowers brightening the day. They matched the spotted ladybird beetles coloured yellow and black, dark blue, or red with black spots feeding on the aphids and scale insects.

Vegetables were grown in a cultivated patch near the perimeter hedge, where a troublesome pig had met its end four years earlier. Tomatoes did very well, and carrots gave promise of a good harvest with a fine show of greenery. Imagine the disappointment, when it was discovered that the rapid growth above ground was not matched by a stunted root, where a healthy carrot should have been. At a time when I was eating the roots of bitterness (Exodus 12:8), it was the outward show of the Church in Samoa, which impressed casual onlookers. Lack of depth and substance was what I saw. The quality of the carrots,which grew below the surface, was also disappointingly small. I thought again of people who lived in the colder climate of northern Britain and what they said about someone mainly concerned with their appearance. 'She was all fur coat,and no knickers.'

Out of the loop

Removal from the Bookshop was intended to strip me of any 'mamalu' or standing that I might have had in the eyes of American Samoa people.. Having discovered over the years that the people with whom I lived and worked had a proverb for every eventuality, I was not surprised that one in particular described my condition perfectly. 'O le pola motu i tua', means that you place damaged and torn blinds at the back of the house where nobody can see them. Passers-by see only the front of the house. It is unnecessary therefore to pay any attention to the things at the back. 'O le a le mea tou te amanai'ia le pola motu i tua?'

One consequence of the dismissal from the Bookshop and District responsibilities was that I was no longer invited to take part in ceremonial or official occasions, such as the annual Gift Day event in each sub District (Pulega). Required to be present at Induction services of ministers to pastorates, or speaking at Church Openings was a thing of the past. The long wait for the starting bell to sound from the church tower summoning all to perfunctory performance,had at least been preceded by camaraderie. Overlooked a year later when President Lyndon B. Johnson visited American Samoa in October 1966 for two packed hours of high rank ceremony and celebration, I was a 'has-been'. Not welcome at ceremonial occasions, I experienced, to a limited extent, what it meant to be an outsider in Old Samoa. With nowhere to go when ostracised, the pressure to conform must have been intense. Knowing expulsion to Tonga, or a faraway island, had also been a possibility.

Standing up to sing the opening hymn as a member of the congregation in the Town Church of Fagatogo on Pulega Gift Day, I had mixed feelings watching the procession of those leading worship (Solo a le 'Au Failotu). I was genuinely glad to see Fiti Sunia, a trusted colleague, and now the Senior Minister of Fagaloa ma Ituau (mainly the Pago Bay Area), emerge as the honorary Leader of the District. Another's increase and my own demise, was not without its bitter sweet thoughts.

However I was not the only one to experience rejection. Several Samoan ministers discovered that an agreement made between them and a village council, had not been renewed. An obligatory three month long sabbatical from the pastorate, recently introduced, provided an opportunity for a village to get rid of an unsatisfactory- or demanding incumbent. The new rule was designed to break the grip of the ancient lifetime Covenant (Feagaiga) between a pastor and a village. I had argued loud and long for the change!

Backroom tasks done to keep the Bookshop in business for the past eight years needed attention, and Ioane the Manager was pleased that we were willing to help unofficially with stock control, and the ordering of books, stationery and educational materials. He understood that we were unable to assist with the accounts, sales and financial transactions. According to the Church Auditor, the Bookshop had made a profit of $3,000 on the years trading ending March 31st 1965, which provided a sound financial basis for future business.

Four months after my removal from the Bookshop, Dr. Raymond Gray, Director of Churchman Overseas, a division of the US National Council of Churches based in New York, wrote on September 14 1965 to say that the subject of a closer connection with the Church in the USA had not slipped from his attention.' I am planning to visit Pago to explore with you and leaders of the District the needs of the American community, and the possibility of an expert in Christian Education giving his attention to the Samoan churches.' (I did not take part in those discussions).After his visit early in January Dr. Gray wrote on the 31st of that month in 1966 to express his gratitude for the welcome given to him by American Samoans. He suggested that, 'A joint committee of people from the American and Samoan churches be formed to discuss matters of common interest regarding a pastor, who would serve both groups'. The visit confirmed that there was strong support among the pastors and people in Tutuila and Manu'a for a closer link with the Church in the USA.

In the meantime I had received a letter from the Prime Minister of Western Samoa, Fiame Mata'afa written on January 13 1966. The letterhead showed that he was now the Chairman of the Church, which demonstrated again the strong link between Church and State. Mata'afa wrote 'The Church Assistant Treasurer for Tutuila (Tulafono F.S.) has advised me that you have received rental money from the Atauloma School property, and has paid it into an account other than the Church General Account. This move is not in accord-ance with our Church Constitution, page 31 sub clause (h), which reads, 'All monies received must be sent without delay.' Although Mata'afa was writing as the Chairman of the Church, he allowed a copy of his letter to be sent to the Attorney General of American Samoa, Owen S. Aspinal. Clearly Inter governmental pressure was being applied. The letter addressed to me had come as a bolt out of the blue for I had begun to come to terms with a limited pastoral role, mainly with the American / English speaking congregation.

I replied to Mata'afa's in a letter written on January 17, that I had no knowledge of the reported misdemeanour, but because he had written to the American

Attorney General, his assertion was slanderous. I reminded Church officials in Western Samoa through him, that property in American Samoa, including Atauloma, was registered at various times between 1913 and 1948 in the name of an incorporated body known as the Congregational Church in American Samoa. According to the laws of Incorporation in an American territory, only an officer of the Tutuila and Manu'a District such as Panama Mutu, its present Secretary, and an American national, could receive any payment of money. I stressed that it was unlawful for an alien person,(Englishman or Western Samoan),to receive any payment from a lease made in the name of American nationals.

The substance of Mata'afa's letter reminded me of the resentment expressed ten years earlier by Americans who made an accusation directed at me, that large amounts of dollars were siphoned off to the L .M. S. Church, (with its British Colonial connections). This was done through a favourable exchange rate for pounds sterling which had been fixed 30 years earlier. In 1966 I heard nothing further from those who had considered legal action against me, and concluded that this had been an inept attempt to discredit former Church servants in American Samoa. It was another example of officials in Western Samoa being preoccupied with financial control. They remained unwilling to recognise the groundswell against such heavy handedness in financial relationships between Eastern and Western Samoa. The move towards Inter-dependence had been crushed, yet a growing number of church members in American Samoa remained reluctant to pay for church institutions wholly based in Western Samoa, and were exploring the possibility of stronger links with the USA.

Tourist connection

On November 8 1965 the luxury liner 'Statendum', an enormous Holland-America cruise ship with mostly American passengers on board, used every inch of available space to berth along the Pago dockside. The day long stopover was one stage on a sixty day 'Pacific Adventure Cruise'. Normally such visits lasted only half a day, but from 1965 onwards a steady trickle of tourists stayed for a longer period. 239 tourists in 1966 had become 667 by January 1967, and this number increased to 1032 by July 1967. A steady trickle became a flood, before the tours moved on to other exotic places.

The Office of Tourism was created in 1965, and Fofo Sunia was appointed Director six months before the Pago Pago Inter-continental Hotel opened its doors in December. Travel agents and writers in the USA and Australasia sprang into action. Governor Lee wanted the American Samoan Development Corporation to be responsible for the first luxury hotel in the territory. Set up to give local Samoans an opportunity to make a worthwhile investment, the incorporated body became the owner of a 101 room luxury hotel. The venture didn't realize its potential.

During the 'worst hurricane of the century,' that is according to 'old timers' quoted in the newspaper Samoana on February 2 1966, 100 mph gusts caused widespread damage and some loss of life. The recently constructed 'Samoan style' buildings using modern materials, stood up well to the test.

They also withstood the hurricane of October 1967,which many thought was far worse than the previous one. Our home at Fagalele lost part of its roof on both occasions, water and power supplies stopped for a week, and the mark of flooding in two successive years, can be seen on old books and papers referred to in this book. Tafuna airport was closed because of the hurricanes, but the number of aircraft bringing tourists in 1966 doubled in 1967 to 1,268. Numerous U.S. Air Force flights during those Cold War years were a reminder of a grim reality waiting in the wings.

'Fickle glamour is the face of tourism'. Governor Rex Lee used these words when he spoke to 200 travel executives, transport representatives and government officials meeting in Western Samoa in May 1967. He began by saying that tourism was similar to many other industries in creating both material benefits, and harmful by products. Hotels and resorts should reflect the unique culture and characteristics of the people. It was therefore necessary for Governments to provide safeguards against unscrupulous speculators. Developers emulating hotels in Middle America with their huge advertising billboards,should be sent packing. Simpler entry forms and custom regulations were needed and Governments should find ways of protecting tourists from exploitation, cheating and overcharging. Hygiene was important because 'a tourist with an upset stomach is not going to advocate the charm of the South Pacific to those back home.' Government interference did not go down well with many tour operators present.

In the course of his speech Lee stressed the need for uncontaminated water supplies, with beaches and public places cleaned up. The East-West Centre in Honolulu would provide help for those people working in the service sector of a Samoa's economy. Hospitality was to be a keyword, but added that tourism was not a magic cure-all for an Island people's economic problems. Cheap sexual innuendo, gambling and making the Polynesian way of life a mere commodity, would attract an undesirable element. It was a glamorous industry, but it was usually skin deep.

Lee knew the dangers inherent in tourism as a primary industry, but was well aware of the limited options open to Tutuila, a small island of 76.2 square miles (18 miles long, 5 miles across at it widest), most of which was mountainous, and unsuitable for agriculture. Two American tuna canning firms, Starkist and Van Camp, between them provided work for 830 employees working in processing and maintenance positions. Tourism would provide work and an opportunity for visitors to appreciate the island's natural beauty. However locals advised visitors to avoid places down wind from the Van Camp canning factory. The stench could be overpowering.

Wide sandy beaches at the eastern end of the island at Alao and Tula, gave an opportunity for swimming and snorkelling. A sensible regulation prevented visitors from attempting the hazardous passage to Aunu'u, which I had done on a yearly basis in the 1950's. Instead it was possible to have a boat trip to empty golden beaches along the north coast between Afono and Vatia underneath the sheer 100 metre high cliffs. The reef heron, (Matu'u), and various wader birds, (Tuli), on Pola Island were seen feeding nearby. Ten years earlier I had trekked through the rain forest over the mountain pass to Afono. It was there that I first met my friend Ioane, who had been the villager's pastor before he was invited by the District Meeting to become Assistant, then Manager of the Bookshop.

Whereas in the 1950's, it had been a steep climb to A'olo'au Fou, in 1966 it was possible to travel by bus to the mountain village. From that vantage point it was a relatively easy to walk on to A'asu and the monument commemorating the massacre of 12 French mariners in 1787 (p9). For most tourists abiding memories of American Samoa were the sight of the magnificent Pago harbour, a bus trip through villages towards Leone, or over the mountain pass to Fagasa, plus a ride on the two-mile long aerial tramway that stretched above Pago harbour.

The trip on the longest single-span aerial tramway in the world, when built in 1965, was for the transportation of T. V technicians and equipment to the transmitters atop Mount Alava. A signpost next to a transmitter at 535 metres had one arm pointing southwesterly towards Leone Bay and the far distant city of Sydney, Australia, 2377 miles away. Another arm pointed north-easterly to Manu'a, 60 m. Honolulu 2276 m. and Los Angeles 4,782 miles.

According to the Director of Tourism the two questions most frequently asked by USA travel agents were 'How do pronounce Samoa? His answer was that the first part of the word. Sa, meant sacred, and was pronounced as in 'Sarm' not 'sum' but most visitors still say 'Sumoa. The other question was 'Does it rain there all the time?' 'No. Most of the rain falls at night!' (Ahem!) was the diplomatic answer. It was best not to mention the high humidity to package tour operators. Television engineers had discovered that transformers given a tropical coat, had proved unequal to the task. An Educational Television system provided two hours of teaching through five channels on each school day,with all instruction revolving around the TV lesson. Lessons in English were prepared at TV studios, by Stateside teachers on two year contracts. Texts were sent to the Samoan classroom teachers several days before being broadcast. Principals appointed came mostly from California, and lived at each school site to advise classroom teachers on how to prepare lessons,what to watch out for, and how to ensure follow up.

Officials of the Department of the Interior in Washington, and members of the House of Representatives and Senate in Samoa, supported the spending of $ 2 million on a 6 channel television system, and financial provision was made for replacing individual village schools by 18 new Consolidated Schools costing a further $3 million. Junior High Schools were eliminated, and young children from Grade 1 upwards to Grade 8 pupils, were to attend new consolidated elementary schools of roughly 200 pupils each, with an average class size of 30, before they moved on to 1 of 4 proposed High Schools. Ili'ili in the county of Tualauta, Western District, which brought together the villages of Faleniu, Pava'ia'i, Tafuna and Vaitogi near to the village of Leone our home, was the location for one of the 18 new Consolidated Schools It was ready to use televised instruction in 1966 and I was able to observe the radical development for 2 years.

With 2 High Schools nearly finished in 1966, 60% of a large construction programme had been completed. A further substantial grant of $2 million over the next 3 years meant that 4 High Schools for 7,500 students, and a total of 24 Consolidated Schools were operational in 1969. Lessons in the High

Schools appeared on large television screens in front of an assembly of nearly 200 pupils seated in a massive 'Samoan style' bee- hive shaped classroom/ lecture theatre. The completely restructured school system reflected the finest style of Samoan architecture, and made use of the best available equipment and technology.

Viewing the intense activity at the emerging television studios, I thought of a Samoan humorist in an educational radio broadcast which I heard in 1955, who began his lesson. 'Yesterday your teacher told you that you were to have a lesson this morning on fish, and he told you each to bring along a small fish. Now, look at the fish that your teacher told you to bring. If the teacher forgot to tell you to bring a fish, well, look at the fish he has drawn on the blackboard. If he forgot to tell you to bring a fish ,and if he has not drawn a fish on the blackboard, well just look at the lazy face of your teacher'. It was hoped that the new system would counteract a local teacher's lack of preparation in front of a blackboard.

Television was to carry the core of curriculum, rather than supplement what went on in the classroom. In essence, all instruction was conceived, re-searched, and written by 50 skilled professionals and disseminated from what critics called a 'Command Centre'. The foot soldier on the front line, or in this case the teacher in the classroom, carried out received instructions to the letter. Those directly involved and sympathetic to this major new educa-tional project preferred to talk about a 'Resource Centre', which depended on cooperation from the entire teaching team, research teachers, television teachers administrators, cameramen, producers directors, technicians and classroom teachers. Following a telecast, a local teacher gave added expla-nations, followed by supervised exercises based on the telecast. Television it was claimed was the modern 'Magic Lantern', and would make it possible for a skilled teacher to teach a standardized curriculum throughout the territory.

To meet the daunting challenge of providing what sounded like a mainland USA standard of education for pupils throughout the islands of Tutuila and Manu'a, one question was often put to the Government's Educational Department.'Would large numbers of relatively ill prepared teachers be able to handle mountains of photocopied supplementary material accompanying Television lessons?' A local reality check showed that teachers often wrote answers on the board for students to copy instead of carrying out suggested experiments. Asked to use bundles of sticks to get across the idea of sets of ten sticks in simple arithmetic, no effort was made to collect easily found materials.

Anecdotal evidence of this kind agreed with our early experience of teaching in Fagalele School. Although a minority of teachers appreciated guidance, and improved upon it, our experience was that constant supervision was needed. Feedback given to those who monitored the Educational Television project indicated that it was as difficult as ever to encourage young pupils to ask questions, and older students appeared inhibited when asked to express their own point of view on any given topic. A standardised response was as predictable as ever.

Resistance to a form of Educational Television which put 'all the eggs in one basket' was expressed most forcibly by those teachers who thought that they would eventually lose their jobs. Moreover they were uneasy about being known as a 'receiving' teachers, because it suggested an inferior status. In a hierarchical society, where one's standing within it was 'registered', such a designation amounted to downgrading, which was only put right when it was known that the local teacher worked occasionally alongside someone seen on television.

Those who remained dissatisfied with being receivers, were capable of sabotaging the effort involved in preparing material presented in front of the television camera. However the main opposition to the new system came from a group of stateside educators, including the Director of Education and his deputy, who said that not enough time had been given to planning curriculum before the new system began, and that the classroom teacher was devalued. Basically they said that the scheme wasn't going to work, and should be radically cut back. They were sacked

It would have been impossible for such a major upheaval to take place in American Samoa's education system without a Governor who was determined to make 'all out' television instruction succeed. Within the constraints imposed by a fixed budget, Rex Lee became a compelling influence on U.S. policy towards the territory. Competing educational bureaucracies, such as the previous Department of Education and Teacher Training School, were swept aside, or made impotent. An autocratic administration was able to get things done, with opposition reduced to little more than angry words.

High expectations surrounding the educational television project had been evident when President Lyndon Johnson visited American Samoa for two hours in October 1966 when Mrs. Lady Bird Johnson gave her name to the Manulele Tausala (Ladybird) Consolidated School near Tafuna Airport. In her speech she declared that, 'the television transmitters on Mount Alava would become a beacon of understanding to shine around the world'. A desire to develop an Educational Television programme,which could be transplanted to 'undeveloped' countries, seemed to fuel the interest of the Presidential party in the project. (Photo of President Johnson p200)

This suspicion was confirmed when I received a letter from Governor Owen Aspinal, (successor to Rex Lee).In May 1969 he wrote about the termination of the contract between the Government and the National Association of Educational Broadcasters, who from 1963-69 had been the consultants of the project. Aspinal in his letter wrote, 'The Director of Education never knew whether he was in command of the education program in Samoa, or if N. A. E. B. in Washington was in effect establishing the policies that controlled us! You will be aware that many of the Samoans were not in favour of the E. T. V. Program and the way that it was being handled. Hopefully I will soon be able to enter into a new contract with the University of Southern California.' Reading Aspinal's letter I thought of the growth of a banyan tree.

The Strangling Fig (banyan) tree begins life as a seed deposited in the top of a palm tree by a flying fox, or other fruit eating bird, where it germinates. Several aerial roots are sent downwards entwining the trunk in the manner of a botanical boa constrictor. As the growing palm swells, the banyan's death grip tightens, helped by sustenance received from roots that have gone to ground, spreading out through leaves and shoots. When the supporting tree dies, the Strangler takes its place in the sun.

Despite what has been written above the death-dealing banyan, it can also be the means of prolonging life. Some human ailments respond positively to chemicals in the bark of trees found in Samoa. Slender banyan roots (Ficus prolixa),produce a substance used in treating skin cancer, and the milky sap contains Ficin verminfuge, to expel worms from the intestines. In a similar way Educational Television acting on its own became a strangler, but when used later alongside conventional teaching and learning methods, it became a valuable 'Sorcerers Apprentice'. 'The all or nothing' emphasis on television was in effect a programme of social control similar to the ancient hierarchical structures that had operated in Samoan society. Both top / down systems, assumed to be self sufficient, had passed their 'sell by' date.

Programmed sexuality

Living in a Girls Boarding School(Atauloma), for 3 months in 1955, and on a Boys School campus (Fagalele) for the next 13 years, I knew about a controlled environment. The staff at the Girls School supervised students day and night, whereas the routines of the young men (14-19 years), allowed brief opportunities to get outside the system in the hours of darkness. Both male and female students found that one way of resisting restraints imposed upon them, was to withdraw into a prolonged sulk. Being 'musu' expressed a mood of non co-operation, and being emotionally unresponsive. To an outsider like myself it looked as though the person's 'moodiness' was a retreat into a self imposed isolation in order to get some personal space.

Atauloma girls were groomed for the lifestyle of a chief's wife (Faletua ma Tausi), or that of a Pastor's partner. This was done under the 'all seeing' eyes of Fuluiole Meleisea, the joint Headmistress,born into an aristocratic family, who at that time was in her mid 50's. During village tours in school holidays, I met Atauloma schoolgirls acting as hostesses for visitors to the Pastor's home. Built by order of the Council of Chiefs, they were well furnished to provide hospitality for honoured guests to the village. During Boarding School holidays Atauloma students lived with local girls of a similar age in a dormitory area inside the Pastor's house. He and his wife acted as the teenager's guardians. The arrangement was similar to an ancient custom, in which a special house, 'fale tali malo', was reserved for girls of high rank, who were protected virgins eligible for marriage to aristocratic males.

In Old Samoa, a network of connected aristocratic families formed the ruling class, and marriage was intended to produce a new exalted lineage. George Milner, the compiler of the (Oxford) Samoan Dictionary, referred to the family history of the Paramount Chief of Manu'a, and his marriage to Sina. 'Sa usu Tui Manu'a ia Sina'. The physicality of the word 'usu' is clear. It is about conquering a female through sexual intercourse. Marriage was not about forging a relationship, but creating a dynasty. An arranged marriage would never measure up to the deeper bonds of loyalty and love found between sisters and brothers.

In Old Samoa no such formal marriage procedure existed for the lower orders, who cohabited by mutual consent. The experience of visitors to pre-Christian Samoa suggested that unmarried women were free, even expected to have sexual relations as part of local hospitality. From 1830's onwards, Christian churches, promoting monogamy and premarital female chastity managed slowly and surely to alter such attitudes.. Building on the long established link between marriage and family honour among the Upper class, lesser mortals were encouraged to imitate them. The gap between the ideal and the actual could be monumental, in the same way that the English aristocracy expected people 'Downstairs' to behave properly. Sexual liaisons and marriage between people living in a closely knit community was discouraged through strict rules intended to prevent quarrels. Consequently men sought favours further afield. Eighteen year old Fagalele schoolboys were often missing early morning before lessons began.

In the 1960's it was still taken for granted that brothers of young women protected their sisters from the attention of male admirers. Just as Samoan rugby players do not take prisoners on the field of battle, the behaviour of guardians of sisters was often violent, the precious honour of the family name being at stake. Honour crime was a fairly common occurrence. I witnessed an ambush ending in violent payback time outside the village of Taputimu in 1960. The warrior disposition of males meant that high risk stratagems were used by those seeking a conquest.

Disguised admiration of adventurous males by young women, the thrill of the chase and the fear of being discovered, both deterred and encouraged young males. Because it was relatively easy in village life to see what others were doing at any time of the day or night, close neighbours were aware of whispers and movement. Gossip was a powerful deterrent of errant behaviour although it didn't stop sexual encounters taking place. Samoans spoke of a secretive world in which a nod was as good as a wink regarding some pillars of their society. Lifted eyebrows or sly hints could begin a trail of blame for the untitled leading to fines, ridicule or banishment. These were enforced by the Village Council, the arbiter of morality.

Chiefs acting through Village Councils were capable of prohibiting the wearing of immodest shorts and jeans by women,and long hair by men. Pregnancy outside marriage, adultery, and sexual assault were punished. Fines were often paid by the chief representing the family of the offender and church discipline added to the burden and shame of individuals and their families. This happened because a large majority of chiefs were deacons of what had become the Church of the Establishment. The expulsion of sexual sinners from receiving Communion for a specified period, was a 'double whammy'. Love of power was a sufficient aphrodisiac for the elite.

Although I was never involved in deliberations at a village level, I shared with five Senior ministers,(Au Toeaina) the oversight of ministers,which meant that I knew about some male sexual offences. Shame on the man's family,and removal from pastoral charge for a year was regarded as a sufficient discipline. Sensing that I was chasing shadows, I was regularly confused in these meetings by the expression of both legalistic and permissive opinions Who do you believe when you hear that both men and women are expected by to be chaste before marriage, and continue faithful afterwards, whilst 'off the record', it was said that 'Men were expected to be potential predators'? In the 1960's I understood from unguarded comments that surreptitious rape took place despite protective measures being taken.

Thirty years earlier, Margaret Mead (1901-1978), a 23 year old American anthropologist, had done research about Samoan culture on the island of Ta'u in the Manu'a group. Being a young person she had a good opportunity to get alongside Samoan young people during her field work, which lasted 6 months. Her study was about the teenage years of Samoans,and she compared these with her own experience of adolescence in the USA. She lived in a village of 600 people, close to 68 young women aged between the ages of 9 and 20, and they provided the material for a book entitled 'Coming of Age in Samoa'.

Mead came to a view that among Samoan young people there was absence of the usual traumas associated with growing up. The emotional confusion and distress attributed to raging hormones, or the pressure of parents and elders was avoided. One result of her research suggested that the smooth transition from child to adult in Ta'u was due to acceptance of an assigned role in village life. Allegiance to the system gave adolescents a sense of identity. Expected to put the good of the community before private and personal satisfaction, they seemed to have accepted such behaviour.

Controversy was sparked,then fanned into a blaze by Mead's other assertion that chastity only applied to a relatively few young women of high rank. Her adolescent informants told her that casual sex was normal among most young women in Ta'u. This was put forward as an alternative explanation for the absence of upheaval as Samoan adolescents grew into adulthood. Readers of her book in Europe and the USA concluded that teenage Samoans were spared the aggravation of growing up in the Western world. Not quite in the same bracket of notoriety as 'Lady Chatterley's Lover', the thesis attributed to Mead nevertheless caused a stir earlier in the century.

Writing in the mid 1920's the anthropologist went on to say that there was a

price to be paid for a detached attitude to sexual activity. Mead wrote.'The facts of life and death are shorn of all mystery at an early age. Likewise children and young people come to see sexual intercourse as nothing out of the ordinary. Consequently doing what comes naturally, or too casually, could lead led to indifference about another's personality. Far from being about individual sexual freedom, Mead thought that the sexual drive of Samoan young women owed much to community values. The westernised interpretation of her views was a distortion but widely accepted.

Twenty years after the book was written, thousands of U. S. Marines occupied the Samoan Islands in the 2nd World War, and as a result the number of children of mixed race increased, especially in the semi-urban Bay Area. In the majority of villages however, the traditional Samoan social system of tightly knit communities held firm, despite being tested by the presence of large numbers of male troops living in nearby camps. In-built conservatism ensured that village life was orderly and well managed, which included the protection of young women from sexual predators. Strictly enforced curfews, and laws governing all aspects of local life continued to be the responsibility of the Village Council. The penalty of banishment was an instrument of last resort to instil conformity.

It was a different matter if a couple agreed to elope with the intention of settling some distance from the young woman's home village, after sexual intercourse had taken place, Could this have been what Mead's informants had in mind when they spoke about the prevalence of casual sex? To 'come of age' did not mean being obsessive about it. The male was expected to take the initiative in sexual acts, and there was no denying their powerful urgency, but other matters could also be on his mind. Casual sex did happen, yet a Samoan male's priority in life was to become a chief, preferably a high chief, not one of the large number of lesser ones . The procuring of a suitable partner was a step on the way to fulfilling that ambition. Daring to have a view, Samoans possibly regarded me as a gullible 'palagi'(white man).

I was baffled by polar opposite attitudes towards sexual conduct where permissiveness existed side by side with harsh discipline and punishment. On the one hand I saw that Samoan young people shared the world wide characteristics of their age group. Teenagers everywhere have a preference for novelty,excitement and particularly the company of their own peer group to confirm their generation's attitudes. At the same time outward conformity and a need to be conciliatory were deeply ingrained.

The importance of status was another example of the co-existence of a similar contradiction. Status was passed on through the right family connections based on heredity. At the same time it was expected that a highly regarded blood line should be validated by high achievement. Both were necessary. Was an ability to hold together apparent opposites written into a Samoan's genes through their upbringing? Does the social order and behaviour of young Samoans 'coming of age' provide clues for understanding the ability of adults to hold together what seem to be contradictory attitudes and views ?

Highly treasured days in a Samoan child's life are those spent sleeping in the home of the biological parents during the first 2 years of life. Surrounded by adoring adults, illegitimate children are also welcome. The first impression on meeting most Samoan adults, a sunny smile and cheerful disposition, owes much to 24 months of living in a land of milk and honey. Suddenly it comes to an end, and despite whining,clinging to clothes,crying and screaming, the firmness of parents means that the child turns to other adults in the first instance, but increasingly to older brothers, sisters, and other kinsfolk.

Growing up in the midst of a large family of several parents,uncles aunts,brothers and sisters extending in all directions, meant that an adolescent felt secure in the midst of a wide range of different peer groups. They learned to know their place. Parenting by various groups meant that children learned from an early age to hold together ways of thinking and behaviour. It could be that competitive and cooperative solutions to problems, or democratic and autocratic ways of arriving at decisions became enmeshed. Many outside observers comment that Samoans seem to be natural politicians, in Village Council, or in the Legislative Assembly Hall. This rather fanciful explanation of a slippery disposition came to me as I listened to the conversation of

Senators and Representatives calling in the Bookshop following Government Assembly Meetings.

Search for responsible government

In late 1966 the Bookshop provided a grandstand position to view a slow procession of chiefs in ceremonial attire walking across the Malae o le Talu (sacred ground), a grassed oval shaped arena in the capital. In ancient times the malae had been set aside for sacred purposes. Government buildings, the Bank, shops and bars stood on the opposite side of what had been a special enclosure in Old Samoa. Nowadays large crowds gathered at this central location for the annual Flag Day celebrations (April 17) to mark the beginning of the U.S. Navy Administration in 1900. Chiefs of American Samoa in 1966 waited in line outside the Bookshop ready to walk forward to sign the document ratifying a new Constitution.

One Article agreed to the creation of a Senate elected by Samoan custom, that is by the votes of chiefs, or talking chiefs. Each of the 14 political counties had a member. At the same time a democratically elected legislative body, the Samoan House of Representatives, having 17 members,was confirmed with due solemnity. The minimum age for voting was lowered in 1966 from 20 to 18 years, Seen as a momentous occasion, the New Constitution was the culmination of long drawn out discussions designed to link two contrasting systems of government, ancestral and democratic.

Governor Lee had been able with the Department of the Interior's backing, to recommend that the Legislature,(Senate and the Representatives together), be given power to appropriate funds raised from local revenues. In addition to being asked to take part in preparing the territory's budget, members of the Legislature had the authority to require the Governor to submit a preliminary budget plan for their consideration. In some cases they could pass bills to override the Governor's veto. The views of the two Houses were expected to be passed on to those responsible for determining the detailed budget of the Department for U.S. Territories when it met in Washington D.C..

Basically American Samoans were still dependent on the mainland US taxpayer for meeting the cost of high spending departments such as Education. Asking for accountability in the spending of public finance set aside for local enterprises was difficult to enforce. The observance of Samoan customs regarding hospitality expenses led to overspending the amount of money set aside in the Budget for such purposes. Vigorous questioning by officials in Washington with different priorities was resented. Samoan dignitaries expected large expenses to meet the cost of traditional events which might include events in the social calendar such as an important marriage or funeral. In addition Washington officials knew that money intended for a village health project had been swallowed up in some previous cases by an unexpected demand for storm repairs. Maintenance grants for school buildings had been used to entertain a V. I. P. arriving unexpectedly in a village.

During my years in Samoa there were several high profile cases of misuse of public money under the control of Samoan officials, one of which stands out in my memory. He was a Church Deacon and a friend. A top man in the Bank of American Samoa, he was found guilty, with other Samoan colleagues, of embezzling $ 40,000. One consequence of the fraud was that Treasury officials from the U.S. Department of the Interior found it necessary to advice caution in devolving financial responsibility to the Island government. Inordinate pressure from family members to siphon off funds money inappropriately, was the reason given for delaying the transition. In the blame game that followed, Government fiscal discipline was often construed as Washington holding on to political power.

Before 1958, decisions on priorities and allocations in Government spending, had been in the hands of the Governor. Lee in 1961 went further than previous administrations in accepting that political advancement was linked with responsibility in handling large amounts of money. In 1959 members of the Legislature learned the hard way that the Copra Fund, (money raised locally), was not a revolving fund that filled up automatically to enable copra producers to be paid cash on delivery. Previously it had often been regarded as a slush fund for bribing officials, or raided at will for ceremonial occasions.

As members of the Samoan Legislature began to work in closer contact with executive officers of the central government, it became possible for a committee system in both Houses to be formed.. It became the backbone of political advancement. Lauvao Lolo was Speaker of the House of Representatives in the early 1960's pleading the cause of democratic rights A few years later he became a High Chief, and afterwards the President of the Senate advocating completely different, elitist values.

Lauvao came frequently to the Bookshop for his copy of the Time and Newsweek magazines, along with requests for additional reading. In conversation he showed that he was alive to the economic realities facing the territory, and the complexities of government as the old world met the new. Lauvao also demonstrated the continuing hold of elitist attitudes on the Samoan psyche, despite the earlier appeal of democratic principles. As a sophisticated political operator he was able to hold together apparent opposites with consummate ease.

Governor Lee was more straight forward. Although he had powerful critics, others felt that the wide sweeping measures taken at the outset of his term of office, 3 years earlier, had been necessarily 'bullish'. Lee had been authorised to prepare the way for a greater measure of self-determination in government. At the end of his term in office, what was an admittedly limited transfer of power had taken place based on a partially sustainable economy. Lee gave a sense of confidence and drive to his Government, which contrasted favourably with the drift experienced under the Navy's control before 1950. U. S. Navy appointed Governors were not prepared to put painful choices before the Samoan people. A casual 'hands off' approach had been symptomatic of successive civil administrations before Governor Lowe's appointment in 1953 led to the introduction of the tuna cannery.

When Lee arrived in American Samoa during 1961 he persuaded a tightfisted U.S. Government Select Committees to release millions of dollars for development purposes. He provided long-term goals for the territory, and a comprehensive, year-by-year plan of action to realize such aims. He showed great tenacity of purpose over an unusually long six-year term in office attending countless hearings in order to obtain the necessary support from the 'powers that be' in Washington Arresting drift in Samoan society as a whole, and village communities in particular was a constant challenge to responsible leaders in Government and Church. Those who accepted the mantle, had to expect a rough ride.

Deserving the criticism that he was guilty of autocratic government when he thought it was necessary, Governor Rex Lee's action in ensuring the renewal of local ramshackle buildings, of encouraging local pride in a distinctive culture, and prompting greater efficiency in public services, had been long overdue. In addition he faced up to alcoholism among leading chiefs,who consequently neglected the well- being of their village communities. Confrontations over the gradual devolution of responsible executive power required a measure of flexibility, but mainly the attribute of persistence. Local business leaders were challenged to become more involved in sponsoring sports facilities and scholarships as Lee attempted to provide decisive leadership in a era of rapid transition.

Although the Governor often overruled thoughtful opposition to his proposals (Educational Television), he was respected for his genuine concern about the steady deterioration of a cherished culture with sound Christian roots. He believed that the Samoan way of life would benefit from a 'short sharp shock', and that American Samoans would wake up to the intrinsic value of their shared community life, expressed in the eloquent language, and deeply held sentiments of her finest orators. 'O le fa'aaloalo ma le fa'atauaina o tagata uma, o se uiga fa'atamali' i, ma le tausa'afia o le atunu'u.' (That is respect and honour being accorded to all. An enrichment that comes through social solidarity).

Following the Governor's departure from Samoa on July 17 1967, the President of the Senate, Lauvao Lolo, elected by fellow chiefs, made the headline in the local newspaper by stating that the Samoan way of life would probably not survive. He went on to say, 'The corrosion of our culture is moving very fast through the weakening of the Matai (chiefly) system, with the resultant increases in crime, delinquency and drunkenness. The new attitude of individualism where people do not want to hand over their paychecks to the family head but want to keep it for themselves will mean the end of the family system. In addition these individualists want to own their own land, and cut away from the family.' The same person, Lauvao Lolo, the former leader of the democratically elected House of Representatives, went on to say that he liked the remarks of the incoming Governor Owen Aspinal, who intended to strengthen the traditional Matai system, and to slow down the pace of change.

In the following week's edition, the Senate President seemed to reject his appeal to traditional values made a week earlier, because he was now reported as saying that he was in favour of a change of policy on the preservation of Samoan land rights 'American Samoa should seek to become an organic territory of the United States similar to Guam'. Despite calling for full citizenship of the USA, he then proceeded to feed his own fears, and those of his fellow chiefs by saying, 'that such an Organic Act for American Samoa would mean that our land tenure laws, designed to protect Samoan ownership of land, would be unconstitutional and illegal in American law. If American Samoa became an American territory, in the full sense of the word, such safeguards would be removed.' The same circular argument which preoccupied an earlier generation continued to spin round.

When I returned to Britain in 1968 it seemed that the group who wanted to cling to elitist patterns of local government had won the argument, However the issue would not go away. Would the Senate members always uphold the ancient system of chiefs acting on behalf of family groups, or would they move towards the ownership of land based on democratic principles? The dominant concern was that powerful U.S. business interests would move in immediately to ensure that American Samoa became a miniature version of the Hawai'ian Islands, which became a State of the USA in 1959. Many Samoans living there became U.S. citizens.

The Samoan chiefly system had always been adept in balancing opposing views, but this particular issue facing politicians in American Samoa defied resolution. When I returned in 1993 and again in 2005, Independent Samoa, formerly Western Samoa, was designated a Self Governing Territory by the United Nations. An elitist style of government was accepted by that body. American Samoa on the other hand is presently listed as a non Self Governing Territory administered by the U.S. Department of the Interior. The Governor and members of the Legislature,with limited powers, are elected by American Samoans.

Working the system

Early in March 1968, 'Air Force One' landed at Tafuna Airport,Samoa, bringing President Johnson to the territory. This was the second visit within 14 months. On both occasions the President praised the American Samoans serving in the Vietnam War. Formed long before the Second World War, Samoans had enlisted in the Fitafita Guard as a part of the U.S. military system. Pago Pago Naval Station had been an essential link in the network of bases protecting American interests in the Pacific. Samoans were attracted to military life by several factors including a Naval family link, a structured system similar to their village life, secure employment and a steady income, with improved job prospects on leaving the service.

Max Galea' i was a 5 year old boy living in my home village, Leone , at the time of the President's second visit in 1968. The same boy became Lieutenant Colonel Max Galea' i, aged 42, who was killed in Fallujah, Iraq when meeting with tribal leaders. A suicide bomber dressed as a security officer infiltrated into their company, and detonated an explosive belt killing 20 in the group. Compared with residents of other U.S. territories or states,a disproportionately large number of Samoan soldiers were killed,or received horrific injuries in Iraq and Afghanistan. Ioasa Tavae was a mature, trustworthy student at Fagalele School in 1959 whose open friendly manner and helpfulness was always welcome in our home, when he lived with us for over a year. Staff Sergeant Ioasa Tavae, killed in 2005 near Mosul Iraq, aged 19,was the son of the Ioasa Tavae of Fagalele School. Father and son both served in U.S. Marine Corps.

American Samoans arriving in California in growing numbers, often settled in military establishments, or nearby cities stretched along the western seaboard of the USA from San Diego in the south to Alaska in the north. Their descendents often enlisted, were married and then spread to central and east coast cities, through military service. Family members moved from their homeland in the Islands to be near them, and a mushroom development of Samoan communities took place, especially on the West Coast.

Many in the next generation enlisted and were stationed in Germany, along with more than 54,000 U. S. Servicemen. Japan had bases for 35,000, and Afghanistan 71,000 in 2010, and groups of American Samoans were among them. Military personnel with a common Samoan ancestry, living in Korea and other East Asian countries kept in touch with each other with the help of the paraphernalia of modern communication systems. American Samoans took full advantage of an extensive military system already in place. Throughout history, people 'going places' to find employment, or start a new life overseas have made use of existing networks to assist their movement.

London Missionary Society missionaries from 1795 onwards, recognised and used colonial systems of trade expansion to propagate the Christian faith and values. Tradesmen, joiners, engineers, merchants conversant with money markets, men capable of using the latest technology (eg print), came together in an organisation representing many occupations. Connected by a common purpose, the different parts were expected to work together as a whole. Critics of the missionary movement of the 19th century claim that it was an agent of British imperialism, and an investment for future British trade worldwide. John Williams known as the Apostle to the South Seas appealed directly to merchants for financial backing. David Livingstone, the pioneer L. M. S. Missionary in Southern Africa, spoke of Christianity and commerce going hand in hand. We should not be surprised.

The need for overseas markets attracted some merchants to support mission-ary enterprise, especially if they were already sympathetic to the 'unwearied diligence and application' associated with Nonconformist Christianity in Britain. Daniel Defoe, an early admirer of the Puritan creed created 'Robinson Crusoe', a book first printed in 1719. He wrote that when Crusoe arrived on an island in the middle of nowhere, he went through all the basic production processes of Britain's business world. Economic Man was applauded as a great export to other lands. Exploiting the islands resources, he also treated Friday, the local native who saved his life, in the manner of a benevolent slave owner. When the modern missionary movement hitched herself to the star of business enterprise, it took a calculated risk. It could be compared to an American Samoan joining the military to defend democracy, and finishing up in endless overseas conflicts.

Missionaries with trading instincts, bought and sold copra, which enabled growing churches to be engaged in works of mercy, and to mount a challenge against an established slave trade practiced by cruel Blackbirders. The supporters of the L. M. S. also brought the attention of Parliament to the ruthless exploitation of the Islanders by the Sandalwood pirates. The obscenities committed in the name of the Whaling Industry were also highlighted. Together with supporters of other organisations, these agitators for reform had been deeply affected by the Evangelical Revival in 18th Century Britain. William Wilberforce in his work as an M .P. on behalf of African slaves, was a prime example.

The scandal of British traders committing murder in the South Pacific gave rise to a Parliamentary Act of 1817. This was the direct result of the reports written by L. M. S. missionaries in the South Pacific, particularly Thomas Powell living in what became American Samoa. Missionary supporters in Britain exerted political pressure on H. M. Government to instruct the Royal Navy to stop the activities of slave masters. In the 19th Century, the Navy played a big part in spreading the influence of the British Empire. However using the existing systems of commerce or colonial expansion, did not stop missionaries biting the hand that fed them.

Thomas Powell, a former resident of our Fagalele home, criticised merchants involved in the exploitation of Islanders as slave labour. Missionaries spoke out against the exercise of British military power to crush legitimate local aspirations throughout her Empire. Constant heart searching accompanied the missionaries use of ready made systems lest those vested interests spoiled their essential task of spreading goodwill. In today's world widely scattered colonies of American Samoans exist within the U.S. Armed Services. A military super power's system of policing some of the world's trouble spots raises questions about when to be 'In' and when to be 'Out'.

Independent Samoa in the 1960's provided an illustration of making use of a system of government indebted to colonial ties with the U. K. and New

Zealand. Recently Samoan leaders had sought to take advantage of China's global economic expansion to receive substantial material assistance from an influential Super Power of the 21st century. The construction of an impressive Government Centre, a building for the Justice Department and a National Hospital depended on Chinese money. Clearly the Samoans have seen the need to 'work the system'.

Another example of reading the 'signs of the times' was the decision of the Samoan Government to 'lose' one day from the calendar in the year 2011. When the clock struck midnight in the capital, Apia on Thursday, 29th December, time jumped forward 24 hours to Saturday the 31st. The movement westward across the International Dateline enabled government and commercial interests in Samoa to transact business with China and Pacific Rim countries, such as Singapore and Australia, on the same day. Previously Samoans had been singing hymns at Sunday church services during the hours after the Monday money markets had opened in the Asian Pacific time zone. In the 19th century it had been beneficial for trading interests in Europe and the USA to locate Samoa east of the Dateline.

Systems come and go. Pacific Island church organisations have moved away from 'colonial' missionary systems in the direction of regional groupings. For example the administrative centre of the World Council, which grew out of the London Missionary Society, previously located at Livingstone House at the hub of the old British Empire in Westminster, London SW1 moved to Singapore in 2012. Not for the first time the centre of gravity for Christian missionary activity appears to have changed. There will be opportunities for growth along with the need to deal with harmful viruses at work within any system.

Benefits and curses co-existed within the British Imperial system, which meant that honourable and disreputable traders went about their daily business. Bigots existed alongside fellow missionaries possessing diplomatic skills. Men with guns selling cheap liquor to make money out of others misery lived cheek by jowl with teachers, artisans, linguists, and printing press operatives all of whom played a part in the massive upheaval,which brought the Pacific people into the modern world. The pioneer missionaries had rough workmen's hands, and if their supporters had the audacity to regard them as angels,they had to admit that also possessed dirty faces. These messengers, for that is the meaning of angels, were prepared to be soiled by an association with the Empire's systems in order to get their message across.

Inevitably the White Man's arrival was a mixed blessing for Pacific people. Chicken pox was not the only alien virus that adversely affected the people of Oceania. Could the same be said about the spread of literacy?

Universal literacy in Samoa brought about a transformation with both gain, and loss. An ability to memorise information gained through many generations of oral tradition was lost. Exceptional navigational skills based on environmental awareness almost disappeared. Inflections in the voice, ringing the changes on word endings,recognising emphases, inner harmonies and conflicts in speech, these could not be caught in print. The use of picture language, (eg proverbs) to engage the mind and imagination of the listener, was replaced by print and strings of words. Nuances of meaning found in everyday conversations and sensitivity to what was going on beneath what was being said in group conversation before action was taken, gave way to bookish learning. Sadly the new learning encouraged individualism and self promotion. The search for balance and consensus was compromised.

Nevertheless the gains and losses of the encounter between European and Polynesian cultures, plus the uneasy compromise with polluted yet still serviceable colonial systems, has resulted in a vital spark of life being spread across the Pacific. At least, that is the claim made by the author who also looks for inspiration in the experience of the Apostle Paul also journeying across vast distances. Paul used his citizenship of the Roman Empire, a magnificent yet often corrupt world wide system, to tremendous effect.

At all times Paul wanted to press forward, (punou a'i i mea o lumana' i.) Philippians 3 :13. He had lit the light of Christian faith across a deep and wide Roman world, yet he was convinced that the light would spread without his assistance. A prisoner in Rome, Paul was true to his watchword, 'Keep going forward !' and planned to use his Roman passport to take him to Spain. It didn't happen. Paul knew that systems were to be used. However it was the message proclaimed,and the life lived,that had a vitality to outlive both system and bearer.

Reappraisal needed

On the night of Saturday August 13 1797 customs officials looking for illegal goods or immigrants, boarded 'The Duff' in the Thames Estuary. Safeguarding the interests of a trading nation, the captain was asked 'Whither bound?' 'O Taheite' was the reply. 'What cargo?' 'Missionaries and provisions.' Cleared for passage, Captain Wilson navigated The Messenger of Peace' down the English Channel towards the Needles.

215

According to an entry in the ship's journal noted later in the month, 'An English man of war drew alongside and gave the crew information about a French privateer lurking in the offing'. The Duff's journal also mentioned that the ship had to wait for a convoy of the East India fleet including The Adamant of 50 guns. Finally the Missionary Ship was allowed to leave home waters on the 22nd September,the fleet having provided protection. A much appreciated naval system could take them so far, but no further.

Compelled to sit for long hours in darkness because the oil on board fed the lamps required for navigation,the voyagers relied on a vision that was by no means blindingly obvious to others. The journey took 7 months and provided one of the first slender strands in what became a World Wide Web. Most of these tradesmen/ evangelists set out a journey into the unknown with 'a concern in their hearts, not a bee in their bonnets'. At a time (late 18th Century), when sectarianism divided families, villages and towns in their home country, Britain, members of the Missionary Society explicitly stated that they would not export church denominations competing with each other.

The Lotu Tahiti, the Pacific Islander's Mission, which grew out of the work of the L. M .S. was an inter racial enterprise with Polynesian missionaries being drawn from various island groups such as Tahiti ,Samoa and the Cook Islands. Their work was among the many islands, large and small, in Melanesia where their task was to live in one of two contrasting worlds. On the one hand some would serve in the unexplored and unknown equivalent of 'Darkest Africa'. Others would have an important role to play in the ports associated with the growth of colonial power, and the spread of commercial empires with improved communications. Port Moresby was such a place..

For more than a century the missionary movement gathered pace in the Pacific. During a similar period of enterprise and hard graft, a shared vision of lives transformed by The Good News of Jesus Christ spread through India, Southern Africa, China, South East Asia, and the Caribbean. Nowadays a Council of World Mission is drawn from 31 regions worldwide whose members are committed to share global resources of money,people,skills and insights to strengthen particular local ventures, some of which are described below. As will be seen cross fertilisation, or experiencing cultural diversity is encouraged, and much of the training is targeted at youth.

A global family, including United Churches such as those found in populous North and South India, C. W. M. is nevertheless a minuscule organisation among commercial conglomerates, and combined armed forces. It is like a grain of mustard seed,which, when sown in the earth is less than all the seeds in the world. (Mark's Gospel 4:31)

In the 1990's students, representing member bodies of C. W. M. in different parts of the world, travelled to Taiwan to spend a year exposed to the social problems facing the Taiwanese people. These issues included migrant labour, rebuilding confidence in the wake of typhoon named Morakot, disclosing the horrors of human trafficking, and sexual exploitation,which cross every national frontier. They were able to take advantage of in-service training in local Churches,which supported senior nursing homes with teams of physicians and care workers. When they returned to their own homelands representatives were expected to encourage their compatriots to widen their horizons, and learn from the deeper experience of their universal family.

Siulepa Fa'alinga, a young man from American Samoa participated in the Taiwanese programme in 2006, when the impact of typhoons on densely populated areas was high on the agenda. Post disaster rebuilding included the havoc caused in people's domestic lives. Three years later following a magnitude 8.1 earthquake close to Siulepa's island home in the Pacific created huge tsunami waves causing substantial damage and loss of life. His contribution to the work of slow and steady recovery was appreciated. Less than a year afterwards in February 2010, an 8.8 earthquake in Chile was an anxious reminder to Samoans, and other island people of the ring of fire around them. Member bodies were quick to respond with practical help. Awareness of what was required in caring for stricken communities was available immediately.

Botswana, a land locked country in Southern Africa,70% of which is covered by the Kalahari Desert, provided a different in-service training exercise for today's heralds of world wide enterprise. David Livingstone of the London Missionary Society began his work here. 150 years later Botswana people have their own strong tradition of representative democracy. Environmental concerns remain drought and communal grazing. 50% of all households own cattle. Getting to know the problems of overstocking and overgrazing required constant travel for the visiting team. They found that indigenous knowledge and traditional management of 'Wetland' would decrease poverty. Caring for God's world was still a global mission.

New Delhi was the destination for members of C. W. M.'s Global Youth programme combating Human Trafficking. A visit was made to a nursery run by the Church of North India for the children of women working as prostitutes in a brothel. Victims of human trafficking, (that is the mothers waiting for clients to arrive),had their children looked after in a confined space where no natural light came in. The most vulnerable and innocent in society were paying the price for sexual exploitation. Heartbreaking as the work is, the United Church of North India attempts to prevent and combat the abuse of children, the corruption of pimps in procuring,and the complicity of bystanders in a system of degradation.

A final pen portrait of C. W. M. 's work comes from the East Asia and Pacific regions. Hong Kong, Kuala Lumpur, and Pago Pago . Christians seek to address young people's downward spiral into despair, demonstrated by a growing rate of suicide and intentional self harm. Earlier chapters in this book have drawn attention to the clash between Western and Samoan culture,which can place young people at odds with a strict family hierarchy. Often a lack of accomplishment fails to satisfy family pride. Pregnancy outside marriage brings an overwhelming sense of shame. The Council tries to answer a cry for help. (Between 1990 and 1996 144 suicides were recorded by the Samoan Department of Health. 97 of them were aged between 18-24). To proclaim and practice a life-affirming message is made possible through a tough, flexible network of support.

This chapter began with the drag fishing net (tapo) being used in front of our Fagalele home in Samoa. None of the original material strands remain after constant use. As the plaited sennet (afa) disintegrates, strips of the same strong yet supple coconut fibre replace the gaps in the network. Again and again the yarn is torn and shredded by rough usage before being renewed for further fishing. Material that made the net serviceable for many years wore out several times, yet the same net endured. Capable of being strengthened and adapted by succeeding generations, the net speaks volumes about the Christian Faith's endurance, - and the need for constant renewal.

Welcoming the 'otherness' found in different cultures has meant that the expression of missionary enterprise by Europeans has been transformed by that encounter. Using the language of the Internet, Loop, Connection, Default, Programme, System,Search, Web, an attempt has been made in this final chapter to understand and engage with the modern world.

Beginning with those 'who go down to the sea in ships, doing business on the great waters' (Psalm 107:23) seven chapters in Part One of this book describe successive waves of navigators, explorers, traders, missionaries and Empire builders. They provide an account of expeditions requiring a large canvas. Events recorded in the five chapters of Part Two revolve around raw recruits 'Learning the ropes', Avoiding shipwreck, Riding the waves, Plunging to the depths to await rejuvenation. A small scale world, it describes a Samoan experience, which together with Part One is intended to help readers understand and value Pacific People. It is 'A Vision Shared'.

Chapter Headings

Hung out to dry - Out of the loop - Tourist connections - Educational T. V. Default - Programmed sexuality - Search for responsibility - Working the system - Reappraisal needed.

www.ingramcontent.com/pod-product-compliance
Lightning Source LLC
La Vergne TN
LVHW051505080426
835509LV00017B/1920